KU-240-685

EFFICIENCY & EFFECTIVENESS
IN THE PUBLIC DOMAIN

Edited by T.P. Hardiman and Michael Mulreany

INSTITUTE OF PUBLIC ADMINISTRATION

338.45 / 328699

First published in 1991
by the
Institute of Public Administration
57-61 Lansdowne Road
Dublin 4
Ireland

© 1991 with the authors of their respective chapters

All rights reserved. No part of this publication may be reproduced
or transmitted in any form or by any means, electronic or
mechanical, including photocopy, recording or any information
storage and retrieval system, without permission in writing from the
publisher.

British Library Cataloguing in Publication Data
Efficiency and effectiveness in the public domain
  (Proceedings of IPA public finance conferences; vol. 5)
  I. Hardiman, T.P. II. Mulreany, Michael, 1954–
  II. Series
  338.45

ISBN 1 872002 06 4

Cover designed by Butler Claffey Design, Dún Laoghaire
Typeset in 10/11 Times Roman by Computertype Ltd., Dublin
Printed by Leinster Leader Ltd., Naas

Contents

Contributors

Bertie Ahern is Minister for Labour

John Blackwell is Principal Administrator, Social Affairs and Industrial Relations Department at the Organisation for Economic Cooperation and Development, Paris

C.V. Brown is Professor of Economics at the University of Stirling

T.P. Hardiman holds directorships in industry, commerce and banking. He is chairman of the Irish Institute for European Affairs at Louvain

Anthony G.J. Haselbekke is Associate Professor of Public Sector Economics at the Erasmus University, Rotterdam

Peter Kemp is Second Permanent Secretary in the Cabinet Office (Office of the Minister for the Civil Service), London, and Project Manager for 'Next Steps'

Dermot McAleese is Whately Professor of Political Economy at Trinity College, Dublin and a Director of the Central Bank of Ireland

Michael Mulreany is Lecturer in Economics at the Institute of Public Administration, Dublin

Arie P. Ros is Assistant Professor of Public Sector Economics at the Erasmus University, Rotterdam

Peter Saunders is Director of the Social Policy Research Centre at the University of New South Wales

Joseph E. Stiglitz is Professor of Economics at Stanford University

Thomas Swartz is Professor of Economics at the University of Notre Dame

Norbert Vanhove is General Manager of the Regional Development Authority of West Flanders

Preface

THE search for improved public sector performance is a key concern of modern government and the search for efficiency and effectiveness intensifies as the public sector is confronted with ever increasing demands for services. The oil crises of the seventies shook the existing consensus on the role of government in the modern economy and OECD analyses in the eighties emphasised the importance of an increasing reliance on the market. This shift to a greater reliance on the market has been accompanied by renewed emphasis on both value for money and management accountability in the public sector.

The search for increased efficiency and effectiveness has brought with it the need to clarify objectives and set priorities, to evaluate outputs rather than concentrate on controlling inputs, to improve managerial information and develop concepts of managerial accountability, and to take account of consumer satisfaction with the quality of the services delivered. New techniques in public sector output and performance measurement have necessarily been developed in many OECD countries.

As deregulation and liberalisation proceed in the developed countries, the role of direct state involvement in some sectors is increasingly in question and privatisation of state-owned enterprise is now a commonplace feature of public policy.

These currents in national economic affairs deserve serious enquiry by the public and private sectors in Ireland. What precisely is meant by efficiency and effectiveness? To what extent can the efficiency and effectiveness of government services be measured? Is it possible, advisable or, indeed, necessary for the public sector to apply market-determined techniques of measurement and evaluation? Are the new management techniques likely to be effective?

These are some of the questions that impelled the Institute of Public Administration to organise a conference on efficiency and effectiveness in 1990. This book contains the revised conference papers. Two extra chapters have been specially written for inclusion in the book; one provides a foundation to the book by reviewing key issues, the other examines the evaluation of public investment projects.

Throughout the book, in the course of discussing efficiency and effectiveness, we will naturally treat the related area of economy. Hence the scope of the book encompasses the '3 Es' – economy, efficiency and effectiveness. The 'fourth E' – equity – is also dealt with but considerations of space preclude an in-depth treatment.

Chapters 1 and 2 provide an overview of the main issues in the efficiency and effectiveness debate. Chapters 3-5 deal with efficiency and effectiveness in specific areas – taxation, social policies, and industrial policy. The techniques of project appraisal and of performance measurement are treated in Chapters 6 and 7 respectively. The significant changes designed to ensure economy, efficiency and effectiveness in the UK civil service are discussed in Chapter 8. Efficiency and effectiveness issues and the relationship between central and local government are considered in Chapter 9. The final chapter raises issues of efficiency and effectiveness of particular concern to Ireland.

The book provides a mixture of overview, technical and case material and draws on a wide range of international experience. We hope that it provides a useful coverage of this increasingly important area.

T.P. Hardiman
Michael Mulreany
September 1991

Introduction

BERTIE AHERN, TD

Efficiency and effectiveness in the public domain

THE public domain is of direct relevance to people, as taxpayers, as citizens, as customers of the public service, as well as to those who work in or closely with it. And it has a major effect on the economic and social performance of the country.

The efficiency and effectiveness of the public sector therefore have profound and far-reaching effects on the economic and social well-being of the whole community. The growth in the number of functions provided by the state, in Ireland as elsewhere, has been a very significant feature of the second half of this century. Its influence is now felt in virtually every facet of national life.

It is therefore important to everyone that the public sector should provide the services required of it in the most effective and efficient way possible – in other words that it should provide the highest quality service at the least possible cost.

The macro level

I would like to deal with the subject at three levels; macro-economic, micro-economic, and social. First, the macro level. The sheer size of the public sector makes it one of the dominant influences on the prosperity of the whole nation. The money it spends affects the performance of the whole economy. The revenue collected to finance it affects such areas as investment, the labour market and consumer spending. And the services it provides affects every aspect of our economic and social life.

Practically every aspect of our everyday life – including communication, travel, health services, education, and business development – is influenced in some way by the public domain. Central and local government affect economic life in many other ways. To a large extent the public domain provides the environment within which the economy functions.

Through the impact of legislation and regulations, the government determines the framework within which activities are carried out by individuals or companies. Government action can have a direct personal effect: for instance in the labour-market sphere, legislation administered through or by my department gives statutory

1

protection to workers while at the same time facilitating job creation.

It is the task of the government, at the heart of the public sector, to ensure that the right balance is struck between sometimes conflicting functions. The importance of this framework is very clearly demonstrated in the success of the present government's policies. We have followed two over-riding priorities: control of public expenditure; and improved social equity. Since 1987, these priorities have been addressed fairly and squarely.

Our success in controlling public expenditure, well ahead of target, has enabled us to reverse the spiral into debt and to make significant headway in reforming revenue collection. And, with the assistance of the consensus in the Programme for National Recovery and the Programme for Economic and Social Progress, we have been able to make a start in addressing inequities in our society which have built up over decades. These are historic achievements. Indeed, I welcome the international recognition which these achievements have generated in organisations such as the OECD.

Developments in the European Community, particularly the single market and the community support framework, add a further dimension to the role of the public sector. On the one hand, the public sector has the prime responsibility for the effective and efficient use of the major investment which the Community is making through the structural funds. These are intended to help Ireland to overcome its disadvantages of location and relative under-development. And on the other hand, the government and the public sector have a major role in preparing the economy for the new conditions in the single market. Indeed, in a sense the public service will have to become competitive with its counterparts in the other EC countries to ensure that we are not left behind.

The public sector has in the past been criticised for not using opportunities as well as possible. While there are many factors involved, we have to admit that some of the blame can be laid at our door. Too often short-term goals have taken priority over long-term national and EC priorities: Ireland is likely to have to pay a price, for instance in the agricultural sector, because of the temptation in the past to rely too heavily on the intervention system rather than on market development.

But I welcome the greater public debate on the development of long-term policy strategies; it is too easy merely to criticise politicians and the public sector for following policies which have not been generally challenged or even discussed. The Programme for National Recovery was itself one result of the growing public appreciation of the need to drop *ad hoc* measures in favour of an overall strategy. I hope that the Programme for Economic and

Social Progress will be successful in enabling us to continue this healthy development.

In overall terms, the creation of wealth and jobs can best be achieved by planning at national level – as we have done in the Programme for National Recovery and the Programme for Economic and Social Progress. The first of these programmes has been uniquely successful in Irish economic history in achieving tough economic objectives while at the same time creating greater economic growth and social equity. Indeed, *The Economist* recently cited Ireland as having pulled off the three-card trick: low inflation, robust growth and a current account surplus.

It must be acknowledged that the new programme faces difficulties. The external environment is more difficult now because of the recession in the UK, the difficulties in the US economy, volatility in the Gulf, problems arising from the GATT talks and new competition from Eastern Europe for mobile investment. And of course there are the implications of the unstoppable moves towards economic, monetary and political union in the European Community. Furthermore, we cannot forget the enormous debt problem which still remains. I need only remind you that our national debt is still over £25 billion and the cost of servicing this still accounts for 80 per cent of income tax receipts. This burden diverts resources and needs further remedial action.

But while the world situation makes life more difficult, and while we have our own internal constraints, I believe that these are the very reasons why we must have a further successful programme. Give and take is needed from all the interest groups. Each of us will have to tailor our own objectives, whether on tax, jobs, social services or pay, to fit in with the good of all. Indeed, the idea of a ten year plan, in which several programmes can be fitted, is a most useful idea from the Irish Congress of Trade Unions. I strongly welcome it as a basis which can be used for more long-term planning, which as I said earlier is sometimes neglected in the heat of current developments.

The micro level

I mentioned above that I wanted to look at the efficiency and effectiveness theme at three levels. I would like now to turn to the micro level. By this, I mean the efficiency and effectiveness of the public sector in itself, rather than as part of the overall economy, although of course the two aspects are closely linked.

Each of us pays, directly or indirectly, for the services of the public sector. We all pay taxes and we pay for the use of services such as transport or energy. We all have, therefore, a keen interest in seeing that the money we contribute is used in the best possible way. We want 'value for money' in the public domain, in the same way as in any other aspect of our lives.

It is the special responsibility of public sector managers to ensure value for money. This is far from being an easy task. In fact, it is in many respects more difficult for public sector managers than it is for their private sector counterparts. The 'bottom line' of profits, or even survival, is the acid test for private sector managers. Many managers in the public domain do not have this powerful discipline of the market place. They provide services which are essential and for which there is often no alternative. And yet they must achieve similar 'value for money' results. How to achieve this, how to develop a new discipline equivalent to the market place in the private sector, is the crucial task facing public sector managers.

The government has the leading role in determining the overall thrust of developments in the public domain. It has set about this task with vigour. For instance, it has laid down stricter financial targets for state trading bodies. It will no longer automatically bail out those that fail to perform in accordance with these targets. Where appropriate, it is prepared to consider private sector involvement. It has rationalised the number and role of many state bodies; this has produced more structured and sharply-focused organisations. The structure and financing of the health services is under review following the report of the Commission on Health Funding, and the government is also reviewing the structure of local authorities. In my own area, I have reorganised the manpower bodies into a single, client-centred body, FÁS, with a heavy emphasis on the goals of efficient and effective operation and giving the best possible assistance to the client, the unemployed. All these moves are designed to produce a more efficient and effective public sector which will be better attuned to the emerging needs of the community.

I referred earlier to the size of the public sector in relation to the whole economy. Because of the government's success in controlling public expenditure, a climate of expectation is appearing that, with the worst over, we can now go back to our old ways. This would be a very dangerous delusion. Notwithstanding the hard-earned gains, we still face an uphill battle.

It is against this still sombre background that public sector managers must continue to operate. Given this scenario, what can be done to improve efficiency and effectiveness in the public domain? The experience of recent years has, I think, sharpened up the approach of public sector managers. Faced with limits on their resources, they have started to re-assess priorities and devise different ways of managing. This must continue. The difficulty now is to

4

maintain and improve services with, at best, existing resources.

Within central government, a number of initiatives have been taken. The Efficiency Audit Group, which has been expanded to include top managers from the private sector, has embarked on a programme of reviews of the work of government departments. We expect this to lead to greater efficiency and effectiveness. In fact, it was this group which had a major input to the development of administrative budgets for departments.

Administrative budgets are based on the principle that front-line managers know best how to allocate limited resources to deliver the required level of services. Departments are being given delegated budgets to cover administrative costs for a three-year period. They will have considerable flexibility but within an overall requirement to achieve savings in real terms. It is expected that this freedom from detailed central control will release the undoubted talents of managers in line departments. Furthermore, the concept of performance pay may have a role to play in rewarding and inspiring good deliverers of the required services.

Information technology is another area in which rapid strides are being made. Considerable sums have been invested in this and the level of sophistication and skill is rising rapidly. This will pay dividends in the form of better quality services and decision making. Without information technology, the public service would have been unable to maintain and develop services in the light of the financial cutbacks.

Social equity

Lastly, I would like to turn to the third major aspect of efficiency and effectiveness in the public domain. So far I have concentrated on the economic and financial aspects of public sector activities. I would like to finish by making a brief mention of the effect of efficiency and effectiveness in achieving social goals.

For many years it has been clear that the major socio-economic problem facing this country has been the appallingly high levels of unemployment. For all of the earlier part of the 1980s, we had the dual problem of a growing labour supply and an insufficient number of jobs. Young people, the long-term unemployed, and women faced immense difficulties in getting jobs. Many left the country in despair and others just gave up, sliding into poverty and lethargy.

Despite the need for rigid financial controls, we have been able to make a start at tackling many of these problems. By creating a climate favourable to investment and expansion, we have reversed the decline in jobs and have seen a 40,000 increase in net jobs between

1987 and 1990. We have introduced new social welfare and manpower opportunities for full-time and part-time work and training. We have improved by a staggering 35 per cent the levels of social security for the long-term unemployed. We have taken action to tackle the 'poverty trap' and to ease the tax position of the lower paid.

The achievement of all these goals simultaneously, the control of the public finances and the improvement of the position of the more disadvantaged in our society, has been no easy task. An integral part of the success of these measures has been the increase in the efficiency and effectiveness of the public sector.

1

Economy, Efficiency and Effectiveness in the Public Sector: Key Issues

MICHAEL MULREANY

Introduction

CONSIDERATIONS of economy, efficiency and effectiveness may appear cold, calculating and relentlessly functional. Yet they are at the heart of controversies over matters ranging from the relative merits of market and state resource allocation to the results of public policies and, even, to the performance of national economies. Hence, considerations of economy, efficiency and effectiveness are central to decisions about privatisation, the retreat from central planning, the pursuit of a single European market, the reform of agricultural and industrial policies, the reform of taxation, and the level, quality and pricing of government services. This is a formidable list but not an exhaustive one.

This chapter aims to explore major issues that arise in the literature on economy, efficiency and effectiveness. Broadly, we will consider issues of definition, of performance measurement and of management reform in pursuit of value for money. What emerges will provide both an overview of a complex area and a backdrop for subsequent chapters.

Because of the complex and wideranging nature of economy, efficiency and effectiveness the treatment in this chapter will necessarily be selective. Every effort is made in what follows to minimise complexities and, where possible, technical matters are confined to endnotes.

Clarifying concepts: efficiency

The words economy, efficiency and effectiveness are sometimes used imprecisely. We will proceed by clarifying the meaning of efficiency and then identifying the interrelationship between efficiency, effectiveness and economy.

A central concern for any society is the efficiency with which it produces and distributes goods and services.

Efficiency in production

Efficiency in production is labelled variously as productive efficiency, technical efficiency, x-efficiency, managerial efficiency and internal efficiency but here we will use the term productive efficiency.[1] Whatever the label, the emphasis is squarely on the supply-side of the economy. Production is efficient if there is no waste: in other words if it is impossible to increase the output of one good without reducing the output of another. Conversely production is inefficient if by simply reallocating inputs it would be possible to increase the output of one commodity without reducing the output of another. The input-mix is therefore important in productive efficiency. The happy condition of productive efficiency is achieved when firms and industries produce at the lowest possible cost.

In essence, the idea of productive efficiency is relatively straightforward. It focuses on the internal process of firms and industries and exists when a given output uses the minimum amount of inputs. Viewed in a slightly more positive light, productive efficiency leads to the maximum output that could possibly be produced from given inputs.

What causes an enterprise to produce inefficiently, ie above minimum cost? The reason is waste in any of its forms – overmanning, carrying excess stocks, overgenerous expense accounts, low productivity and so forth. Waste exists in the private as well as the public sector. The Commission of the European Communities (1988) has indicated that the elimination of waste in private sector enterprises is an important benefit deriving from the increased competitive pressures in the single European market. Particularly in large firms there may be a divorce of ownership from control and a consequent threat to productive efficiency. The owners (or 'principals') may seek maximum profits and minimum costs but the managers (or 'agents') who are in control may pursue other goals, such as an 'easy life', which involve production at higher than minimum costs. In order to impose their wills the owners will need to monitor, at a cost, the behaviour of managers. Because information about particular circumstances and about managerial behaviour is skewed in favour of managers, then owners may have to offer incentives in order to change managerial behaviour. This is a variation on the 'principal–agent' problem, other aspects of which we will encounter in due course.

Of course, waste also exists in the public sector and the question naturally arises whether one sector is likely to be more inefficient in production than the other. In the public sector there is no easily identifiable equivalent to the private sector shareholder to appropriate the savings from reduced waste. For this reason and because of the absence of threats of take-overs and bankruptcy, the public sector might be expected to be more prone to inefficiency. However, much depends on the degree to which competition exists. If, for example, we were to compare a monopolistic private sector firm with a public sector equivalent then it may not be clear-cut which has the most 'organisational slack'. This is a matter to which we will return, in slightly greater depth, below.

Leaving aside, for the present, the question of comparative public–private sector efficiency, some of the methods for improving productive efficiency in the public service are worthy of note. Particularly in the past decade, market disciplines have been introduced to the public sector. For example, contracting out of government services has been instituted in many OECD countries and savings have ensued (Oxley *et al.,* 1990). Competition such as exists between suppliers where there is a choice between health care schemes or between schools (or where vouchers allow consumers of public services to make direct choices) will also tend to improve efficiency. Another method aimed at improving productive efficiency in the public sector is the process of efficiency 'scrutinies' or audits designed to uncover wasteful practices. Indeed the movement described by Kemp (Chapter 8 in this volume) towards increased accountability based on decentralised authority combined with clear objectives and priorities, can be expected to lead to improvements in productive efficiency. More immediate and crude methods exist. For example 'budgetary stress' and consequent pressure for efficiency could be induced by setting reduced expenditure targets or by restricting the income of a government agency or of local government. Such was the case in the UK when, at various times, central government reduced grants to local authorities, penalised authorities which exceeded expenditure targets and placed a limit or 'cap' on incomes from local rates.

Before concluding this section it is well to emphasise that inefficiency in production is not exclusively associated with problems of the 'time-and-motion' type. There are many current examples of waste associated with centrally planned economies. Indeed, even in the Western democracies, government intervention can lead to problems. For example, regulation by placing a ceiling on a firm's profits may in certain circumstances reduce the incentive to seek economies in production.

Unquestionably, unemployment is the greatest waste of resources inasmuch as the resources are left unused. There is no scope in this text to develop on this, other than to note that in the desired eventuality of fully employed resources there would still be a need to pursue productive efficiency, ie production at the lowest possible cost.

Efficiency in distribution

Even if goods and services are produced at lowest cost, resources can still be used inefficiently if the output-mix contains too much of one product and too little of another. Efficiency in distribution, or allocative efficiency, takes account of consumer preferences. The emphasis accordingly shifts from the supply-side to considerations of demand. At the extreme, if goods and services are being produced which no one wants to buy then clearly there is an inefficient use of resources. Such was the case in some centrally planned economies where there were examples of production of extremely thick glass and very heavy nails which technically met plan requirements but were unusable.

Allocative efficiency exists where it is impossible, by redistributing products among individuals, to make one person better off without making someone else worse off. The condition which guarantees such efficiency is that the cost of an extra unit of output should be equal to the consumer's willingness to pay.[2] If, for example, consumers are willing to pay more for an extra unit of output than it costs then the product is underproduced and there is allocative inefficiency. We cannot here go deeper into the technical properties of allocative efficiency. Rigorous treatments can be found in introductory and intermediate economics textbooks (eg Begg *et al.*, 1991; Koutsoyiannis, 1979; Stiglitz, 1988). However, our limited treatment does bring out essential features of allocative efficiency by emphasising the concern about whether too little or too much is being produced. By taking account of consumer preferences allocative efficiency is concerned with markets, in contrast with productive efficiency which is concerned with the internal processes of enterprises. In the public sector, allocative efficiency prompts questions such as: do the services financed by public expenditure acutally meet the public's demands? A different type of question is asked about productive efficiency in the public sector; a typical question might be whether too many people are employed in producing public services.

It is, unfortunately, much more difficult to answer questions about allocative efficiency in the public sector. It may be hard for consumers to specify, for example, what level and quality of defence they require or what amount and quality of graduates they expect from universities. Quantification and specification are easier in the case of productive efficiency where questions about the least cost combination of inputs arise.

The difficulty in quantification associated with questions of allocative efficiency helps explain why management reforms, such as efficiency scrutinies, in the public sector have been largely confined to matters of productive efficiency. This is not to deny that greater attention is being paid to consumers of pubic services; we have already alluded to the movement towards greater consumer choice between schools and health care schemes. The efficiency gains from improved consumer choice complement the productive efficiency gains as suppliers compete for consumers free to exercise a measure of choice. Moreover, greater account is taken of the consumer of public services by such methods as consumer surveys and analyses of complaints by the public. Yet it is wise not to be overoptimistic due to the difficulties, already noted, in quantifying consumer preferences in the public sector. We will return to this matter later in the chapter.

Productive and allocative efficiency: privatisation
The distinction between productive and allocative efficiency is useful in a number of ways. We have just seen that it can explain why some efforts at public sector reform may be more effective than others: it is easier to quantify inputs than outputs in the public sector.

The distinction between productive and allocative efficiency also informs the debate about privatisation. Vickers and Yarrow (1988) examined the case of privatising a public sector monopoly. They show that in the private sector the monopolist in pursuit of monopoly profit will increase price above and reduce output below the levels associated with allocative efficiency. However, privatisation will also affect the pattern of management incentives and thence the tendency to monitor costs; hence managers in the privatised enterprise may achieve greater productive efficiencies than when the enterprise was under public control. A privatised monopoly, therefore, may bring improved productive efficiency but reduced allocative efficiency and the overall effect on efficiency will depend on the relative size of these countervailing effects. Of course, in this example we are examining the case of a monopoly transferred from public to unregulated private ownership. Indeed Vickers and Yarrow show that the degree of competition and the effectiveness of regulation may have more important effects on performance than does the form of ownership, ie public or private.

Competition is particularly beneficial inasmuch as it leads to improvements in both allocative and productive efficiency. Vickers and Yarrow (1991, p. 116) draw particular attention to potential for improved productive efficiency under competition due to the possibility of performance comparison. Contracting-out is especially interesting because it combines privatisation with competition. We have already noted that savings from contracting-out have been identified in several OECD countries. However, contracting-out is not without it hazards including the possibilities of collusion at the tendering stage and the running down of quality during the execution of the contract. An important question that arises with contracting-out, and indeed with any form of privatisation, is how sustainable are any initial gains?

Modern theories of competition have an important bearing on efficiency. The theory of contestable markets argues that even in a market with a few relatively large firms there can be a threat of competition if new firms can enter and, if they wish, exit the market without losing the money they invested. By extension the theory of contestable markets would imply the imposition of competitive disciplines on privatised monopolistic firms where liberalisation measures allow potential rivals freedom of entry. If this were so then we might hope for efficiency gains when measures to improve liberalisation accompany the privatisation of monopolistic firms. It is, however, difficult to be enthusiastic about these prospects when one considers the likelihood that existing dominant firms may seek to protect themselves against new entrants.

Leaving considerations of competition aside we can turn briefly to an examination of the argument, already encountered, that privatisation leads to greater monitoring of costs and hence greater productive efficiency. This argument rests on a key assumption, namely that the monitoring of public sector managers by politicians is weaker than the monitoring of private sector managers by shareholders. Politicians may indeed have other priorities besides monitoring state-owned enterprises, though some degree of monitoring will always be present, particularly if tackling perceived inefficiency either seems to be necessary for meeting budget targets or appears politically popular. However, the seemingly severe monitoring of managers in private enterprises may be deceptive. Effective monitoring by shareholders would necessitate 'efficient markets' in which information about performance is easily acquired. However acquiring information is costly and this alone can engender shareholder inertia. In such a case the managers may pursue matters not likely to be approved by shareholders. Nonetheless there does exist a potentially powerful check on private managers through the buying and selling of shares, particularly in cases where shareholders specialise in holding certain types of shares and hence are likely to react against any perceived poor decisions by managers. The prospect of profit is a powerful incentive to monitor and it is natural to expect some gains in efficiency as a result. One should guard, however, against simplistic expectations of inevitable substantial gains.

From this brief review of efficiency issues arising out of privatisation some of the complexities of comparing public and private enterprises emerge. It is not surprising therefore that empirical work on the relative performance of public and private enterprise is less than fully conclusive. Surveys of comparative studies can be found in Millward and Parker (1983), Levitt and Joyce (1987) and Vickers and Yarrow (1988, 1991). Millward and Parker found no systematic evidence that public enterprises are less cost effective than private enterprises. Levitt and Joyce found evidence of faster productivity growth among some public sector workers than among comparable private sector workers. In general, they found that among the organisations studied, the performance of government departments was not inferior to that of comparable private sector organisations. Vickers and Yarrow found that where enterprises had market power, neither public nor private enterprises had a clear edge in efficiency. Private firms tended to show an efficiency advantage in conditions of competition but this was not a consistent finding in all studies. The evidence, it seems, is as conclusive as that.

Productive and allocative efficiency: bureaucracy
The distinction between productive and allocative efficiency is again useful in understanding the analysis of bureaucracy. This analysis is based on the proposition that it is difficult for the legislature to control the permanent administrative machinery of the state. This echoes modern analyses of the private sector firm which stress the separation of ownership from control and the possibility of managers pursuing objectives other than those of the owners. The modern analysis of bureaucracy dissents from the idea that policy implementation follows on slavishly from policy formulation. Instead, those who implement policy are assumed to act out of self-interest and to possess considerable discretion. Bureaucrats, rather than being neutral, are seen as forming with politicians a bilateral monopoly.

What emerges from this conception of public sector resource allocation is that fabled economic potentate, the 'budget-maximising bureaucrat'. Niskanen (1971) saw the factors motivating bureaucratic behaviour as 'salary, perquisites of office, public reputation, power, patronage, output of the bureau, ease of making changes, and ease of managing the bureau.' He argued that all but the last two of these were positively related to the total budget and of the bureau and that accordingly each bureau would seek to maximise its budget.

It is easy to see elements of reality in this view. Certainly the superior information posssessed by bureaucrats could provide scope for the pursuit of self-interest. However, there are also defects in the Niskanen approach. Cromien (1986) pointed to the counter-vailing forces of internal departmental controls and concern for the national interest. It could be further argued that under some of the public sector management reforms, which we discuss in a later section, success in cutting costs would be, for some public servants, an indicator of achievement and an avenue for promotion.

The Niskanen model, though flawed, has clear implications for efficiency. A bureau which maximises its budget will produce more output than the public is willing to finance: the services provided are not what consumers prefer. The Niskanen model, therefore, points out a potential source of allocative inefficiency.

A related problem arises with instances of 'supplier-induced demand'. Examples can be drawn from either the public or the private sectors. In essence the argument is that professional 'agents', such as doctors, lawyers and financial consultants, often make decisions on behalf of their clients or 'principals'. This is, therefore, a variant of the principal–agent problem. If the professional provides more than the client needs then allocative inefficiency results. Brown and Jackson (1990, pp. 204-5) extend this type of reasoning to encompass the relationship between voters and politicians and argue that where the latter do not implement the preferences of the former there is allocative inefficiency.

The Niskanen critique of bureaucracy emphasises allocative inefficiency but there is also the possibility of productive inefficiency. Costs may rise above their minimum because in a non-profit-making organisation which cannot go bankrupt and in which salaries may be restricted, there may be little incentive to minimise cost. Indeed, as is the case in private enterprises, there may be difficulties in monitoring performance to ensure that costs are reduced to a feasible minimum.

Bureaucracy therefore is a potential source of productive and allocative inefficiency in the supply of public sector goods and services. But considerations of supply alone provide too narrow a perspective. Government (representing the public) provides the demand for public services and the analysis of the demand process is underdeveloped. Among the unanswered questions on the demand-side are whether local government will respond better than central government to the public, and whether voter pressure on politicians to tackle inefficiencies is a significant countervailing force to the inefficiencies arising on the supply-side. Furthermore, according to the foregoing Niskanen critique, it would appear that public sector budgets are too big. There is some support for this conclusion on the demand-side. For example, Buchanan and Tullock (1962) argued that politically active interest groups cause upward pressure on expenditures and that this is not counteracted by pressure from taxpayers who are less likely to form groupings. This view stands in opposition to Downs (1960) who argued that taxpayers keenly feel the impact of taxes but that the benefits of expenditures are widely spread and that accordingly budgets would be too small. Quantification in this area presents major difficulties, but where the Downs type argument prevails there will be pressures offsetting inefficiencies on the supply-side. Where the Buchanan and Tullock type argument prevails in conjunction with the Niskanen scenario, then budgets would seem to be on an upward trajectory that could be described as *expansio ad absurdum.*

Some reassurance that pressures for growth are more temperate is available by looking at the process of decision-making underyling budgets. This process tends to build fresh allocations on top of each previous year's budget outcome and is commonly known as 'incrementalism' (Wildavsky, 1964). Under this process each bureau applies for more than it expects to get; after negotiations to trim the excess, each bureau hopes to emerge with more than the previous year's allocation. Attempts to alter the process, so as to impose greater rationality of choice, have been unsuccessful. For example, zero-based budgeting which required fresh justification of each expenditure item each year, foundered for a variety of reasons including the difficulties of acquiring and processing information. The incrementalist process is certainly less demanding, and less expensive, in the use of available resources but is inefficient where an original misallocation of resources is carried forward annually. Jackson (1982, pp. 146-64) provides a detailed treatment of incrementalism not possible within the confines of this chapter. It will not further detain us except to add that re-evaluations of base-line expenditures at intervals longer than one year, ie a less ambitious type of zero-based budgeting, might help address inefficiency due to compounding original misallocations over time.

Market and state failure

Market failure

Competitive markets generate efficiency. Under perfect competition the pursuit of self-interest by profit-maximising producers will also promote the public interest by yielding an outcome in which no one person can be made better off without making someone else worse off – an outcome known as Pareto-optimal.[3] However, perfectly competitive markets presuppose a range of restrictive conditions, such as that there are a large number of buyers and sellers and that information is easily accessible. These conditions are not frequently encountered in the real world and hence efficient outcomes cannot always be attained by the free play of the market. Where markets fail to promote efficiency governments may intervene. We will briefly consider the most common forms of market failure in what follows.

Firstly, imperfect competition in markets leads to losses of efficiency. Monopoly, the extreme form of imperfect competition, is associated with higher prices and lower output than competitive markets. Monopoly is allocatively inefficient, as we have previously noted, because it entails production where the consumer's willingness to pay is not equal to the cost of an extra unit of output. Consumers willing to pay more than the cost of the extra unit of output are not supplied. Governments may intervene in such circumstances to prevent abuses of dominant position and to break down barriers that may exist against potential entrants to the market.

However, intervention to promote competition in a market may be inappropriate in certain circumstances. Perverse as it may seem, a monopoly may be the most efficient way of structuring some markets. Telephones, electricity, natural gas and water are examples of industries where there are cost advantages associated with large-scale operation. Such industries are known as natural monopolies. In a natural monopoly the advantages of producing on a large scale may allow a single firm to produce the total industry output at lower average cost than a number of competing firms. In such circumstances there may be a trade-off between the allocative inefficiency associated with monopolies and the scale economies generating lower costs. Several electricity grids or many competing networks of telephone cabling would be inefficient. In such cases the appropriate government intervention would be to regulate the conduct of the natural monopoly rather than to promote competition.

A second cause of market failure is the lack of full information. Information is costly and consumers may not be adequately knowledgeable to weigh up accurately the costs and benefits of their purchases. For example, consumers acquiring fuller knowledge about the costs and benefits of consuming convenience foods might reallocate their purchases in favour of fresh food. Similarly there may be less than full information in the markets for alcohol or cigarettes. Government may intervene to improve efficiency in such markets by issuing information about health and safety. In a similar vein governments may license certain professions and thereby inform consumers of the standards of service to expect. Alternatively government may prohibit the use of commodities such as food additives.

A third cause of market failure is the existence of transaction costs, in other words costs of using the market. For example, there are costs involved in identifying potential customers or suppliers, in time spent in negotiation, and in drawing up contracts. If these costs are too high then transactions might not take place and the market will fail.

A fourth cause of market failure arises in situations where the activities of some consumers or producers have an effect on others. These effects are called externalities and may be positive (eg where a person is treated for an infectious disease) or negative (eg where a producer pollutes the environment). Free markets will under-produce goods and services which confer positive externalities (because inadequate emphasis is laid on the social benefits) and overproduce goods and services which produce negative externalities (because inadequate emphasis is laid on the social costs). To correct these inefficiences governments may intervene by, for example, subsidising the commodities which confer positive externalities and taxing the commodities which produce negative externalities.

A fifth cause of market failure arises with goods and services such as street lighting and defence. Goods and services of this type have two properties, namely that one person's consumption does not deplete the amount available for others; and that it is impossible to exclude someone who does not pay from enjoying the benefits. Commodities possessing these properties are termed public goods. The free market will not provide public goods because consumers, knowing that they cannot be excluded from benefit, will opt to 'free-ride' rather than pay. Government intervention in this case will take the form of direct provision.

A sixth form of market failure may be termed 'missing markets'. For example, private markets may fail to provide many types of insurance. Two forces can work together to deter a market in insurance, namely that the people wishing to insure are those at greater risk (called adverse selection); and that people, once insured, may make less effort to avoid the feared threat (called moral hazard). Government may wish to intervene where some insurance markets are mising, for example by providing unemployment insurance against loss of income.

We have examined just some of the causes of market failure. Many other sources exist, including inefficient allocation of resources between the present and the future (eg because of distortions to investment caused by interest rates or because people fail to take proper account of the future); inefficiencies due to speculative litigation to win control of profit-making opportunities (such

17

unproductive activity – called rent seeking – causes delays in private enterprise decision-making and wastes resources); and inefficiencies due to the business fluctuations associated with the market.

In this brief survey of sources of market failure the emphasis has inevitably fallen on failures with implications for efficiency. The market may also fail to contribute to greater equity in a society and governments may intervene in markets in order to redistribute income. Our focus, however, is on efficiency and effectiveness and limitations of space preclude consideration of equity at this juncture.

State failure

The market has its advantages and disadvantages and so also does state intervention. We have already discussed a major source of state failure in our treatment of bureaucracy and its implications for allocative and productive efficiency.

Parallel to developments in the market, there is also rent seeking in the public sector domain. The latter form of rent seeking takes the form of lobbying to influence the nature of state intervention and, as in the market, it is associated with delays and wasteful resource use.

A further problem area – the unbalanced growth of costs in the service sector – is common to both the public and private sectors. Whereas improvements in technology have yielded significant gains in labour productivity in the manufacturing sector, there has not been an equivalent development in the service sector. Because of the direct personal contact involved in most services, a reduction in labour input will reduce the quality of output. The result is an imbalance between the services and manufacturing sectors with services becoming more expensive compared to manufactured goods. There is therefore a sort of relative inefficiency between services, both market and state, and manufacturing.

Other sources of state failure include: instability due to the political business cycle (whereby the economy may be stimulated prior to elections with adverse consequences thereafter), the difficulties faced by government in trying to combine individual tastes into a consistent ordering of social preferences,[4] and the inefficiencies due to errors in the design and implementation of state interventions. We have treated just some causes of state failure and have concentrated on those with implications for efficiency thereby neglecting issues such as the effects of government intervention on individual liberties. The important point to emerge from the discussion is that inefficiencies can arise in both the state sector and the market. The inefficiencies in one domain should not be considered in isolation.

Economy, efficiency and effectiveness: the '3 Es'
Thus far we have concentrated on efficiency; we now widen the discussion to include effectiveness and economy. In order to distinguish between the three concepts it is useful to think in terms of the familiar economic model of an enterprise based on inputs, throughputs (sometimes called intermediate outputs), outputs and effects (or outcomes). Economy is exclusively concerned with inputs, efficiency relates inputs to outputs and effectiveness relates outputs to effects, or desired outcomes. Each concept is more fully described in what follows and greater detail is provided by Haselbekke and Ros in Chapter 7 of this volume.

Economy is the purchase of inputs at the lowest cost. There is an improvement in economy if actual input is less than planned input. A shift to cheaper inputs, for example of staff, premises or energy will promote economy.

Efficiency can be viewed either as obtaining the maximum output from given inputs or as achieving the minimum level of inputs for a given level of output. This is a fuller concept than economy inasmuch as it relates inputs to outputs. Efficiency may, for example, be measured by utilisation rates such as the utilisation of hospital beds, or recreational facilities.

Effectiveness is the extent to which outputs achieve objectives or policy aims. The actual output may differ from the planned output or outcome. For example, if mortality rates are higher than expected or if examination pass rates are lower than planned, then certain health and education outputs may be said to be ineffective.[5]

This formulation of economy, efficiency and effectiveness covers familiar ground. Economy and efficiency are broadly equivalent to productive efficiency; effectiveness, and its corollary of the appropriate output-mix, is broadly equivalent to allocative efficiency. There is a change of terminology rather than of substance. In what follows it may help to think of economy and efficiency as indicators of productive efficiency and of effectiveness as an indicator of allocative efficiency. All three concepts – economy, efficiency and effectiveness – are commonly collectively termed value for money.[6]

Interest in value for money in the public sector is not new but it has acquired a new lease of life in recent years in line with attempts both to control public expenditure and to allocate this expenditure among ever increasing demands for services. Progress in achieving value for money has, however, been uneven. It is relatively straightforward to acquire information on economy and efficiency but measurement of effectiveness has proved elusive. Data on inputs and on the relation between inputs and outputs are internal to an organisation and hence readily available. By contrast, data on effectiveness is external to the organisation and accordingly difficult and expensive to acquire. Moreover, difficulties may arise if, in order to establish the effectiveness of a public service, consumers are consulted about their preferences: we have already noted the example that many people may not easily be able to formulate preferences about the level and quality of defence. Consumer preferences are, by contrast, much easier to establish in a market system.[7]

Fundamental problems in assessing effectiveness centre around the specification of objectives. It is notoriously difficult to specify the objectives of public sector organisations – objectives such as promoting the public interest are difficult to pin down. By contrast, in private sector enterprises objectives such as improving profitability seem unambiguously clear.

Even when, at first sight, the objectives of public sector organisations seem obvious there may be problems in store. We may think it obvious that the objective of hospitals is to improve health. Roberts (1990, p. 87), however, points out that there is no simple definition of health: health may be defined negatively as 'absence of disease' or positively as 'optimal physical, mental and social well-being'. Similarly, we might ask whether the objective of education is to prepare students for the jobs market, to improve students in a cultural and social sense, or to somehow combine the economic and cultural purposes.

If there are combined or multiple objectives then a question arises about the relative importance of each aim. Failure to establish this will confound attempts to gauge effectiveness. To some extent the problem of multiple objectives may be shared with private sector organisations but there the underlying pursuit of profit provides a benchmark of effectiveness.

One can easily conjure up other potential hazards posed by the specification of objectives in public sector organisations. It may be that some objectives conflict as in the case where a state-owned enterprise combines economic objectives with social objectives such as providing services to remote areas. Difficulties may also arise if objectives change over the period of time in which effectiveness is being assessed. Alternatively, it may be the case, if objectives are not clearly stated, that a sponsoring state department may have a different conception of objectives than a state agency which delivers a service. Indeed an underlying problem besetting the assessment of effectiveness is, as noted by Tomkins (1987, pp. 54-5), that there are several 'stakeholders' – such as managers, consumers and service professionals – with an interest in a service whose views may need to be consulted before policy-makers set strategic goals.

Looking beyond the specification of objectives, other important questions arise in dealing with effectiveness. Concentration on whether outputs meet objectives should not displace due attention to strategic questions such as whether the objectives are appropriate or worthy. Moreover, the problems do not just apply to the objectives side of the effectiveness ratio; there are also problems with outputs. It is not always easy to specify the output of public service. For example, part of the output of the police service is crime prevention. It is obviously difficult to quantify and assign a relative importance to this facet of police work compared to, say, crime detection.

There may even be difficulties in distinguishing outputs from effects. Roberts (1990, p. 88) makes the rather macabre observation that death may be both an 'output' and an outcome of hospitalisation. In a similar fashion one might ask if patient satisfaction is a throughout or an outcome of health care.

Effectiveness relates actual output to planned output or effects. However, there may be unplanned effects. Jackson (1988, p. 14) notes that the measurement of performance can change behaviour which yields unintended effects. For illustration, he notes that a police force whose success is judged by the number of arrests may have a high incidence of wrongful arrest; similarly schools whose success is judged by the number of high level grades attained may emphasise cramming by students rather than personal development.

The pursuit of economy and efficiency may also have unintended consequences. If, for instance, hospitals are required to be cost effective in terms of bed use, they may either release patients prematurely or perform certain types of surgery designed to speed up the rate of bed use. High rates of readmission or instances of patients succumbing to the risks of surgery would be unintended consequences of the pursuit of efficiency. This example also serves to illustrate possible conflicts between efficiency and effectiveness. Short-term efficiency gains, in terms of improved rates of bed use, which lead to long-term consequences of a high readmission rate is most probably not the effect intended by policy-makers.

Measurement and measurement problems
Output and performance measurement enable the monitoring of value for money in the public sector and therefore perform a roughly similar task to measures of profitability in the private sector. Economists have traditionally used variables such as productivity or unit costs as indicators of efficiency.[8] This tradition is carried on in the public sector by measurements such as the total factor productivity index which in mathematical form relates inputs such

as wages, rents and capital costs to outputs such as planning applictions processed and library loans (Daffern and Walshe, 1990, pp. 146-51).

For reasons already given in the previous section, measurements of economy and efficiency are more advanced than measurements of effectiveness. There has, however, been some progress in analysing effectiveness, with the development of measures of some outcomes or of proxies for outcomes. In education, for instance, there are measures of income differentials enjoyed by graduates as well as monitoring of their employment record, and in health there are measures such as immunisation take-up rates. In policing, the final objective might be to reduce burglaries but a measurable intermediate objective might be to sensitise the public to the risk and to persuade them to use more alarms and locks.

Returning to considerations of efficiency, a similar use of proxy may be appropriate if there are difficulties in measuring outputs. In such cases intermediate outputs, such as the grades achieved by students or the number of patients seen by doctors, might be used. However, the use of intermediate outputs or objectives is a less than fully satisfactory substitute for final outputs and objectives.

Public sector output has been measured over a long period in national accounts. Beeton (1988) provides a brief summary of developments in measurements of public sector output. Of particular interest is the convention adopted in the national accounts to value public services by the cost of the input (predominantly wages and salaries). This convention can be justified on the basis that there are difficulties in pricing public sector output where it does not pass through the market. This convention is, however, an abstraction from reality. If the value of a service is identical to the value of the manpower employed in its delivery, then any improvement in the productivity of that manpower will not be reflected in the value of output. In other words, there is an implicit assumption of zero productivity growth and hence any improvements in productivity, such as those associated with management reforms in the public sector, will not register in the national accounts. Oddly, measured output will increase if a public servant gets promoted onto a higher pay scale and then works less hard. This assumption of zero productivity growth also has the unfortunate effect of distorting comparisons between the public and private sectors. Productivity increases in the private sector will reduce unit costs but similar increases in the public sector would leave unit costs unchanged. This distortion is sometimes referred to as 'the relative price effect'.

In the remainder of this section we will move on to consider some of the difficulties encountered with output measurement, performance measurement (ie precise measures of performance), and performance indicators (ie less precise or indicative measures of performance). A knowledge of these difficulties is important inasmuch as it helps prevent falling into traps in measurement.

Double counting is a common problem encountered in economic measurement. In education, for example, research income might be seen as an indicator of performance because such income implicitly attests to a good research record. If research income is also seen as an indicator of input then there will be double counting with the same income registering twice as a positive indicator (see Cave and Hanney, 1990, p. 71).

A further pitfall to be aware of in economic measurement is the assumption that in the absence of a policy intervention there would be no improvement. To avoid this pitfall analysts ask what would most likely have happened without the policy intervention. In the case of an industrial grant the analyst would attempt to anticipate what development would otherwise occur. A 'with–without' test of this nature will give an estimate of the net benefit of the grant. Similarly in assessing the benefits of industrial training we might ask what level of skills might be acquired by other means in the absence of an industrial training service.

A recurrent difficulty which arises in the literature on output and performance measurement is that of allowing for changes in quality. If the interval at which refuse is collected were to be extended, with the consequence that the same volume of refuse was collected but less regularly, then the output measurement for the service might not change but the quality of the service would deteriorate. Sometimes output and performance measures are adjusted by a quality factor, such as class-size in the case of education, but such adjustments are inevitably imprecise. Apart from quality there may be other immeasureables. It would be difficult to measure an intangible output like disease prevention. How could one measure the output or performance of a public art gallery or museum? A proxy such as number of visits or charge per visit is a poor indicator.

Another family of problems arises out of the probability that the existence of output and performance measures may change the behaviour of those being assessed. There may be an understandable inclination to skew effort towards those activities being measured. If, for example, a university department is being judged by the amount of published research produced or the number of citations of work published by staff, then a possible reaction could be that research work would displace preparation for, and number of, lectures. Alternatively, staff may be tempted to publish incomplete or trivial work or may engage in excessive self-citation of their

23

previous work. Moreover, a large volume of published work or a high rate of citation is not *ipso facto* an infallible indicator of the value of the research (Cave and Hanney, 1990, pp. 60-1). Other forms of 'gaming' may include the performance of the more easily achieved tasks at first, perhaps in the hope of moving elsewhere before the harder tasks become inevitable. Yet another form of gaming is illustrated by Jackson (1987, pp. 14-15) who notes that, in the absence of proper scrutiny, measured results such as reductions in maintenance costs per square metre might be achieved by deferring spending into the future. This may lead to the unintended consequence of a more pronounced deterioration of the capital stock.

Among the other unintended consequences of measuring output and performance may be to encourage short-term thinking in an effort to satisfy measures taken on an annual basis. This in turn may, for instance, lead to a reduction in initiative or innovation. Yet a further unintended consequence would be if the existence of measures led both assessors and assessed to assign lower priority to the less easily measured activities. Alternatively, the existence of measures might lead to a defensive attitude among those assessed resulting in wasteful efforts to sabotage the measures. The reactions of employees and service professionals has, therefore, significant implications for the process of management.

Another set of problems arises out of the need to disaggregate. If there are a number of people working together on a project it may be difficult to disaggregate the efforts and productivity of individuals. If, for example, there is joint research it may be that one person had a disproportionately large input. Other problems of the same nature arise if there is joint output such as crime prevention and crime detection; or where there are joint objectives such as, in education, to promote personal development, to provide cultural enrichment and to prepare students for the job market.

A final set of difficulties centres around the need to compare like with like. Clearly if output and performance measures are to be used to compare organisations at a given point in time or to compare a given organisation over a period of time, then it is necessary to compare organisations of the same scale, producing similar outputs in similar areas. It is also important to allow for the possible influence of other factors. In assessing health care, for example, life expectancy may increase for a particular age-group over a period of time but the improvement may in part be due to factors external to health care such as improvements in public sanitation and public housing, or improvements in food and in attitudes towards exercise.[9]

In the light of these difficulties and the problems with assessing effectiveness dealt with in the previous section, it is not surprising to learn that continual efforts are being made to improve measurement of value for money. Barrow and Wagstaff (1989, p. 78) argue that performance indicators are 'singularly inadequate' in gauging inefficiency. They criticise not only the weakness of performance indicators in dealing with outcomes but also the *ad hoc* nature of indicators chosen with little basis in economic rationale. They demonstrate the potential of efficiency measurement using statistical and quantitative techniques. Measurement of inefficiency based on economic theory, which clearly specifies the type of efficiency being analysed, would appear to have decided advantages over the more 'scattergun' approach associated with performance indicators.

The most developed and soundly based economic evaluation of efficiency is to be found in investment appraisal. Techniques such as cost benefit analysis are employed in investment appraisal to assess the efficiency of alternative projects and policies. The rational weighing up of costs against expected benefits is an important aspect of the process of public and private management. A detailed treatment of public investment appraisal is provided by Blackwell in Chapter 6 of this volume. Even allowing for the sophistication of investment appraisal techniques, there is still a need for careful design of evaluations in order to avoid common pitfalls and to make effective choices. In the case of industrial grants, for example, it is proper to ask questions such as whether a project would proceed anyhow even in the absence of grant aid, whether a project is likely to fail prematurely, and whether a grant-aided project contributes to national output and national efficiency. Addressing this type of question raises evaluation above the mechanical application of techniques.

Management reforms in the public sector
Public sector management reforms have gathered pace over the past decade and the pursuit of value for money has been central to these reforms. Notable developments have occurred across OECD countries in the fields of information, incentives, devolution of responsibility, and accountability (Oxley *et al.,* 1990). There have been improvements in the costing of activities and in the dissemination of information to management. Efficiency incentives, such as performance related pay and promotion, have developed, though not dramatically. Devolution of responsibility for budgets to spending departments and agencies has relieved central budget departments of detailed control and freed them to set targets and to order priorities. Spending departments have acquired greater

control over the allocating and timing of expenditure. Accompanying the devolution of responsibility has been the heightened emphasis on managerial accountability which in turn has spawned independent audits and efficiency review units. Value for money audits requiring assessment of economy, efficiency and effectiveness have taken root alongside the more traditional audit which emphasised the accuracy of financial statements and compliance with legal requirements. Public servants are seen not just as administrators but increasingly as managers of resources.

The experience of management reform in the UK public sector illustrates many of the foregoing developments. There, despite some disappointments with attempted management reforms in the early 1970s, a number of new departures took hold in the 1980s. Firstly, efficiency scrutinies (sometimes called Rayner scrutinies after the head of the Efficiency Unit) were established to identify cost reductions. The scrutinies were conducted within three month periods and focused on particular programmes and areas.[10] Secondly, the Financial Management Initiative in 1982 decentralised budgets to spending departments. It required departments to develop management systems containing clear objectives and the means of measuring the attainment of these objectives. Emphasis was also placed on the specification of responsibilities for efficient resource use, and on information and expert advice to assist in exercising the responsibilities.[11] Thirdly, value for money auditing was instituted and as part of this process, performance indicators were introduced. Fourthly, the Next Steps project was launched in 1988 with the intention of separating the policy advice functions of government departments from the service delivery functions. By the end of the 1990s the majority of UK civil servants may be working for semi-autonomous executive agencies responsible for service delivery. The underlying objective of the project is to improve management and produce gains in efficiency and effectiveness along with better service to the general public. A detailed description of the Next Steps project is provided by the project manager Peter Kemp in Chapter 8 of this volume. Fifthly, there have been attempts to introduce market forces by methods like compulsory contracting-out of services such as refuse collection.

The efforts to introduce market forces underscore an important point, namely that competition has a prominent role in engendering efficiency. Contracting-out is just one of a number of attempts to promote the ways of the market in the public sector. For example, market disciplines are represented by the increasing resort to user charges in various OECD countries and by the movement in the UK to enable health authorities to buy health care from a number of competing providers.

In commenting on the range of reforms just outlined, it is appropriate to recall that improvements are more likely to result in gains in productive efficiency than in allocative efficiency. It is easier to specify and pursue improvements in economy and efficiency than in effectiveness.

It is important also to take serious account of the culture of the public service. Crude and insensitive implementation of economic mechanisms or cost accounting techniques can evoke defensive reactions. We have already noted some of the problems associated with reactions by service professionals to performance measurement. If management reforms are perceived as mere devices for cost cutting there may be resistance. Moreover, there may be difficulties in the relationship between central and decentralised control. Previous initiatives such as Planning-Programming-Budgeting Systems (PPBS, of which more below) and Zero Based Budgeting (ZBB) encountered difficulties with internal organisation 'politics' and interdepartmental 'politics' (Tomkins, 1987, p. 16).

Allowance must also be made for the diversity of the public sector. The service delivered by the police force is quite different from the more administrative type service provided by a social welfare department. Some departments have closer relations than others with their clients: the relationship between a Department of Agriculture and farmers is unlikely to be the same as the relationship between tax authorities and taxpayers. These diversities in type and complexity of service, and in relationships, may have implications for economy, efficiency and effectiveness and consequently for the choice of method to promote value for money.

Transplanting private sector management practices and market processes to the public sector requires long-term commitment and perhaps political will. In the absence of either or both, the transplant might be rejected. Alternatively, subtle and adverse dynamics may arise in the process. If private sector methods are applied without, as some might see it, commensurate private sector rewards then there may be a loss of able public sector staff to the private sector.

In general the management reforms are positive. Performance measurement enables the identification of good and poor performances and helps indicate operational improvements. Devolved spending authority, improved incentives, better information, greater accountability and the use of cheaper private sector suppliers will all contribute to economy, efficiency and effectiveness.

Management reforms in the Irish public sector

As elsewhere, management reform in the Irish public sector is not novel. The Devlin Report (1969) contemplated devolution in the form of separation of policy from executive activity and looked beyond traditional audit to effectiveness audit of programmes. The White Paper *Serving the Country Better* (1985) emphasised the importance of clear objectives and performance monitoring. It advocated some decentralised management controls to government departments and noted that a major purpose of the proposed changes was concern for value for money.

Over the past twenty years there have been a number of developments in pursuit of economy, efficiency and effectiveness. In the early 1970s Ireland in common with many other countries experimented with Planning-Programming-Budgeting Systems (PPBS). These systems attempt to establish objectives for major operational areas, to identify alternative methods for achieving the objectives and to choose the most efficient and effective method. The Department of Finance established a section to promote and develop PPBS throughout the civil service and designed programme structures, objectives, outputs and plans for most government departments. However, PPBS makes considerable demands in terms of the acquisition and processing of data and, furthermore, these systems require time in order to become accepted. In common with the experience in other countries, PPBS faltered in Ireland and was abandoned in 1977.

In 1982 the government published the discussion paper *A Better Way to Plan the Nation's Finances*. It made a number of proposals for the reform of financial procedures: one such proposal was that estimates for public expenditure be presented in programme format. Commencing in 1983, the government has published *Comprehensive Public Expenditure Programmes* on an annual basis. This publication gives an outline of programmes, their objectives, their main components and the associated public expenditure. Information on costs and outputs in this format is an important input to the evaluation of economy, efficiency and, to a lesser extent, effectiveness.

In 1983 the Department of Finance issued circular 1/83 (subsequently restated in the 1984 Public Capital Programme) which laid down procedures for the evaluation of investment in public projects. The circular required that appraisals of public investment in a project contain clearly-defined objectives, a statement of alternative methods of meeting the objectives, an identification of constraints affecting the project, a listing and quantification of benefits and costs associated with the project, and a recommendation about the preferred alternative. These requirements provided, for the first time, a systematic basis for planning and implementing public projects. Blackwell in Chapter 6 of this volume provides more detailed comment on both the requirements for public investment appraisal and the programmatic approach to public expenditure.

In 1984 the Department of Finance issued 'Guidelines for Financial Management' to all government departments. In essence the guidelines attempted to fix responsibility for costs and budgets at the lowest possible management level. The guidelines to a large extent echoed the Financial Management Initiative in the UK in emphasising clarity of objectives, the specification of responsibility, the need for greater financial control, the importance of improved information systems and so forth. The guidelines are important for their formal recognition of the need for improved financial planning and control systems and were largely restated in the 1990 government publication *Public Financial Procedures: An Outline* (Department of Finance, 1990). The latter document also emphasised the importance of output and performance measures in monitoring the achievement of results. It further emphasised the need for each government department to develop its own procedures for measuring results against targets, thereby enhancing efficiency and effectiveness.

In 1988 the government established an Efficiency Audit Group to enquire into methods to reduce costs and improve efficiency. Alongside all the foregoing attempts at management reform to improve efficiency and effectiveness, there has been increased recourse by government to competitive market forces in the form of contracting-out and privatisation of selected state enterprises.

Recently there has been a significant new departure in Irish public sector management with the introduction of a system of administrative budgets on the recommendation of the Efficiency Audit Group. Here we concentrate on the broad outline of the system: a fuller account is provided by Moore (1991). The administrative budget system, announced in 1989, is to be extended to all government departments. It is based on the familiar rationale that value for money improvements will result from delegation of responsibility for resource allocation and from greater accountability for results.

Administrative budgets cover pay, costs of premises, information technology, training and such like. These are quite separate from programme budgets covering industrial grants, social welfare benefits and so forth. The new arrangement operates within an agreed three-year budget framework and accordingly allows some extension of usual departmental planning horizons. Departments are, however, expected to achieve real reductions of 2 per cent annually over the three-year period. Within these constraints, departments are allowed greater freedom of decision over some elements of staffing and over the switching of funds between activities (eg between training and information technology). Departments are also allowed to carry forward funds not used in one year into the following year. Under the administrative budget system value for money benefits are expected as public service managers are put in the front line of resource allocation with heightened cost consciousness and with greater freedom to adjust resource inputs to achieve results. There may also be gains to the Department of Finance as it becomes freer to evaluate progress and to concentrate more on strategic matters.

A further notable development has been signalled in proposals for value for money in the higher education system. There have been proposals, in line with developments in the UK, to establish in universities cost centres (such as arts, medicine, engineering and so forth) with separate budgets and also to allow greater discretion in the use of funds. There has also been consideration of performance indicators such as student intake, course completion rates, staff student ratios, percentage of honours degrees, research work and so forth.

In many ways therefore developments in Ireland have paralleled developments in other OECD countries though, in general, progress has tended to be more slow and there exist some gaps (such as the lack of comparative data on local government performance from which 'best practice' can be identified and promoted). The advantages and disadvantages associated both with performance measurement and management reform that have been previously discussed must also be borne in mind in the Irish case.

Equity — 'the fourth E'
The scope of this chapter does not extend to encompass a detailed coverage of equity but some comment is possible.

Where economists confine themselves to analysing changes which make at least one person better off without making anyone else worse off, they are attempting to exclude from analysis any subjective comparison which would arise if one person's gain was contrasted to another's loss. Economists must however enter the area of interpersonal comparison when dealing with many economic policies but in so doing must relinquish somewhat the comfort of objectivity.

Efficiency is not an exclusive criterion to be applied in policy formation: considerations of income distribution are also important. Policies which improve efficiency may increase inequalities in income distribution. Conversely, attempts to increase equity, for example by progressive taxes and redistribution by social welfare transfers, may detract from efficiency if those who pay taxes reduce work effort or investment and if the level of social welfare transfers deters some from seeking work.

There is often a trade-off between efficiency and considerations of equity and equality (see Okun, 1975). At the level of the enterprise this may be manifested in multiple objectives, for example, where a state agency is expected to pursue commercial objectives including efficient operation as well as non-commercial objectives such as widespread or low-price provision of services. Political decision-making on the role of public enterprises in economic and social development may have significant implications for efficiency. Also in the political domain, Flynn *et al.* (1988, p. 40) note that account must be taken of yet another 'E', namely electability, and that considerations of efficiency may have to pass the 'electability indicators' test.

The concern for equity is one of the factors which differentiates the public from the private sector. It is also one of the reasons why private sector management techniques may not automatically transfer to all areas of the public sector.

Macroeconomic efficiency

Thus far we have adopted a microeconomic view of efficiency. Efficiency is also of central importance to the national economy. Adopting a 'bottom-up' perspective, we can note that efficient and effective government interventions, such as industrial policies, will increase GNP. Alternatively, government interventions which promote equity at the expense of efficiency may reduce GNP. We have already seen that the national accounts convention, whereby productivity increases in public services are not counted, will leave measured GNP the same despite public sector productivity gains.

There is also a 'top-down' perspective inasmuch as budgetary constraints in the macroeconomy lead to budget cuts and enforced economies in the public sector. Indeed short-term efficiencies will result from such cuts but longer term improvements are probably best based on delegated responsibility and increased accountability as discussed earlier in this chapter.

Looking at efficiency at the macroeconomic level also brings out some important interactions between the public and private sectors. To the extent that resources are wastefully used in the public sector there is a 'crowding out' of resources from the private sector (assuming that the resources would not be wastefully employed there). 'Crowding out' takes many other forms such as where high taxes reduce work effort and investment in the private sector. Alternatively, where high levels of exchequer borrowing reduce national savings and thereby cause upward pressure on interest rates there may be a 'crowding out' effect on the private sector. To preserve some sort of balance we must also allow for the possibility that efficient public services, such as industrial and agricultural advice or improved transportation infrastructure, may have a 'helping out' effect on the private sector.

Macroeconomic efficiency is particularly important to a small open economy like Ireland. The reduction of economic frontiers in the single European market brings the matters of economic efficiency and national competitiveness more and more into centre stage. More detailed comment on developments and challenges in the Irish macroeconomy are provided by McAleese in Chapter 10 of this volume.

Conclusion

This chapter has distinguished between different types of efficiency, examined major aspects of performance measurement and highlighted some major developments in the reform of public sector management designed to promote value for money. We have also examined some aspects of equity, of macroeconomic efficiency and of market and state failure.

Gothic excursions into the precise meaning of efficiency or the design problems of performance measures are of little use in their own right. It is important to understand these matters in order to assess where progress has been made and where it remains to be made. We have repeatedly seen that allocative efficiency, or considerations of effectiveness, have been virtual orphans in the movement towards value for money. The 'evaluative state' is likely to remain a major economic and political preoccupation but adequate weighting of allocative efficiency is necessary in future developments. Furthermore, existing public sector reforms have achieved relatively modest improvements in efficiency (Oxley *et al.,* p. 21). The design of public service reforms may have an important bearing on future improvements.

This chapter has also emphasised that public sector management reforms such as decentralised budgets, performance measurement and value for money auditing, run just part of the efficiency and effectiveness gamut. Competition, whether in the form of contracting-out or increased choice of public services, is also important.

We have also noted that matters of operational efficiency should not detract from strategic thinking. Economic integration in Europe, increasing environmental consciousness, the ageing of populations in developed countries, along with many other developments, place burdens of adjustment on both public and private sectors. Increased public sector efficiency is a necessary part of the adjustment process but is not in itself sufficient.

Notes

[1] There are nuances of difference between some of these terms. Technical efficiency relates input combinations to output. There may be a number of technically efficient combinations which lead to maximum output. Full productive efficiency will require choosing from a number of technically efficient combinations that which involves least cost.

[2] The strict condition for allocative efficiency is that price equals marginal cost. Price indicates the value to the consumer of the last unit consumed and marginal cost indicates the value that inputs to the extra unit would have in their best alternative use. Therefore (using 'A' and 'B' as designations of alternative uses) if the price of good 'A' is (i) greater than or (ii) less than the marginal cost of good 'A' then resources should be either (i) moved from good 'B' into good 'A' or (ii) moved from good 'A' to good 'B'. Under conditions of perfect competition price is equal to marginal cost and allocative efficiency is ensured.

[3] Pareto efficiency is found under conditions of perfect competition. In perfectly competitive equilibrium there is: (a) efficient allocation of resources among firms, ie efficiency in production; (b) efficient distribution of goods between consumers, ie efficiency in exchange; and (c) joint efficiency in production and exchange.

Where this beneficial trinity exists it is impossible to make any one person better off without making at least one other person worse off. This is so because the rate at which a person is *willing* to substitute one good for another is equal to the rate at which the person is *able* to substitute that good for another. A rigorous treatment of Pareto-optimality can be found in almost any introductory or intermediate economics textbook (eg Begg *et al.,* 1991; Koutsoyiannis, 1979; Stiglitz, 1988).

[4] This is more formally known as Arrow's impossibility theorem. Arrow showed that it was impossible to draw up a consistent 'welfare function' for society on the basis of combining individual preferences.

[5] Definitions of economy, efficiency and effectiveness can be more firmly established by looking at a more formal presentation of value for money (see Daffern and Walshe, 1990, p. 144).

Value for money =

$$\frac{\text{Actual Input}}{\text{Value of Input}} \times \frac{\text{Planned Input}}{\text{Actual Input}}$$
$$(1) \qquad (2)$$
$$\times \frac{\text{Planned Output}}{\text{Planned Input}} \times \frac{\text{Actual Output}}{\text{Planned Output}}$$
$$(3) \qquad (4)$$
$$\times \frac{\text{Value of Output}}{\text{Actual Output}}$$
$$(5)$$

Economy is represented by (2) Planned Input/Actual Input.

Effectiveness is represented by (4) Actual Output/Planned Output.

Planned Efficiency is represented by (3) Planned Output/Planned Input.

6 Two further concepts, namely service level and take-up, are sometimes encountered. Service level relates resources to the target population, for example by relating the number of leisure facilities to the population in a catchment area. The take-up of services relates the target population to outputs, for example by estimating the proportion of the population in a catchment area who use a leisure facility.

7 In establishing consumer preferences in the public sector it is necessary to bear in mind that direct consumers of public services are not synonymous with the taxpayers who fund the services. There is therefore an important question to address: are there different types of 'consumer' of public services? Another problem will arise where surveys are used to establish consumer preferences if such surveys are seen as a form of complaints procedure.

8 Productivity is not the same thing as efficiency. Productivity will take the form of a ratio such as the annual output per person employed. This differs from productive efficiency which imposes a condition, such as that for a given output the least cost combination of inputs be used. It is also worthy of note that high productivity is not synonymous with profitability. A firm with high levels of productivity may be unprofitable if consumers are unwilling to buy the product. Productivity and profitability, though not the same thing, are related and can both be used along with unit costs as indicators of efficiency.

9 A further difficulty arises if the information provided by performance indicators is wrongly used in allocating resources. Cave and Hanney (1990, p. 78) note that there may be a misallocation of resources if data on average returns are used in allocating marginal resources.

10 The efficiency scrutinies associated with Lord Derek Rayner and his successor Sir Robin Ibbs are sometimes criticised for their almost insignificant impact (less than 0.5 per cent) in reducing public expenditure. This criticism is somewhat harsh: the savings should also be related to the running costs of central government (which was approximately 15 per cent of public expenditure in 1983-84) and there were unquantifiable effects such as the impact on organisational 'culture' and the unearthing of new talent in the civil service. The impact of the efficiency scrutinies is better described as modest than as insignificant.

11 Sir Roy Griffiths in his 1983 Review of the UK National Health Service advocated a changed management system and echoed many of the features of the Financial Management Initiative such as improved delegation and increased accountability.

References

A Better Way to Plan the Nation's Finances, Dublin: Stationery Office, 1982.

Barrow, M., and Wagstaff, A., 'Efficiency Measurement in the Public Sector: An Appraisal', *Fiscal Studies,* Vol. 10, No. 1, 1989, pp. 72-97.

Beeton, D., 'Performance Measurement: the State of the Art', *Public Money and Management,* 1988, pp. 99-103.

Begg, D., Fischer S., and Dornbusch, R., *Economics,* Third Edition, Maidenhead: McGraw Hill, 1991.

Brown, C.V., and Jackson, P.M., *Public Sector Economics,* Fourth Edition, Oxford: Basil Blackwell, 1990.

Buchanan, J.M., and Tullock, G., *The Calculus of Consent,* Ann Arbour: University of Michigan Press, 1962.

Cave, M., and Hanney, S., 'Performance Indicators for Higher Education and Research', in M. Cave, M. Kogan and R. Smith (eds.), *Output and Performance Measurement in Government: The State of the Art,* London: Jessica Kingsley, 1990, pp. 60-85.

Commission of the European Communities, *Research on 'The Cost of Non-Europe' Project,* Luxembourg: Office for Official Publications of the EC, 1988.

Cromien, S., 'Comment', in J. Bristow and D. McDonagh (eds.), *Public Expenditure: the Key Issues,* Dublin: Institute of Public Administration, 1986.

Daffern, P., and Walshe, G., 'Evaluating Performance in the Department of·the Environment', in M. Cave, M. Kogan and R. Smith (eds.), *Output and Performance Measurement in Government: The State of the Art,* London: Jessica Kingsley, 1990, pp. 143-64.

Department of Finance, *Public Financial Procedures: An Outline,* Dublin: Stationery Office, 1990.

(Devlin) *Report of the Public Services Organisation Review Group* (Chairman: L. St. J. Devlin), Dublin: Stationery Office, 1969.

Downs, A., 'Why the Government Budget is too Small in a Democracy', *World Politics,* Vol. 12, 1960, pp. 541-63.

Flynn, A., Gray, A., Jenkins, W., and Rutherford, B., 'Making Indicators Perform', *Public Money and Management,* 1988, pp. 35-41.

Jackson, P.M., 'Performance Measurement and Value for Money in the Public Sector: The Issues', in *Performance Measurement in the Public and Private Sectors,* London/Edinburgh: ICAS/CIPFA, 1987, pp. 9-17.

Jackson, P.M., 'The Management of Performance in the Public Sector', *Public Money and Management,* 1988, pp. 11-16.

Jackson, P.M., *The Political Economy of Bureaucracy,* Oxford: Philip Allan, 1982.

Koutsoyiannis, A., *Modern Microeconomics,* Second Edition, London: Macmillan, 1979.

Levitt, M.S., and Joyce, M.A.S., *The Growth and Efficiency of Public Spending,* Cambridge: Cambridge University Press, 1987.

Millward, R., and Parker, D.M., 'Public and Private Enterprises:

Comparative Behaviour and Relative Efficiency', in R. Millward, D. Parker, L. Rosenthal, M.T. Summer and N. Topham, *Public Sector Economics,* Harlow: Longman, 1983, pp. 199-274.

Moore, P.J., 'Administrative Budgets — A New Era for Civil Service Managers', *Seirbhis Phoibli,* Vol. 12, No. 1, 1991, pp. 24-28.

Niskanen, W.A., *Bureaucracy and Representative Government,* Chicago: Aldine-Atherton, 1971.

Okun, A., *Equality and Efficiency: The Big Tradeoff,* Washington: Brookings, 1975.

Oxley, H., Maher, M., Martin, J.P., Nicoletti, G., and Alonso-Gamo, P., *The Public Sector: Issues for the 1990s,* Working Paper No. 90, Paris: OECD, 1990.

Roberts, H., 'Performance and Outcome Measures in the Health Service', in M. Cave, M. Kogan and R. Smith (eds.), *Output and Performance Measurement in Government: The State of the Art,* London: Jessica Kingsley, 1990, pp. 86-105.

Serving the Country Better: A White Paper on the Public Service, Dublin: Stationery Office, 1985.

Stiglitz, J.E., *Economics of the Public Sector,* Second Edition, New York: Norton, 1988.

Tomkins, C.R., *Achieving Economy, Efficiency and Effectiveness in the Public Sector,* Edinburgh: ICAS, 1987.

Vickers, J., and Yarrow, G., *Privatisation: An Economic Analysis,* London: MIT, 1988.

Vickers, J., and Yarrow, G., 'Economic Perspectives on Privatisation', *The Journal of Economic Perspectives,* Vol. 5, No. 2, 1991, pp. 111-32.

Wildavsky, A., *The Politics of the Budgetary Process,* Boston: Little, Brown, 1964.

2

The Economic Role of the State: Efficiency and Effectiveness[1]

JOSEPH E. STIGLITZ

Introduction: the re-examination of the role of government

THE 1980s have seen a marked retrenchment of government, both in the mixed economies of the developed world, with the privatisation and deregulation movements, and in the former socialist economies of Eastern Europe. Two events provide important hallmarks of this changed attitude. The first was in France. There the socialist Mitterrand government not only renounced its nationalisation programme, but also reprivatised several industries which it had nationalised only a few years before. The second was the commitment of the Soviet government to a private market economy on 23 September, 1990. In both instances, avowed socialists abandoned the socialist platform. Socialism as a doctrine seems dead.

The former socialist economies have been forced to re-examine the economic role of the state. Within the established democracies, this is an on-going process. The privatisation and deregulation movements to which I referred earlier are but the most recent manifestation of this process.

The political process responds to perceived successes and failures (or perhaps more accurately, disappointments) in both market and government solutions to society's basic problems. Academics on the other hand attempt to extract from these experiences general lessons and principles, which may enable not only a better assessment of the appropriate role of the state, but equally importantly, the design of public programmes and processes in ways which enhance the efficiency of the government.

Is government less efficient?

There is a widespread view (at least in the United States) that government and governmental agencies are inefficient. While several studies have lent some support to that view,[2] the finding is not universal.[3] One study comparing Canadian National Railroad (a public enterprise) and Canadian Pacific Railroad (a private enterprise) found no significant differences.[4] Many public enterprises in France (such as the Electricité de France) have a reputation for efficiency and effectiveness. British Petroleum, in which the British government has had a majority interest, has an enviable reputation for efficiency – far better, for instance, than a purely private firm such as Texaco.

While the US Postal Service has been unsuccessful in its competition with United Parcel, for the delivery of parcels, and Federal Express, in overnight mail service, it has had an enviable record of increases in productivity during the past decade.[5]

In an earlier day, the belief that governments were inefficient was augmented by the theoretical argument: they should be more inefficient, because of the absence of a profit motive. But this theoretical basis for the distinction between public and private enterprises has been questioned in research during the past fifteen years, emphasising that workers and managers in firms have little if any stake in the profits of the firm. (Why should workers be motivated by profits that they do not receive?)[6]

Herbert Simon, who received his Nobel Prize for his important contributions to understanding how organisations behave, recently put the matter this way:

> Most producers are employees, not owners of firms ... Viewed from the vantage point of classical [economic] theory, they have no reason to maximise the profits of the firms, except to the extent that they can be controlled by owners ... Moreover, there is no difference, in this respect, among profit-making firms, non-profit organisations, and bureaucratic organisations. All have exactly the same problem of inducing their employees to work toward the organisational goals. There is no reason, *a priori*, why it should be easier (or harder) to produce this motivation in organisations aimed at maximising profits than in organisations with different goals. *The conclusion that organisations motivated by profits will be more efficient than other organisations does not follow in an organisational economy from the neo-classical assumptions. If it is empirically true, other axioms will have to be introduced to account for it* (emphasis added).[7]

One of the reasons why it is difficult to find convincing empirical evidence[8] concerning the relative inefficiency of government is that, by and large, the public sector produces different goods and is engaged in different economic activities than the private. While detailed studies of those few instances where direct comparisons might be relevant – such as garbage collection – are of some interest, they do not provide direct evidence about the relative efficiency of government in the kinds of services in which it is primarily engaged. In most of these services, output measures are notoriously difficult to come by. This is not only true of the administrative activities which occupy many government bureaucrats, but also of education, and even defence.

Private sector performance in administrative areas too is often criticised for inefficiency: try getting a refund from an airline or collecting money for lost luggage. The Internal Revenue Service processes claims faster than United Airlines!

There are theoretical reasons why we might not be surprised at the seemingly widespread inefficiency in both the public and private sectors in administrative work. Standard economic theory has emphasised the importance of incentives. If individuals are to take actions which maximise a firm's profits (or pursue whatever other objectives the organisation wishes), they must be rewarded on the basis of their contribution to those profits. While this may be impossible to measure precisely, in many industries, surrogates may be found – the number of widgets that the individual paints or inspects. But when the organisation's output is ill-defined, how can we assess the individual's contribution to that ill-defined output? This is no less true of private than of public organisations.

Among the more important administrative functions in both the private and public sectors are those which I shall simply refer to as *management* – selecting the members of the organisation, organising them in productive ways, assigning them to tasks based on comparative advantage, motivating them to do well (whether by incentive structures or other means), etc. As we noted earlier, the fraction of a firm's incremental output captured by management, that is, the strength of managerial incentives, is quite weak. While there is a wide range in these estimates, the consensus is that at most, managers get but a few per cent of the returns from their efforts.

The take-over frenzy in the United States in the late 1980s provided a unique opportunity to observe managerial behaviour and to assess the extent to which it acted in the interests of shareholders. These experiences have reinforced the long-standing institutional view of the 'managerial firm', first depicted by Berle and Means in their classic study (1933): managers have considerable autonomy to pursue – and do pursue – their own interests, even when those interests are in conflict with shareholders' interests. Managers took actions to entrench their position, to enhance their 'bargaining' power. Take-overs were directed not at firms that were the least competently managed, but in some respects those which were more competently managed – that is, where managers had taken less effective measures, had diverted less of the firm's resources to entrenching themselves. 'Golden parachutes' and 'poison pills' were among the well developed instruments. Who needs a civil service to protect your job, when you can design a golden parachute, giving – as in the case of the RJR take-over – top management $100 million in severance pay![9]

But the problems of managerial efficiency go deeper. So far, we have established that managers in the private sector (just as in the public) have inadequate or inappropriate incentives; and that given the difficulties of measuring any particular manager's contribution, it is difficult to design effective managerial incentive schemes.[10] But other methods of managerial control also have limited effectiveness: both the take-over mechanism and voting mechanisms work imperfectly.[11] There is – with public held corporations, and even with corporations with publicly held debt – a public good problem. All owners of any class of securities benefit when the firm is managed in such a way as enhances the return to that class of securities. *Management* – of private as well as public enterprises – *is a public good* (see Stiglitz, 1985).

One critic, Michael Jensen of Harvard Business School, has estimated that managerial incompetence in the United States costs American firms $600 billion in market value, an astonishing number. I raise this not because I have a great deal of confidence in that number, but simply to re-emphasise the point that efficiency and effectiveness are problems not only in the public sector, but also in the private.

Fundamental differences between public and private organisations

So far, I have argued that there is mixed evidence on the relative efficiency of the public and private sectors. Some of the observed differences in behaviour have to do with the nature of what is being produced and the economic activities in which the individuals are engaged. Much of the older reasoning – the private sector *must* be more efficient because individuals within the private sector have incentives (the profit motive drives them to be efficient) – is simply unconvincing. Managerial incentives are weak within the private as well as the public sector, partly, perhaps, necessarily so, because of the difficulties in monitoring and measuring performance.

Having said this, I do believe that there are fundamental differences between the public and private sectors, differences which affect the efficiency and effectiveness with which they provide goods

40

and services. Some of the differences I view as inherent, arising out of the basic public/private distinction. Others are not inherent, but rather are a matter of common, but alterable, practices. Even when there are inherent differences, the impact of these differences may be changed by altering common practices.

In an earlier essay (Stiglitz, 1989), I attempted to delineate what I thought of as the fundamental distinction between public and private sector activity, and two of the fundamental consequences of that distinction. I asked the question, in what way was the state different from the myriad of other economic organisations within our society?

I put forward the hypothesis that the fundamental distinctions arose from the fact that membership in all other organisations was voluntary; membership in the state was compulsory.[12] The state had powers of compulsion (it could force you to pay taxes, to serve in the army, etc.) including powers of proscription (it could prevent you from selling cigarettes or buying Iraqi oil) that private, voluntary organisations simply did not have. The fact that this was so, meant that the government could do things that private firms could not. It could not only solve 'free rider' problems which would arise in the private provision of public goods; it could, in principle,[13] address problems of externalities through corrective taxation. (My recent work with Bruce Greenwald [Greenwald and Stiglitz, 1986, 1988] has established that whenever markets are incomplete or information is imperfect – that is, essentially, always – market resource allocations are constrained[14] Pareto efficient; these imperfections give rise to externality-like effects which can be partially corrected through corrective taxation.)

But while 'compulsory' membership endowed the state with powers that private organisations do not have (if an individual does not think the dues charged by a private club are commensurate with the services received, he can simply drop out), it also imposed limitations. For example, in democratic societies where leadership is determined by a political process and where public funds, coercively raised, are used, there is an obligation that they be used in a 'fair and equitable manner'.

The consequences of the equity constraint
No one is particularly worried if a private firm, owned by a single individual, pays someone too much – it comes out of the owner's pocket. If he makes a bad business decision, he bears the cost. But taxpayers pay the cost of bad public decisions.

Though the public thus worries about efficiency of government operations, it recognises that monitoring of public officials is, by

41

its nature, weak. The voting mechanism is a most imperfect controller, for votes are cast on the basis of a wide range of issues, of which managerial competency is only one, and which is often of far less importance than other issues.[15] But while voters may be aware of their limited ability to ensure managerial competency, they are even more aware of the possibility, given limited monitoring capacity, of diversion of resources to private uses. While they cannot affect incentives for efficiency, they can affect the diversion of resources, by imposing a variety of constraints on public officials.

Limited incentives

These constraints, as well intentioned as they may be, may at times interfere with the efficiency and effectiveness with which government services are provided. Constraints on salaries, for instance, may inhibit the ability to hire the best individuals for the job and to provide effective incentives for public employees. A large literature (referred to as the efficiency wage hypothesis) has developed within the past fifteen years showing how higher wages lead to higher worker productivity.[16] Henry Ford paid his workers more than three times the going wage, but the increased productivity and lower turnover of his workers more than compensated him for these above market wages. The constraints on government inhibit it from taking advantage of efficiency wage effects, and for good reason. Efficiency wages (particularly the incentive versions) depend on individuals receiving rents, ie wages above their opportunity costs. It is these rents, or the threat of losing these rents, which provides the positive incentive effects.

But it is difficult, if not impossible, to distinguish between rents given to elicit greater productivity, and rents given simply to divert resources to private uses.

Moreover, in the belief that there are, nonetheless, rents in public employment, most governments have established civil service rules intended to ensure that those rents are 'fairly' allocated: everyone must have a fair chance, and, more important for our purposes, individuals cannot be dismissed without good cause. The restriction on dismissals is important, because it limits the extent to which the patronage system can work, that is, public officials cannot redistribute whatever rents are available from the followers of the previous administration to their followers. But at the same time, the restriction on firing means that incentives within the public sector are attenuated. The government, in effect, is not allowed to make use of efficiency wages, with the threat of dismissal for inadequate performance.

Excessive reliance on procedures
The limitations on 'control' and the attempt to restrict the private diversion of public funds within the public sector have two further consequences. First, there is a substitution of monitoring process for output. We may not be able to judge whether performance is efficient or outcomes are fair, but we can judge whether procedures have been complied with and whether the procedures are fair. The procedures are intended to, and undoubtedly do, limit the extent of private diversion of resources. An individual cannot simply divert resources to his own benefit or the benefit of his friends. He must get the acquiescence of others, and the larger the number of individuals involved, the less likely that such acquiescence can easily be obtained. The procedures serve to make sure that all points of view are at least heard, and, together with a watchful public press, make it more likely that egregious diversions of resources are stopped.

I say more likely because, in spite of these procedures, there are innumerable instances of the many paying for the benefits of the few. There is a simple reason for this: in the public sphere, no less than in the private, there is imperfect information, and real difficulties of telling what are the consequences of various government policies. Government support of agricultural programmes benefitting a relatively few rich farmers is partly well intentioned: there is a widespread belief that the consequences of abolishing these programmes would be economically disastrous.

But at the same time that the procedures make it more likely that funds are not diverted to private uses, they make it more difficult for public institutions to respond quickly to changing circumstances, and to adapt well to special needs and interests. They interfere with economic efficiency.

Risk aversion
The other consequence of imperfect monitoring is that enormous emphasis gets placed on the performance signals which are observed. Positive performance – a reduction in the cost of providing a service by 5 per cent from what it otherwise would have been – is often hard to detect; only the manager knows what the costs would have been in the absence of his efforts, and then only imperfectly. Negative signals – the failure to deliver some promised service – is more easily observed, particularly in those cases where a particular individual was supposed to receive those services (as in the case of publicly provided private goods).

Throughout this paper, we have taken the view that it is individuals who are the actors within any organisation, public and private, and that to understand how the organisation functions, one needs to know how the individual behaves; and individual behaviour is affected by the incentives that he or she faces. If, as often seems to be the case, the public sector responds strongly to negative signals, and if, as is generally the case, particularly with government workers, individuals are risk averse, we would expect government workers to take strong actions to reduce the occurrence of these negative signals and / or to reduce the blame which is assigned to them for these occurrences. (The reason that government workers may be particularly risk averse is that there is a selection effect: limitations on promotion and on the threat of being fired mean that public employment is, in some sense, less risky than private employment, and thus more risk averse individuals will be attracted to public employment.[17]) This may partly account for the 'red tape' often associated with public bureaucracies, the seeming excess reliance on 'bureaucratic' procedures. If a mistake occurs, a negative signal is observed, no single individual receives the blame, so long as procedures were followed.

Rent seeking in the public and private sectors

A large recent literature has stressed the importance of rent seeking within the public sector.[18] This refers to the incentive which special interest groups and bureaucrats have to use the powers of the state to divert resources to themselves. Many of the constraints we have been discussing can be interpreted as attempts to limit the rents available, and thus the extent of rent seeking activity.

We now realise that rent seeking also goes on within the private sector. In the older theory, where owners of firms perfectly monitor and control those who work for them, this cannot occur. A worker or manager who tries to divert resources of the firm to his own benefit – to get more than the value of his marginal product – would be instantaneously fired. But in the New Theory of the Firm, emphasising owners' imperfect control over managers, managers can, and do, divert the firm's resources to their own benefit; they are engaged in rent seeking, or in other words in seeking gains to themselves at the expense of shareholders.

Informational constraints not only limit the ability of shareholders to control rent seeking behaviour on the part of top managers, they also limit the ability of top managers to control rent seeking behaviour on the part of their subordinates. How much of the time spent by a middle level manager in preparing a report was absolutely necessary? To what extent was he acquiring information, of marginal value to the firm, but which would make that manager look relatively good compared to other managers?

To what extent are the efforts and resources spent by a manager to cultivate a client really being directed to enhance that manager's job opportunities? Private and organisational objectives are intricately intertwined, and in many cases they are not conflicting. But at the margin, they frequently are, and there seems little reason to doubt that private objectives frequently, perhaps usually, win out.[19]

What, then, is the difference between the public and private sectors, or at least the large corporate part of the private sector?

Bankruptcy and competition: the crucial differences

I would argue that the distinguishing features of the private sector are provided by competition and the threat of bankruptcy.

Competition is important both as an incentive device and as a monitoring mechanism. Having different organisations involved in similar activities provides us with a basis of comparison. Without such a comparison, how do we know whether the telephone company has been efficient? With such a comparison, at least we have the basis of a judgement.

Firms face hard budget constraints: if they are unable to compete effectively, to sell their goods at prices which exceed the average costs of production, they cease functioning. Incompetent firms thus get eliminated. There is no automatic selection mechanism working within the public sector. Indeed, in the case of many public enterprises, financial and social objectives get mixed up, making it difficult to tell whether a firm is being efficient. If a steel company is instructed to keep a plant open, to avoid the loss of jobs, and then records a loss, it will try to attribute its loss not to a lack of efficiency, but to the external constraints imposed upon it. We then replace hard budget constraints with soft budget constraints: the firm appeals to the government to cover any losses.

Reconciling organisational objectives with individual incentives

We are left with something of a mystery. We have argued that what matters for organisational performance is individual incentives. We have just described how the organisational incentives differ in the public and private sectors. We need to see how these organisational incentives get translated into individual incentives.

A number of writers, most recently Akerlof and Simon, have argued that one cannot really explain individual behaviour within organisations on the basis of incentive systems alone. These academic writers are perhaps particularly attuned to the limited importance of incentives: few of them receive any financial rewards for any of the myriad of activities which they undertake. What is their incentive for supervising a mediocre student? They could easily either refuse to supervise the student, or make life so unpleasant for the supervisee that he would look elsewhere. Why do they go to department meetings and provide the other public goods required for the running of a successful department? There is considerable evidence that free rider problems are not as serious, at least in many cases, as economists have long contended.

Individuals identify with the organisations of which they are a part. Simon has described the ability of individuals to do so as *human docility*, and argues that there are strong evolutionary forces giving those with this attribute a selection advantage. I have noted (Stiglitz, 1979) that in many circumstances, another often noted trait, *human sociability*, must be invoked to account for individual behaviour within organisations, and the consequent organisational design. To put it perhaps oversimplistically, individuals like to please those around them.

While many individuals are best motivated by goals, maximising their income is only one of the objectives which they are interested in pursuing. Traditional economists would respond to this by saying, 'Yes, of course! They maximise their utility, whatever that entails.' But traditional theory has focused on one aspect of individual behaviour, the individual's selfish pursuit of self-interest – usually interpreted in narrow financial terms – without worrying about how that self-interest gets defined. It is treated as an exogenous variable, outside the control either of the individual or the organisation.

But those in management positions recognise that one of their objectives is to induce those who work with them to adopt, as their objectives, the objectives and goals of the organisation. Again, there is not necessarily a conflict between individual and organisational goals, in this respect: workers often believe that if the organisations of which they are a part do well, they will prosper, and managers seek to reinforce that belief. But for traditional economists, this link would not be enough: because each worker would like to free ride.[20] The perspective for which I am arguing here holds that the individual actually adopts, as part of his own source of utility, the organisational goals. Whether he does this, as Simon suggests, because his preferences are easily malleable or because he simply wishes to please those around him, to be part of a winning team (as Stiglitz suggests), makes little difference for our analysis.

In this view, then, competition has an important incentive effect, not only because it allows for high marginal returns to effort to be associated with relatively low variability in rewards (risk),[21] but also because it facilitates individuals within the group identifying with the team's (the organisation's) objectives, and indeed helps to crystalise what those objectives are: doing better than the rival. In this respect, competition between organisations is markedly different from competition among individuals within an organisation. Competition within firms induces individuals to think of their own interests, and to focus on the differences between these interests and those of other members of the organisation. This, it seems to me, provides part of the explanation for the puzzle: Why is it that we see (in spite of the strong incentive/risk advantages of relative performance schemes, to which I referred earlier) relatively little use of contests *within* organisations?

Lessons for public organisations
What does all of this have to do with the central theme of this paper: How can we explain differences between the efficiency and effectiveness of public and private organisations? And what can we do to improve the efficiency of public organisations? A great deal!

I have argued that public organisations have greatly attenuated financial incentive structures, and, by traditional economic reasons, one would expect individual incentives to be correspondingly attenuated. But then we noticed that private organisations have attenuated individual incentive structures as well. Perhaps individual incentive structures in the private sector are not as attenuated as those within the public sector, but they are weak nonetheless.

Part of the success of the private sector lies in the 'improved' organisational environments – the competition and hard budget constraints to which private firms are subjected. But these organisational objectives have to motivate individual behaviour, using limited financial incentives; and this entails, in one way or another, having individuals adopt the group's objective.

Many public organisations fail in both steps. First, the organisations are not subjected to hard budget constraints. Part of the reason for this has to do with the difficulties governments have in making commitments, in binding their own hands. Democratic governments cannot bind their successors. Though there are actions which one government can take which can affect the 'transactions' costs of, eg subsidisation, and thus make soft budget constraints less likely,[22] they are much less binding than the constraints facing firms. This in turn has much to do with the innate differences between the private and public sector: the power to tax almost necessarily implies a weak budget constraint; the fact that in the private sector, all transactions must be voluntary necessarily implies a hard budget constraint. In a sense, then, the greater powers of government necessarily weaken the effectiveness of incentives.

The second important attribute of the organisational environment to which we referred, competition, also distinguishes the public
from the private sector. In much of what the government does,
it is immune from competition. But unlike the first problem, this
is not, in most instances, an innate difference.

Here, the issue is frequently one of trade-offs. The government
can create either internal or external competition. It could, for
instance, establish two mail services, or it could allow the entry
of new firms. Indeed, in the United States, there is now extensive
competition both for the delivery of parcels and for overnight
(express) mail service. The government has retained a monopoly,
however, for ordinary first class mail.

Competition has had healthy incentive effects. In the case where
there are some increasing returns, *in the absence of incentive effects*
having two mail services would be inefficient. But the loss from
the inability to exploit fully economies of scale may be much less
than the losses from the absence of competition (see, eg Nalebuff
and Stiglitz, 1983b).[23]

The absence of competition not only impairs organisational
incentives, it even impairs, as we have said, the ability to judge
whether or not the organisation is efficient.

We also argued that competition may have positive effects by
helping clarify or focus organisational objectives, and by helping
individuals to identify with those objectives. Of course, competition
is only one way of doing this. Some units of the US government,
such as the FBI and the Park Service, have had remarkable success
in this area, a success which is widely believed to be reflected in
the success of those organisations. The methods by which they have
succeeded in doing this warrant further study. What I want to stress
for now, however, is the seeming absence, in some branches of
government, of focus on these concerns.

Customer relations and monitoring
Earlier in this paper, I noted that in many of the activities of
government, monitoring is difficult; it is difficult to measure
productivity, and to assess performance.

This is not true of all the various activities of government workers,
or at least of all aspects of those activities. For instance, it is possible
to monitor the length of time it takes a document to get processed.
One can monitor the frequency of errors detected in encoding a
form. It is even possible to assess, perhaps imperfectly, the
friendliness with which a government worker deals with a 'customer'.

Firms within the private sector have recognised this. They
recognise that there are many dimensions to transactions with their

customers. The speed with which transactions are completed, the courtesy with which they are dealt, and the frequency of errors are important components in choosing a supplier. Competition helps focus attention on these attributes, attributes which go beyond the simple product description and price. The absence of competition has, in many cases, insulated government agencies from these concerns. Government agencies tend to narrowly focus, for instance, on the private costs of processing, not taking into account the costs borne by their 'customers'. Economic efficiency – and private markets – take into account all such costs.

In these aspects, firms make use of customers as monitors: customers may be very effective monitors because they have an incentive to monitor. In the case of pure public goods, no one has an incentive to monitor. But much of what is provided publicly is not a pure public good. Introducing more competition – more scope for choice – (or even more vehicles for 'voice', to use Hirschman's insightful term) would allow more effective private monitoring of public agencies and officials.[24] At the same time, there are important feedbacks: the positive interactions, and the fact that a choice was available and has been made, may help with 'organisational morale' – with the workers' identification with the organisation's objective.

Recognising human fallibility

Whatever the form of monitoring, mistakes will be discovered. Workers have to be provided with an incentive to avoid mistakes – or perhaps more accurately, I should say that they have to be provided with appropriate incentives to avoid mistakes. Mistakes are inevitable. It is prohibitively costly to avoid them.

Organisations need to be designed in such a way as to mitigate the consequences of individual mistakes. But again, this needs to be viewed as an economic decision. More mistakes can be avoided, but only at greater costs, eg in monitoring.

In recent work with Raaj Sah, we have focused on the question of the design of economic organisations (what we call the architecture), taking into account human fallibility. We have contrasted the performances, for instance, of hierarchical and polyarchical organisations. In the 1960s, management consultants were wont to draw up neat organisational charts: if duplication could be avoided and tasks clearly assigned, organisational efficiency would be enhanced.

We have already seen one set of reasons why this view is wrong: competition among units may have strong positive effects which more than offset any losses from duplication. But the recognition of human fallibility provides another reason why this is wrong: the average performance of the organisation as a whole may be enhanced by polyarchical organisational structures, in which, for instance, several subunits may be assigned the task of reviewing similar projects for approval. 'Failures' or delays in one subunit will not then have the disastrous effects on the overall organisational performance that it would in the absence of this seeming duplication.

The public outcry when a mistake is detected is understandable: it is their money that is being wasted. They do not see the costs which would have to be incurred – and are incurred – to make such mistakes less likely. Businesses can take a more cold-hearted look at the matter. They balance out the costs and benefits of mistakes. In some cases, they can be quite explicit about the trade-offs: one can obtain a more reliable product, but at a higher cost. The market responds to consumer evaluations of the trade-off. But in the public sphere, the link is harder to see, partly because costs and benefits are often borne by different individuals.

In an interview with one major manufacturer of jet engines for airplanes, the firm reported significantly higher costs for making precisely the same engine for the government than for the private sector. Government engines cost 30 per cent to 50 per cent more. These engines were of exactly the same design. The government, however, wanted to make sure that there were no mistakes, and that none of the money that was to be spent on the engine was spent on anything else. The government monitored the private firm closely and imposed many rules designed to prevent waste and mistakes. The lesson seems to be that it is expensive to save money: one can spend more than a dollar to ensure that a dollar is not wasted.

The excessive stress on equity

Among the 'mistakes' which most arouse public ire are those associated with inequities. Any of us with more than one child knows the importance of issues of equity. No charge is heard more often than 'It's not fair.' (Indeed, I cannot recall an occasion in which I heard the complaint, 'It's not efficient.') And most of us – having passed on to the role of the parent – quickly grasp that fairness, like beauty, is in the eye of the beholder. All sides can, simultaneously, and quite righteously, claim to have been unfairly treated.

We saw earlier that the greater powers of government – its power to tax – lead to a strong obligation, in democratic societies, that the funds so raised be spent equitably. No one wants – or would stand for – his or her child being treated differently from another child of equal ability. To ensure that funds are spent equitably, we impose significant constraints on government, constraints which, in many cases, interfere significantly with economic efficiency.

The absence of competition exacerbates concerns about equity. There is a choice of airlines. If a person thinks that an airline has unfairly treated him or her – being assigned an undesirable seat, for example – the option is open to use another airline. The fact that such inequities may also arise in the private sector may teach an important lesson: perceived (and perhaps actual) inequities are inevitable. But when the government has a state monopoly on some activity, there is nowhere to turn in the event of an inequity.

Again, the issue is one of trade-offs: if we were somewhat more relaxed about possible inequities, that one person might get a little more than another, might we gain significantly in economic efficiency? We have no hard evidence on this matter, but I am inclined to believe that we have indeed gone too far. Just as greater tolerance of mistakes – or more accurately, the recognition that mistakes are inevitable and costly to avoid – would enhance the efficiency and effectiveness of public organisations, so would greater tolerance of inequities, or more accurately, the recognition that (perceived) inequities are inevitable and costly to avoid.

Education: a case study
Many of the issues I have raised in this paper are well illustrated by education. Whether in the public or private sector, financial incentives play a relatively small role, either for the workers (teachers) or the managers (principals and superintendents). Almost no one's pay is based on performance – in either the public or private sector.

Because the output of educational institutions is difficult to observe, 'mistakes' and inefficiencies – in the conventional sense of those terms – are hard to detect. Inequities in resource allocations are easy to observe, and hence attention is directed to avoiding those.

In the United States, there has been a small but determined effort to introduce a voucher scheme – the vouchers could be used at either public or private schools – which would allow individuals to make choices. Proponents argue that one should let the market work.

Markets for education, critics claim, are not like markets for the standard goods. In this, they are undoubtedly right. The assumptions of well informed consumers buying homogeneous commodities in perfectly competitive markets, necessary to obtain the standard efficiency results associated with competitive markets, simply do not seem relevant to education markets.

In arguing for competition, I have not relied on the weak analogy

51

between education and other commodities, for which competition can be shown to ensure efficient outcomes. My arguments have used competition as a way of resolving what would be viewed, in conventional terms, as market failures. These market failures include the inability to design financial incentive schemes which effectively reward either inputs or outputs, and the lack of information about technology making it difficult to know whether or not an organisation is or is not efficient.

We now understand clearly the distinction between public funding and public production. While there are good arguments for public funding for education, the argument that public funds be used almost exclusively (within the United States) for publicly produced education seem far less compelling. And even if, for some reason or other, we restrict funds to publicly produced education, there is no reason why we can't reorganise the educational system to allow for more inter-school competition and choice.

Concluding remarks

In this paper I have attempted to put into perspective the issue of the efficiency of the government sector. Government is different from private organisations. It has powers that they do not have. And the existence of those powers leads to constraints, constraints which the private sector does not face.

These powers and constraints give rise to natural comparative advantages: certain economic activities may more effectively be assigned to one sector or the other. An important objective of the economics of the public sector is to discover those comparative advantages.

At the same time, we have noted that some of the differences between the public and private sectors may have been exaggerated – they are differences among the activities being pursued, not differences of the sector within which they are pursued. Private sector organisations face incentive (principal-agent) problems no less than do public organisations.

And some of the differences are not innate, but are more a consequence of common practice. The most important of these is the absence of competition. Government organisations no less than private organisations dislike competition. The difference is the government has the power to forbid competition, which private organisations do not – and indeed, government sees one of its roles as curbing unfair practices aimed at reducing competition.

We have described how the constraints imposed on government, in response to its greater powers, naturally lead to a focus on equity and avoiding mistakes, concerns which in turn lead to bureaucratic red tape and inefficiency. Because the system does not appropriately take into account the costs of ensuring equity and avoiding mistakes, we have argued that concerns about equity and avoiding mistakes are excessive. I suspect that verbal injunctions to public organisations to be more balanced, that is to take costs as well as benefits into account, are unlikely to have much affect. The economic environment in which they operate must be changed for individual and organisational behaviour to change. The environmental change which would have the most dramatic, and I think, effective, results would be inducing more competition. But even short of that, there are alterations which would improve the efficiency and effectiveness of the public sector. A more widespread recognition of some of the trade-offs that I have identified in this paper would be a good place to start.

Notes

[1] In preparing this paper, I have greatly benefitted from discussions with Jane Hannaway. The influence of her ideas (see, eg Hannaway [1988, 1989]) throughout should be apparent.

This paper represents a continuation of a research programme attempting to define more precisely the economic role of the state. See, in particular, Stiglitz (1989). Financial support from the National Science Foundation and the Hoover Institution is gratefully acknowledged.

[2] Several studies have attempted to compare the efficiency of the public and private sectors engaged in comparable activities. Among the findings (from J.E. Stiglitz, 1988):

* Public housing projects cost about 20 per cent more to produce than comparable private housing (R. Muth, *Public Housing,* Washington D.C., American Enterprise Institute, 1973).

* Public garbage collection costs about 50 per cent more than private garbage collection (E.S. Savas, *The Organisation and Efficiency of Solid Waste Collection,* Lexington, Ma: D.C. Heath, 1977).

* Private fire protection in Scottsdale, Arizona cost approximately 47 per cent less than publicly provided fire protection in comparable communities (R. Alhbrandt, 'Efficiency in the Provision of Fire Services,' *Public Choice* 16, 1973, and *Alternatives to Traditional Public Safety Services,* Berkeley, Ca: Institute for Local Self-Government, 1977).

* Private school bus transportation in Indiana cost 12 per cent less than equivalent district provided transportation (Robert A. McQuire and Norman T. Van Cott, 'Public vs. Private Activity: A New Look at School Bus Transportation,' *Public Choice* 43, 1984).

* Urban public bus transportation costs up to one third more than private bus transportation (James L. Perry and Timlynn T. Babitsky, 'Comparative Performance in Urban Bus Transit: Assessing

Privatization Strategies', *Public Administration Review,* January/February 1986 and Edward K. Morlock and Philip A. Viton, 'The Comparative Costs of Public and Private Transit', in *Urban Transit: The Private Challenge to Public Transit,* Charles Lave, ed. Cambridge, Ma: Ballinger Publishing Co., 1985).

* Contracting out for defence support services generates cost savings of 22 per cent (US Department of Defence, 'Report to Congress on the Commercial Activities Program,' March, 1984).

* Private provision of administrative services is less expensive than public provision, with the exception of payroll processing (Barbara J. Stevens, ed. *Delivering Municipal Services Efficiently: A Comparison of Municipal and Private Service Delivery,* Report prepared by Ecodata, Inc. for the US Department of Housing and Urban Development, June 1984, based on a study of Southern California jurisdictions).

3 Among the areas in which studies find that public provision is as, or more, efficient than public provision are the following:

* Hospitals (L.G. Hrebinia and J.A. Alutto, 'A Comparative Organisational Study of Performance and Size Correlates in Inpatient Psychiatric Departments', *Administrative Science Quarterly* 18, 1973).

* Prices in state-run liquor stores were 4 to 11 per cent lower than those charged by private retailers (Sam Peltzman, 'Pricing in Public and Private Enterprises: Electric utilities in the United States', *Journal of Law and Economics* 14, 1971).

* Administrative costs of the social security administration are less than 2 per cent of the benefit paid; while private insurance companies frequently spend as much as 30 to 40 per cent of the amount provided in benefits in administrative (including sales) costs.

* Private institutions of higher learning have almost 50 per cent more administrators than do public institutions (Lorraine E. Prinsky, 'Public vs. Private: Organisational Control as Determinant of Administrative Size', *Sociology and Social Research,* 62, 1973).

4 D.W. Davies and L.R. Christensen, 'The Relative Efficiency of Public and Private Firms in a Competitive Environment: The Case of Canadian Railroads', *Journal of Political Economy,* 88 (1980), 958-76.

5 In 1950, the postal service delivered 90,000 pieces of mail per employee. By 1960, it was 113,000 per employee. Productivity stagnated for a decade, rising to only 115,000 per employee. But then, over the next fifteen years, it increased by more than 50 per cent, reaching 159,000 in 1980 and 188,000 in 1985.

Studies have also shown that productivity increases in other parts of the public sector may be as significant as in the private. A study by the Office of Personnel Management, covering 65 per cent of US federal employees, showed that productivity increased at an annual rate of 1.4 per cent between 1967 and 1978, slightly higher than the rate of productivity increase in the private sector (Nancy Hayward and George Kuper, 'The National Economy and Productivity in Government', *Public Admin-istration Review* 38 (1973) and US Office of Personnel Management, *Measuring Federal Productivity*, February, 1980).

6 Recent studies have shown that, on average, managers of large corporations receive a minuscule fraction of any incremental profits which their actions might earn for the firm.

7 H. Simon, forthcoming, p. 4.

8 Thus, many of the studies cited in earlier footnotes make a valiant effort to adjust for the differing circumstances of the communities in which public and private services are provided, but the corrections are usually (in my judgement) not fully convincing. The communities in which private provision has been chosen often differ in numerous ways from other communities, and not all of the ways may be picked up in the statistical adjustments used in the econometric studies. (There may, accordingly, be a significant sample selection bias.)

Moreover, a 'Hawthorne' effect may arise in those cases where private provision of public services is being tried on an experimental basis.

Thus, the results on the greater efficiency of fire protection in Scottsdale, Arizona (described in the earlier footnote) might appear to suffer from both sources of bias.

9 In recent years, the anecdotal evidence of corporate mismanage-ment has come to rival that of the public sector – the $400 hammers and the $1,000 toilet seat covers that the Grace Commission in the United States has called attention to. After the RJR take-over, auditors were mystified in looking

at the company records to see a G. Shepherd accompanying the Chief Executive Officer (Ross), *in a separate corporate plane,* on almost all of his trips. G. Shepherd was obviously important, but why should he need to be on a separate plane? And why did he not appear within the company's organisa-tional chart? Indeed, he didn't even appear on the company's payroll. An unpaid consultant?

Eventually, it turned out that G. Shepherd was Ross's German shepherd! Evidently, he (or she) had a nasty habit of biting others, or at least making them suffi-ciently uncomfortable that they would not fly with him.

There is, in addition to this kind of anecdotal evidence, increasing statistical evidence, eg that when managers own a small fraction of the firm's shares, it is more likely that they will engage in take-over activity that actually reduces share values (of the taking-over firm). In one extremely clever study, Andre Shleifer confirmed the hubris theory of take-overs: the likeli-hood of value decreasing take-overs increased with the promi-nence of the CEO in the annual report.

Other evidence on 'managerial incompetence' has accumulated over the years. For instance, Stiglitz (1982, 1987) compared tax behaviour (with respect to divi-dends, executive compensation, inventory policy, etc.) with that which would maximise share-holders' net after-tax return, and found significant departures. Though there are alternative explanations of this (managerial incompetence, shareholder mis-perceptions, etc.), it demonstrates clearly that managers do not always take actions which are in the best interests of shareholders.

[10] That is, it is difficult to assess the contribution of any particular manager. It is even difficult to assess the contribution of the total management team, unless one believes that the stock market accurately reflects the firm's underlying value. There is increasing evidence against that hypothesis; there are a variety of ways by which firms can increase current market value at the expense of future profits. The most dramatic evidence in support of this arises from firm tax behaviour, referred to earlier.

[11] See Stiglitz (1972, 1982, 1985), Grossman and Hart (1986).

[12] To some extent, even this distinction is one of degree: individuals have some choice over the jurisdiction in which they reside.

[13] The exact meaning of this caveat will, hopefully, be made clearer later in the paper.

[14] The term constrained is used simply to remind us that the government can take actions which make everyone better off, making use of the same limited markets and facing the same problems of imperfect information which confront the private sector.

[15] This, of course, is not always true. In the United States, the commissioners of sewage districts are often elected. The range of policy issues is often (but not always) limited. (In some communities, sewage capacity is the binding constraint on growth, so that the issue of expansion of sewage capacity is equivalent to that of the growth of the community.) The commissions are, presumably, chosen on the basis of their competency as managers.

[16] This literature has identified four sets of effects: (a) higher wages enable firms to have individuals of higher ability (see, eg Weiss, 1980, or Stiglitz, 1976, 1990); (b) higher wages induce workers to work harder (see, eg Shapiro and Stiglitz, 1984); (c) higher wages reduce labour turnover (see, eg Stiglitz, 1974); and (d) higher wages have positive morale effects, leading to higher work effort (see, eg Akerlof, 1982). For surveys, see Katz (1986), Stiglitz (1986, 1987), and Yellen (1984).

[17] It is important to bear this selection effect in mind: if the same individuals were put into the private sector, without markedly different incentive structures, their behaviour might be quite similar. A hypothetical switch of individuals between public and private sectors might thus result in increased efficiency within the public, decreased within the private, with little effect on national productivity. This provides an important cautionary note: even were significant differences in public and private productivity observed, it does not mean that changing from public to private control would cause commensurate changes in productivity within the public sector.

[18] See, for instance, Bhagwati (1989), Krueger (1982) and Buchanan (1986).

[19] These points have been emphasised in Hannaway (1989).

[20] Of course, to the extent that there are rents (or transactions costs in switching jobs), the organisation and the individual have coincident interests.

Moreover, individuals may find it costly to calculate what is in their own interests, narrowly defined. Organisations may attempt to convince workers that a good rule of thumb is that the two interests coincide.

21 See Nalebuff and Stiglitz (1983a and 1983b) or Lazear and Rosen (1981).

22 The Gramm-Rudman Bill in the US, which set budget deficit reduction targets, provides an example of how one government can affect the transactions costs, say, associated with a government deficit, and this change has real effects on succeeding governments; at the same time, the subsequent history shows how unsuccessful the bill was in actually binding succeeding governments, as the original deficit reduction targets were successively revised.

23 Allowing competition impairs the government in other ways, some of which may be all for the good. It impairs, for instance, the government's ability to cross subsidise – providing subsidies that might not be acceptable if they were brought out into the open, and made more directly. On the other hand, the restrictions that competition imposes on the prices the government charges mean that the government may not be able

to charge the social welfare maximising prices (see Sappington and Stiglitz, 1987). The importance of charging such prices in economies in which there are effective income tax systems has, however, been questioned (see Atkinson and Stiglitz, 1976, 1980).

24 I should raise two caveats. First, when only some of an individual's activities can be monitored, and rewards (implicitly or explicitly) are strongly based on the monitoring, individuals will have an incentive to divert attention away from the activities that cannot be monitored towards those which can. This may actually impair the overall efficiency of the organisation. Thus, when both the quality and quantity produced are of concern, but only quantity is easily monitored, piece rate systems may be inappropriate, because using them diverts attention from quality towards quantity (see Stiglitz, 1975; these arguments have been substantially extended in Holmstrom and Milgrom, 1990).

Secondly, a firm's agent may place greater value on the ease with which a transaction is accomplished than the firm's owners might; this is but another example of the principal-agent problem underlying much of the discussion of this paper.

References

Akerlof, G., 'Labor Contracts as Partial Gift Exchange', *Quarterly Journal of Economics, 97,* 1982, pp. 543-69.

Atkinson, Anthony, and Stiglitz, J.E., 'The Design of Tax Structure: Direct Versus Indirect Taxation', *Journal of Public Economics,* Vol. 6, 1976, pp. 55-75.

————— *Lectures in Public Economics,* New York and London: McGraw-Hill Book Company, 1980.

Bhagwati, J.N., 'The General Theory of Distortions and Welfare', *International Trade: Selected Readings, 2nd Edition,* Jedish N. Bhagwati, ed., Cambridge MA: Cambridge University Press, 1987, pp. 291-309.

Berle, Adolf, and Means, Gardiner, *The Modern Corporation and Private Capital,* New York: The Macmillan Company, 1933.

Buchanan, James L., *Liberty, Market and State: Political Economics in the 1980s,* New York: New York University Press, 1986.

Greenwald, Bruce and Stigitz, J.E., 'Externalities in Economies with Imperfect Information and Incomplete Markets', *Quarterly Journal of Economics,* May 1986, pp. 229-264.

———— 'Pareto Inefficiency of Market Economies: Search and Efficiency Wage Models', *AEA Papers and Proceedings,* Vol. 78, No. 2, May 1988a.

Grossman, H., and Hart, O., 'The Costs and Benefits of Ownership: A Theory of Vertical and Lateral Integration', *Journal of Political Economy,* 94, 1986, pp. 691-719.

Hannaway, Jane, 'Decentralization and Education', Vice-presidential address delivered to the American Educational Research Association, Washington D.C., 1988.

———— *Managers Managing: The Workings of an Administrative System,* New York: Oxford University Press, 1989.

Holmstrom, B., and Milgrom, P., 'Multi-task Principal-Agent Analyses: Incentive Contracts, Asset Ownership and Job Design', Stanford University, 1990.

Katz, L., 'Efficiency Wage Theories: A Partial Evaluation', *NBER Macroeconomics Annual 1986,* Cambridge, MA: MIT Press, 1986, pp. 235-276.

Kreuger, A., 'The Political Economy of the Rent-Seeking Society', *International Trade: Selected Readings, 2nd Edition,* Jedish N. Bhagwati, ed., Cambridge, MA: Cambridge University Press, 1987, pp. 265-286.

Lazear, Edward, and Rosen, S., 'Rank-order Tournaments as Optimal Labor Contracts', *Journal of Political Economy,* 89, 1981, pp. 841-864.

Nalebuff, B., and Stiglitz, J., 'Prizes and Incentives: Towards a General Theory of Compensation and Competition', *Bell Journal of Economics,* 14, 1983, pp. 21-43.

———— 'Information, Competition and Markets', *American Economic Review,* Vol. 72, No. 2, May 1983, pp. 278-284.

Sah, R., and Stiglitz, J.E., 'The Architecture of Economic Systems: Hierarchies and Polyarchies', *American Economic Review,* Vol. 76, No. 3, September 1986, pp. 716-727.

Sappington, D., and Stiglitz, J., 'Privatization, Information and Incentives', *Journal of Policy Analysis and Management,* 6, 1987, pp. 567-582.

Shapiro, Carl, and Stiglitz, J.E., 'Equilibrium Unemployment as a Worker Discipline Device', *American Economic Review,* Vol. 74, No. 3, June 1984, pp. 433-444.

Simon, H., forthcoming, 'Organizations and Markets', *Journal of Economic Perspectives.*

Stiglitz, J.E., 'Alternative Theories of Wage Determination and Unemployment in L.D.C.s: The Labor Turnover Model', *Quarterly*

Journal of Economics, Vol. LXXXVII, May 1974b, pp. 194-227.

_____ 'Incentives, Risk and Information: Notes Towards a Theory of Hierarchy', *Bell Journal of Economics,* Vol. 6, No. 2, Autumn 1975, pp. 552-579.

_____ 'Contests and Cooperation: Towards a General Theory of Compensation and Competition', July 1979, presented at the Conference on the Internal Organization of Firms, Berlin.

_____ 'Ownership, Control and Efficient Markets: Some Paradoxes in the Theory of Capital Markets', *Economic Regulation: Essays in Honor of James R. Nelson,* Kenneth D. Boyer and William G. Shepherd eds., Ann Arbor, Michigan: Michigan State University Press, 1982, pp. 311-341.

_____ 'Credit Markets and the Control of Capital', *Journal of Money, Credit and Banking,* Vol. 17, No. 1, May 1985, pp. 133-152.

_____ 'Theories of Wage Rigidities', *Keynes' Economic Legacy: Contemporary Economic Theories,* ed. by James L. Butkiewicz, Kenneth J. Koford, and Jeffrey B. Miller, New York: Praeger Publishers, 1986, pp. 153-206.

_____ 'The Causes and Consequences of the Dependence of Quality on Price', *Journal of Economic Literature,* 25, March 1987, pp. 1-48.

_____ 'The Design of Labor Contracts: The Economics of Incentives and Risk Sharing', *Incentives, Cooperation and Risk Sharing,* H. Nalbantian, ed., Totowa, NJ: Rowman and Littlefield, 1987, pp. 47-68.

_____ *Economics of the Public Sector,* Second Edition, W.W. Norton Publishers, 1988.

_____ 'On the Economic Role of the State', *The Economic Role of the State,* A. Heertje, ed., Bank Insinger de Beaufort NV, 1989.

_____ 'Prices and Queues as Screening Devices in Competitive Markets', forthcoming in *Economic Analysis of Markets and Games: Essays in Honor of Frank Hahn,* Peter Diamond and Oliver Hart, eds., Cambridge, MA: MIT Press, 1990.

Weiss, Andrew, 'Job Queues and Layoffs in Labor Markets with Flexible Wages', *Journal of Political Economy,* 88, June 1990, pp. 526-38.

Yellen, Janet L., 'Efficiency Wage Models of Unemployment', *American Economic Review,* 74, March 1984, pp. 200-205.

3

Efficiency and Incentives in Income Taxation[1]

C.V. BROWN

THIS paper is concerned with the effects of income (and other direct) taxes on the incentive to work. In analysing the effects we use three concepts of efficiency, namely incentive efficiency, revenue efficiency and economic efficiency.

Incentive efficiency
When asked what they understood by an ineffecient income tax, many non-economists would say it was an income tax that caused people to work less. In the light of this layman's concern we could define an incentive efficient tax rate as one that did not reduce work effort.

Revenue efficiency
Recently there has been quite an amount of attention paid to the notion that we may be able to increase tax receipts if we lower the rate of tax. This suggests that we could define a tax rate as revenue efficient if a lower rate did not raise more revenue.

Economic efficiency
We will see below that economic efficiency means that even if an income tax was incentive efficient and revenue efficient, it would typically be economically inefficient to some degree.

In what follows I will summarise the British and American evidence concerning these three concepts of income tax efficiency and then discuss their possible implications for the Irish tax system.

In thinking about the implications for the Irish income tax system I am conscious that Ireland retains a top rate of income tax (including PRSI) of approximately 60 per cent at a time when the top rate of income tax in the UK has been reduced to 40 per cent and the top rate of federal income tax in the US is as low as 33 per cent. Given the high rates of income tax in Ireland and the narrow tax base, is there a case to be made for reforming the Irish income tax rate structure?

Incentive efficiency

In thinking about the effects of income taxation on work effort, many laymen recognise the possibility – some laymen might say the certainty – that increased income taxation may cause people to work less. These same laymen may neglect the possibility that increased income taxation may cause people to work more. A simple example will explain why increased income taxation could cause people to work either more or less. Suppose that a worker has a job that pays 10 ECU an hour and is free to work as many or as few hours as choice dictates. Suppose further that in the absence of taxation the worker chooses to work 40 hours a week, and in consequence has a take home pay of 400 ECU a week. If a tax of 25 per cent of all income was introduced into this fiscal Garden of Eden what would the effects be? Would the worker choose to work more or less as the result of the introduction of the tax? To tease out the problem suppose we imagine that initially the worker continued to work 40 hours a week. The worker's take home pay would drop from 400 ECU to 300 ECU. It is not hard to imagine that faced with this drop in income the worker will have difficulty meeting rent, food and clothing bills. In order to at least partially preserve the former standard of living the worker might decide to work more than 40 hours a week. Economists call this effect the income effect. At the same time, however, working more is less desirable. Previously the worker received 10 ECU for giving up an hour of leisure. With the 25 per cent tax the worker receives only 7.5 ECU for sacrificing an hour of leisure. For this reason the worker might decide to work less than 40 hours. Economists call this the substitution effect. Thus we have both an income effect increasing work and a substitution effect reducing work and the balance between the two effects could be an increase in hours, a decrease in hours, or no change.

Because income and substitution effects pull in the opposite direction the net effect can only be settled by studying how people actually behave. Much of my paper will be spent summarising the UK and US evidence on this point. I propose to divide the evidence into three sections: special studies of people facing poverty, general studies where the sample tends to be largely middle income and special studies of high income groups. This three way division occurs partly because special interest attaches to the results for the poor and the rich, partly because special sampling procedures are usually necessary to obtain an adequate sample at the extremes of the income distribution and partly because it is thought that inefficiency may be particularly high when marginal tax rates are highest.

It is by no means universally recognised that the highest marginal tax rates are often faced by people at the two extremes of the income distribution. Figure 1 shows the position in the UK. It can be seen that for people with incomes of around £100 a week the marginal tax rate is just under 100 per cent. This is because of the interaction between income tax, national insurance and the withdrawal of means tested benefits. For a wide range of income (where the bulk of the population is found) the rate is 34 per cent. The rate then drops to 25 per cent before rising to 40 per cent. While this particular graph is for the UK only, a similar roughly U-shaped curve exists in many countries. I understand that the position in Ireland is broadly similar because benefits such as Family Income Supplement are withdrawn as incomes rise.

Figure 1: **Marginal tax rates for married couple with two children, 1988-9**

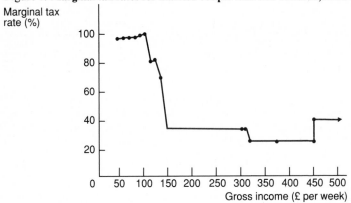

Source: Calculated from *Hansard,* 27 May 1988, columns 423 and 424 for low-income families; also Inland Revenue[2]

Low income groups

For very low income groups the best available evidence comes from the US income maintenance experiments. These studies were commissioned because of an interest in programmes that would substantially raise the incomes of the poorest families coupled with a popular fear that the recipients would react with a massive reduction in their effort. In this case there was a clear theoretical prediction that work would fall because both the income effect (from the higher cash payments) and the substitution effect (from the withdrawal of payments as income rose) pointed to less work. There were four studies: The 'New Jersey' experiment conducted amongst a sample of mixed ethnicity in New Jersey and Pennsylvania, a smaller largely black 'Rural' sample, an all-black sample in 'Gary', Indiana, and a much larger mixed sample in Seattle, Washington and Denver, Colorado — the 'Seattle/Denver' experiment.

In each of these studies the sample was divided into an experimental group and a control group. The experimental group was offered enrollment on an income maintenance plan which provided some income support – the amount being related to family size and earnings. The control group received a token payment in exchange for providing information about earnings, hours worked and so forth, so that the behaviour of the experimental group could

Table 1: **US negative income tax experiments**

Experiment (dates) Sample size Family composition	Race	*Percentage change in hours*		
		Husbands	*Wives*	*Single female parents*
New Jersey (1968-72)	White (32%)	–6	>31	
1157	Black (37%)	+2	–2	
100% husband/wife	Hispanic (31%)	–1	–55	
	All	–1	–24	
Rural (1969-73)	White (65%)	+2	–21	
809	Black (35%)	–8	–31	
85% husband/wife	All	–3	–28	
15% single female parent				
Gary (1971-4)	Black (100%)	–6	+5	–30
1780				
41% husband/wife				
59% single female parent				
Seattle/Denver (1971-82)	White (39%)	–8	–17	–9
4800	Black (43%)	–10	–16	–17
61% husband/wife	Hispanic (18%)	–12	–29	–20
39% single female parent	All	–9	–18	–14
	3-year sample	–7	–14	–13
Weighted average		–7	–17	–17

Source: Adapted from Tables 1 and 2 of G. Burtless, 'The work response to a guaranteed income: a survey of experimental evidence', in A.M. Munnell (ed), *Lessons from the Income Maintenance Experiments,* Federal Reserve Bank of Boston, 1987.

be compared to the behaviour of the control group. Gary Burtless (1987) has summarised the results from all the experiments and his summary is given in Table 1. It will be recalled that income and substitution effects should both lead to a reduction in hours of work in this case and that is what the table shows. It can be seen the husbands' hours fell by 7 per cent overall while hours of wives and single female parents both fell by an average of 17 per cent. While the percentage fall in female hours was much larger it was on a small base as a much higher proportion of females were part-time workers.

Studies of the general population
Turning to more general studies, Gary Burtless has provided weighted average responses from 26 US studies of men and 38 US studies of women. He reports an average price elasticity of –0.10 for men and +1.36 for women – see Table 2. Price elasticity shows the percentage change in hours supplied in a way that combines the income and substitution effects. The –0.10 for men is clearly very close to zero and means that the income and substitution effects very nearly cancel each other out. In terms of our earlier example this implies that the introduction of a single rate of tax *on all income* (technically a proportional income tax) would have a negligible effect on men's willingness to work. The position for women is different. The positive elasticity (+1.36) means than an increase in the wage rate will increase hours supplied. As a tax reduces the wage rate this means that hours supplied will fall. In our example the 25 per cent tax caused the wage rate to fall by 25 per cent. The results reported by Burtless imply that this would lead to a fall in work of over 30 per cent.

Table 2: **Average labour supply elasticities from non-experimental US studies, weighted by size of sample**

	No.[a]	*Price elasticity*	*Substitution elasticity*	*Income elasticity*
Men	26	–0.10	0.28	–0.39
Women	38[b]	1.36	1.37	–0.01

[a] Number of estimates of response used to compute elasticity.

[b] Excludes five estimates with the highest compensated substitution elasticity and five estimates with the lowest compensated substitution elasticity.

Source: G. Burtless, 'The work response to a guaranteed income: a survey of experimental evidence,' in A.H. Munnell (ed.), *Lessons from the Income Maintenance Experiments,* Federal Reserve Bank of Boston, 1987.

Our work in the UK for HM Treasury reported in Table 3 gives very similar results for husbands in Great Britain as the aforementioned studies give for males in the US. Like the US results for women, our results for wives imply that a higher proportional tax would lead to less work, but our results suggest that for the UK the reduction in work would be very much less.

Table 3: **UK labour supply estimates (average of two estimates)**

	Price elasticity	Substitution elasticity	Income elasticity
Two workers or potential workers:			
Husbands	–0.01	0.28	–0.28
Wives	0.23	0.41	–0.22
One worker or potential worker:			
Married couple	–0.22	0.16	–0.38
Non-dependent child	–0.21	0.18	–0.39

Source: C.V. Brown, E.J. Levin, P.J. Rosa, R.J. Ruffell and D.T. Ulph, *Taxation and Family Labour Supply in Great Britain: the Final Report of a Project on Direct Taxation and Short-Run Labour Supply* (funded by HM Treasury), 1986.

These US and UK results have the important disadvantage that they are derived from elasticity estimates of how average people might respond to changes in proportional income taxes. This information is not very useful in telling us how people would respond to changes in the actual tax rates that they pay. There are two important reasons for this. First, Ireland as well as the US, the UK and most other countries have progressive income taxes, ie the proportion of income paid in income tax rises with income. The problem this causes is that a change in a proportional tax has a different effect on people's willingness to work than has a change in a progressive tax. This point can be illustrated by looking at the effects of an increase in tax-free allowances. For a tax-payer who remains in the same tax band this results in higher take home pay with no change in the marginal tax rate. In other words it has a pure income effect that will reduce people's willingness to work. However, suppose we have a part-time worker who works just up to the tax threshold. When the allowance is increased this person could have a pure substitution effect, increasing work.

This leads us directly on to the second difficulty which is that we need to know a lot about the distribution of people in various tax bands (and we may also need detailed information about means tested benefits and overtime payment systems). In terms of the example just given of an increase in tax allowances we have seen that we have a prediction that those remaining in a given tax band will work less, while those just before the threshold will work more. Clearly to know the overall effect we have to know the number in each category.

To get around these two problems with elasticities, economists simulate or predict the effects of tax, often using quite complex programmes to predict how people will respond to particular changes in taxes. As part of our work for HM Treasury my colleagues and I developed two simulation packages for UK taxes. One of these packages which we call the fully constrained package, recognises that people's responses to tax changes may be constrained by the availability of work – for example, someone may wish to work more overtime but more overtime may not be available. In the other package which we call the fully relaxed package we assume that in the long run these constraints will disappear. I would like to report on two of the simulations that we did.

In the first of these simulations we looked at the predicted effects of a 25 per cent increase in allowances. It can be seen from Table 4 that the predicted effect is a very small fall in hours of work – less than half an hour a week even in the fully relaxed package. For purposes of comparison we asked HM Treasury for comparative figures using a simulation package developed by Richard Blundell and his colleagues. It can be seen that there is again a small fall in predicted hours of work.

Table 4: **Predicted effects of a 25 per cent increase in allowances on mean hours of work**

	Change in mean hours of work		
	Blundell et al.	*Brown et al. fully constrained package*[a]	*Brown et al. fully relaxed package*[b]
Husbands	–0.1	–0.1	–0.4
Wives	–0.5	0.0	–0.2
Singles		–0.2	–0.4

[a] In the fully constrained package it is recognised that people may not be able to adjust the amount of work that they do because of employer imposed constraints.

[b] In the fully relaxed package it is assumed that people are able to work as much or as little as they wish.

Source: C.V. Brown, E.J. Levin, P.J. Rosa, R.J. Ruffell and D.T. Ulph, *Taxation and Family Labour Supply in Great Britain: The Final Report on Direct Taxation and Short Run Labour Supply* (funded by HM Treasury), 1986; R. Blundell, C. Meghir, E. Symons and Z. Walker, data supplied by HM Treasury using SPAIN simulation package.

Table 5: **Predicted effects of a cut in the basic rate of tax from 29 to 25 per cent on mean hours of work**

	Change in mean hours of work		
	Blundell et al.	*Brown et al. fully constrained package*[a]	*Brown et al. fully relaxed package*[b]
Husbands	−0.3	0.0	0.0
Wives	−0.4	0.0	0.0
Singles		0.0	0.0

[a] In the fully constrained package it is recognised that people may not be able to adjust the amount of work that they do because of employer imposed constraints.

[b] In the fully relaxed package it is assumed that people are able to work as much or as little as they wish.

Source: C.V. Brown, E.J. Levin, P.J. Rosa, R.J. Ruffell and D.T. Ulph, *Taxation and Family Labour Supply in Great Britain: The Final Report on Direct Taxation and Short Run Labour Supply* (funded by HM Treasury), 1986; R. Blundell, C. Meghir, E. Symons and Z. Walker, data supplied by HM Treasury using SPAIN simulation package.

In the second simulation that I wish to report, we looked at the effects of a cut in the basic rate of income tax from 29 per cent (the level at the time we did the simulations) to 25 per cent (its present level). We predicted no change in hours with both of our packages and the Blundell package predicted a small fall.

Taking the elasticity and simulation evidence from the US and the UK together it seems clear that we can expect little if any change in male hours worked to result from most kinds of direct tax changes. I say 'from most kinds of direct tax changes' because there are special cases such as the income maintenance programmes where there may be noticeable changes in hours worked. The position for women is less clear. Our evidence would suggest some responses from women. However, Blundell's results (and other UK evidence not cited here) suggest a somewhat larger response and US evidence a still larger response.

Upper income groups

The behaviour of upper income groups who tend to pay the highest marginal rates of *income* tax (see above) has become the latest flavour of the month. There are two reasons for this recent increase in popularity. One is that it is increasingly hard to maintain, in the face of the evidence presented above for males, that there is a serious disincentive effect for males who have lower or middle incomes. In this respect it is interesting to note the change in the position of successive British chancellors of the exchequer. In 1979, in the first budget speech of the new government Sir Geoffrey Howe the chancellor said the 'keystone' of the government's strategy was to reduce income tax at *all* levels because that was the only way to restore incentives. In 1988 when Nigel Lawson reduced both higher rates of tax and the basic rate of tax, it is significant that he made no claims about the incentive effects of the cuts in the *basic rate* of tax, which suggests that he was aware of the research findings in this area. However, he made very clear claims about the likely effects of his proposals to eliminate all of the tax bands above 40 per cent. He said:

> It is now nine years since my predecessor ... reduced the top rate of tax from ... 83 per cent ... to 60 per cent. [Tax rates in other countries have since fallen.] The reason for the worldwide trend towards lower rates of tax is clear. *Excessive rates of income tax destroy enterprise, encourage avoidance, and drive talent to more hospitable shores overseas. As a result, far from raising additional revenue, over time they actually raise less.*
>
> By contrast, a reduction *in the top rates of income tax* can, over time, result in a higher, not a lower yield to the exchequer. Despite the substantial reduction in the top rate of tax in 1979, and the subsequent abolition of the investment income surcharge in 1984, the top 5 per cent of taxpayers today contribute a third as much again in real terms as they did in 1978-9, Labour's last year; while the remaining 95 per cent of taxpayers pay about the same in real terms as they did in 1978-9.
>
> (1988 Budget Speech, emphasis added)

What is the evidence to support these claims – assuming that the definition of enterprise includes work effort?

There have been three studies in Britain of high-income individuals, the first two of which are particularly interesting because both studied the same professions. A survey of British solicitors and accountants conducted by Break in 1956 found a small but significant number of persons experiencing net tax effects; but he did not find the disincentive effect (13 per cent of the sample) to be significantly greater than the incentive effect (10 per cent of the sample); see Table 6. He concluded that the net effect, 'be it disincentive or incentive, is not large enough to be of great economic or sociological significance'.

In 1969 Fields and Stanbury repeated Break's study. They found that 19 per cent of the sample experienced disincentive effects and 11 per cent experienced incentive effects (see Table 6). Unlike Break's findings, the difference in these proportions was statistically significant. Furthermore, the difference in the proportions experiencing a disincentive effect over the 12-year period between the two surveys (from 13 to 19 per cent) was statistically significant. Thus Fields and Stanbury's results suggest that, if there is a net tax effect, it it likely to be a disincentive, and also that the disincentive effect is growing stronger over time.

Table 6: **Incentive/disincentive effects on high incomes in the UK**

Incentive/disincentive effects of taxes on lawyers and accountants (per cent)

	Incentive effect	Disincentive effect
Break	10	13
Fields-Stanbury	11	19

Sources: G.F. Break, 'Income taxes and incentives to work: an empirical study', *American Economic Review,* 1957; D.B. Fields and W.T. Stanbury, 'Income taxes and incentives to work: some additional empirical evidence', *American Economic Review,* 1971.

Changes in hours worked by senior managers in past five years

	No.	%
Decrease	11	12
Increase	12	12
No change	33	35
No reply or don't know	39	41
Total	94	100

Source: F.C. Fiegehen and W.B. Reddaway, *Companies, Incentives and Senior Managers,* Oxford University Press for the Institute for Fiscal Studies, Oxford, 1981.

This would have been a reasonable conclusion were it not for problems of comparability between these two studies. Despite Fields and Stanbury's claim to have replicated Break's study they changed both the order of the questions and the wording of the key questions. The changes are of a nature that would lead one to expect a larger disincentive effect.

Fiegehen and Reddaway (1981) have reported on a study by the Institute for Fiscal Studies of the incentives of senior managers. An approach was made to 108, mostly large, companies through introductions arranged by the Institute for Fiscal Studies, and a further 68 smaller companies were approached with the cooperation of the Confederation of British Industry. In all, interviews were held in 94 companies (53 per cent of those approached) during 1978. What is methodologically unusual about the study is that inferences have been drawn about the behaviour of people *not* interviewed. In each company one interview, lasting over an hour, was taken. The interview was with a senior manager – usually of board level – and questions were asked about all senior staff (roughly defined as those earning more than £10,000 a year in early 1978). Table 6 shows the reported changes in senior staff work behaviour. The authors concluded:

> Although a study of this type does not enable precise relative weights to be attached to the various effects of incomes and tax policies, it is clear that in total any disincentive effects that operated on senior managers had a minimal impact on the activities of British industry.

There is a problem with the methodology of this study that makes me reluctant to accept this conclusion, namely that the study wished to find out about all senior staff from a single interview. Given that many of the companies had over 100 senior staff, it seems unlikely that all would react the same way, and that any one manager would know how all staff had behaved. Even when members of senior staff are lower, one wonders how well informed managing directors, personnel managers, or board members would be – all of whom might be involved in promotion decisions. If for purposes of argument it is assumed that taxes did have disincentive effects on senior staff, it seems hard to believe that they would tell their bosses they were slacking off.

In addition to these British studies there have been several American studies of high-income earners. These studies, which have been surveyed by Holland, show little evidence of taxation reducing or increasing productive work, but rather more evidence of taxation causing businessmen to devote time to minimising their corporate and personal tax liabilities.

Given the dated nature of George Break's evidence and the problems with the other two studies, there is clearly a need for fresh evidence and I am in the fortunate position of directing an Economic and Social Research Council financed research project that is designed to collect evidence on the effects of the cuts in the higher rates of tax announced in the 1988 UK budget. In this project we are taking as our starting point the chancellor's claims quoted above.

Cedric Sandford of Bath University and I have interviewed over 300 accountants on the effects of the 1988 cuts in higher rates of tax. We chose accountants for basically the same reasons as George Break three decades ago: accountants know the tax system, are used to dealing with questions involving numbers, many pay higher rates of tax and they are in a position where they could vary their work effort in response to either income or substitution effects. Our questions were almost entirely framed with the chancellor's statement in mind. Our general approach was to ask the partners to compare their behaviour in fiscal year 1987/88 (the last year of the old higher rates of up to 60 per cent) with fiscal year 1988/89 (the first year with the highest rate of 40 per cent). In this respect our methodology was quite different from George Break's because he was trying to find out the effects of higher rates in a period where there was no change. Most of our questions were of the sort:

> Was there any change between tax years 1987/88 and 1988/89 in the number of hours you normally worked each week when you were not on holiday?

If there was a change we recorded normal hours in both years and then asked why hours had changed.

Table 7 is adapted from the study findings and the conclusions we will draw from it are just part of a larger analysis to which the reader is referred (Brown and Sandford, 1990). The table comes from questions right at the end of the interview where we asked the partners their views on the overall effects of the tax cuts. We asked first:

> What are the most important effects of the cuts in higher rates of income tax on your behaviour?

and then

> Are there any effects of the cuts in higher rates of income tax that have affected your own behaviour that we have not discussed?

Table 7 summarises the combined answers to these two questions. The results are reported for the 179 (out of a total of 316) partners whose tax rate in 1987/88 was 45 per cent or more and who therefore faced a reduced higher rate of tax from 1988/89.

It can be seen from the table that the most common responses, other than no effects, are that people are financially better off and that they are happier. Only a very small minority report either incentive or disincentive effects. Just 3 per cent report that they have worked harder. Given the layman's view about taxes, the publicity that accompanied the tax cut and the fact that all the respondents were told both by letter and in person the purpose of the study, this is a surprisingly small figure – well below George Break's 13 per cent. Just 2 per cent (compared to George Break's

Table 7: **Effects of cuts in higher rates of income tax on the behaviour of accountants in Great Britain**

	*Number**	*Percentage***
Work harder/more enterprising	5	3
Do not work harder	13	7
Work less hard/more holidays/ earlier retirement	3	2
Changes in tax planning	17	9
Financially better off	91	51
Happier	20	11
Miscellaneous	46	26
Not even one effect	53	30

*The number is the number of responses. As the table reports the answers to two questions with up to two answers each, the number of responses exceeds the number of respondents. The table is based on 179 respondents – weighted data.
**Total percentages exceed 100 because of multiple responses.
Source: ESRC financed research project, Economics Department, University of Stirling.

10 per cent) report that they have worked less hard, taken more holidays or planned to retire earlier as a result of the higher rate tax cuts. There is no evidence in this table that supports the chancellor's claim about enterprise.

Implications of the evidence on incentive efficiency
At the outset, I said that many laymen would define an efficient tax system as one in which there are no significant disincentive effects. This paper has looked at the evidence *vis-à-vis* the incentive to work (other possible effects, eg on savings and risk taking have been ignored). American and British evidence so far available suggests that for men there are no significant disincentive effects to work. For women, particularly American women, there appears to be evidence of disincentive effects.

What are the implications for the Irish tax system? You may well say that none of the evidence I have presented is Irish and ask if I know if it is relevant to Ireland. I have to say straight away that I have no idea whether or not Irish work incentives differ significantly from British and American incentives. However, I will proceed on the assumption that there are no significant differences between Ireland and the other two North Atlantic countries we have looked at.

This heroic assumption doubtless reminds you of the story about three men on a desert island who had a tin of fruit juice and no can opener. Each of the three was asked to propose a solution for extracting the juice from the tin. When the economist's turn came his suggestion was, 'Let us assume we have a can opener.'

With my can opener assumption I can say that it would appear that the Irish tax system is incentives efficient for men and incentives inefficient, to a debatable degree, for women.

Revenue efficiency

Can we then safely conclude that there is no case for reforming Irish income tax rates along similar lines to the US and the UK reforms? Certainly not on the basis of the argument so far.

Given the inconclusive nature of the three studies referred to above it is perhaps not surprising that the evidence on work incentives was ignored by Nigel Lawson. As the quotation from the 1988 budget speech makes clear, Lawson put great emphasis on the possibility that the reduction in the higher income tax rates would raise more revenue which brings me to my second definition of efficiency – revenue efficiency. This is the revival of an idea that goes back at least as far as Adam Smith's *Wealth of Nations*, and was stated explicitly by Dupuit in 1844:

> If a tax is gradually increased from zero up to a point where it becomes prohibitive, its yield is at first nil, then increases by small stages until it reveals a maximum, after which it gradually declines until it becomes zero again.

A Laffer curve, which might more accurately be called a Dupuit curve, is illustrated in Figure 2. It has the tax rate on the horizontal axis and tax revenue on the vertical axis.

Not surprisingly, attention is most frequently focused on the prohibitive range of the curve and on the possibility that cuts in income tax rates could raise more revenue. There are several reasons why cuts in taxation might lead to more revenue. One is the possibility that cuts in taxation might lead to people working so much more that they end up paying more income tax despite the rate being lower. An example may help. Suppose that the worker in the earlier example who was paid 10 ECU per hour and worked 40 hours had faced a 60 per cent tax rate on all income thereby paying 240 ECU per week in tax. Suppose that the tax rate was then reduced to 40 per cent. If the worker increased the hours of work by half – from 40 to 60 hours a week – the tax bill would remain 240 ECU a week. In this example then tax receipts would rise only when work increased by more than 50 per cent and we have seen that there is no reliable evidence that changes in work behaviour of anywhere near this amount will occur. This suggests that actual

Figure 2: **A Dupuit or Laffer curve**

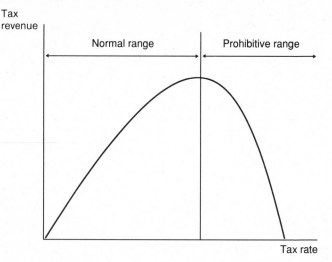

tax rates are well below the revenue-maximising level. Hemming and Kay (1980) have estimated that in the UK the revenue-maximising rate exceeds 80 per cent. Ballard *et al* (1985) for the US have estimated that with a labour supply elasticity of 0.15 the revenue-maximising rate is 70 per cent. Only if labour supply elasticities are as high as 4.0 will the revenue-maximising rate be as low as 30 per cent.

Given the evidence of limited labour supply results, from where did Lawson get his ideas? He appears to have been particularly influenced by two pieces of evidence in making the statement quoted above. The first is the increased share paid by the top 5 per cent of taxpayers in the UK, and the second is the work of Professor Lindsey (1987) of Harvard. Referring to US experience, Lindsey makes it clear that increases in labour supply were not the major reason for the revenue increase:

> Why did upper-income tax-payers pay more tax when the rates were lowered? To some extent, these upper-income tax-payers *may* have earned more by working harder. *But frankly, there aren't enough hours in the week for them to have worked to explain the enormous increase in their taxable income.* A more important explanation is a change in the way these tax-payers chose to be compensated.
>
> (Quoted in the *Sunday Times*, 20 March 1988, emphasis added.)

Higher-rate taxpayers could pay more tax as tax rates fall for several reasons including:

1. Falls in avoidance and evasion and in net emigration – as the chancellor suggested.
2. Switching of remuneration from perks to salary. When the marginal rate of tax was 83 per cent it cost an employer £5.88 (before tax) to pay an extra £1 to an employee. When the tax rate is 40 per cent the cost falls to £1.67. Salaries now become much more efficient relative to perks.
3. Switching of remuneration from capital gains to income. When the top rate of tax on unearned income was 98 per cent a person needed £50 before tax in order to receive £1 after tax. By converting that income to capital gains which was taxed at 30 per cent, the cost of £1 after tax fell by 97 per cent to £1.43.

These are all reasons for expecting that earnings at the top will rise faster than earnings at the bottom. Indeed this is what happened in the period 1979-86 when, according to the New Earnings Survey, real earnings in the top decile rose by 23 per cent compared with a rise of 11 per cent in median earnings. The arguments above depend on the reduction in the ratio between pre- and post-tax income. The force of the arguments is much greater when, for example, rates fell from 83 to 60 per cent than when they fell from 60 to 40 per cent. Does this mean that we should no longer expect rises in tax receipts? No; in the latter situation while the problem posed by the ratio between pre- and post-tax income is much reduced in scope it has not been eliminated.

In addition, a shortage of managerial talent could lead to higher pay rises for managers which would in turn increase the tax paid by those on high incomes. It is also important to note that the share of tax paid by the top 5 per cent will rise even if there are no tax cuts, no changes in the form of payment and no labour supply effects. All that is required is for real incomes to rise while the rates remain constant.

To summarise the arguments relative to revenue efficiency there are no work incentive arguments to suggest that lowering tax rates may actually increase income tax receipts. This does not rule out the possibility of extra tax receipts for other reasons.

Economic efficiency

Because almost all of the groundwork has been laid, I can be quite brief on the final of the three definitions of efficiency given at the start of this paper – economic efficiency. The formal definition of economic efficiency depends on the compensated elasticity of labour supply. Compensated labour supply elasticity refers to the response to a change in the after-tax wage rate if the person is given sufficient compensation so as not to feel worse off after a tax increase. Roughly what this means can be seen by thinking back to the concepts of income and substitution effects. If taxes raise money to pay for something useful like roads or old age pensions, road users or pensioners will be better off. The degree to which they are better off is an income effect and such positive income effects on the beneficiaries of the expenditure will roughly offset the negative income effects on the taxpayers. After cancelling out income effects we are left with substitution effects. It is because there is no offset to the distorting nature of the substitution effect that there is an element of economic inefficiency even when there is no incentive inefficiency and no revenue inefficiency.

Professor Stiglitz in his text (1988) suggests that with a 28 per cent tax on wage income this loss might lie anywhere from a negligible level up to the equivalent of nearly 12 per cent of the total revenue raised – a very high figure. While not wishing to dispute his range of estimates, I would be surprised (and I think he would be surprised as well) if the true figure is anything like as high as 12 per cent. Even if the figure is a high one that does not necessarily mean that immediate steps should be taken to reduce tax rates – that would depend on the alternatives.

You may think that I am about to conclude that there is no case to be made for changing the Irish income tax system, but that is not my conclusion. Remember first that the range of losses that I have just quoted are for a tax rate of 28 per cent and that Irish rates rise to just over 60 per cent and efficiency depends on marginal tax rates. Remember also that one reason for the high rates of tax in Ireland is that the tax base is narrow. My tentative conclusion based on my review of the evidence on incentives is that there is a case for trying to reduce income tax rates by broadening the tax base.

Notes

[1] I am grateful to HM Treasury and to the Economic and Social Research Council (ESRC) for funding some of the research reported on in this paper.

[2] Figures 1 and 2 and Tables 1 to 6 are reproduced from C.V. Brown & P.M. Jackson, *Public Sector Economics,* 4th edition, 1990.

References

Ballard, C.L., Fullerton, D., Shoven J.M. and Whalley, J., 'The relationship between tax rates and government revenue', *A General Equilibrium Model for Tax Policy Evaluation,* Chicago: NBER Monograph, University of Chicago Press, 1985.

Break, G.F., 'Income taxes and incentives to work: an empirical study', *American Economic Review* (September 1957).

Brown, C.V., *Taxation and Incentive to Work,* 2nd edition, Oxford: Oxford University Press, 1983.

Brown, C.V., 'Will the 1988 income tax cuts either increase work incentives or raise more revenue?', *Fiscal Studies* (November 1988).

Brown, C.V. and Jackson, P.M., *Public Sector Economics,* 4th edition, Basil Blackwell, 1990.

Brown, C.V. and Sandford, C.T., *Taxes and Incentives: The Effects of the 1988 Cuts in the Higher Rates of Income Tax,* Institute for Public Policy Research, Economic Study No. 7, 1990.

Burtless, G., 'The work response to a guaranteed income: a survey of experimental evidence', A.H. Munnell (ed), *Lessons from the Income Maintenance Experiments,* Federal Reserve Bank of Boston, 1987.

Fiegehen, G.C. and Reddaway, W.B., *Companies, Incentives and Senior Managers,* London: Oxford University Press for Institute for Fiscal Studies, 1981.

Fields, D.B. and Stanbury, W.T., 'Income taxes and incentives to work: some additional empirical evidence', *American Economic Review* (June 1971).

Hemming, R. and Kay, J.A., 'The Laffer Curve', *Fiscal Studies* (1980).

Holland, D.H., 'The effect of taxation on incentives in higher income groups', *Fiscal Policy and Labour Supply,* London: Institute for Fiscal Studies, 1977.

Lindsey, J.B., 'Individual taxpayer response to tax cuts 1982-1984: with implications for the revenue maximising tax rate', *Journal of Public Economics* (July 1987).

Lindsey, J.B., *Sunday Times,* 20 March 1988.

Stiglitz, J.E., *Economics of the Public Sector,* 2nd edition, Norton, 1988.

4

Efficiency and Effectiveness in Social Policies: An International Perspective

PETER SAUNDERS

Introduction

THE slowdown in economic growth that followed the supply shocks of the 1970s led to a fundamental re-assessment of the economic outlook for all OECD countries. That re-assessment has focused increasingly on the need for structural change rather than on the need for better application of existing economic and social policies. Policy makers accepted that the rules of the game had changed and that what was required was a new strategy rather than just an improvement in tactics and performance. The change in economic thinking has seen increased emphasis given to supply-side and structural issues, a resurgence of belief in the role of unregulated competitive market solutions to policy problems, and, as a consequence, a fundamental questioning of the rationale, role and impact of government intervention. The key to improved economic performance was seen to lie more in tackling micro-economic reform than in achieving greater efficacy in macro-economic policy implementation.

That any re-assessment of the structure of OECD economies would focus on the role of the public sector is hardly surprising. Studies have confirmed that, even when defined as the general government sector, thereby excluding most public enterprises, the share of government expenditure in GDP had increased markedly throughout the post-war period. By 1980, for example, the government expenditure to GDP ratio exceeded 50 per cent in about a quarter of OECD countries and was approaching 50 per cent in another quarter. Furthermore, much of the growth of government since 1960 was attributable to the growth in expenditure on social programmes, defined here following the OECD convention to include spending on health, education, income support and welfare services.

These developments raised both economic and political concerns. The economic concerns included the need to restore financial balance to the government accounts, thereby reducing levels of public debt, and the need to address the detrimental effects on economic performance resulting from the disincentives and distortions accompanying the growth of government. There were also concerns that the growth in expenditure on government programmes in general, and social programmes in particular, had been accompanied by little progress in achieving the goals of those programmes. Some even argued that there was an inverse relationship in some cases between the level of social spending and the achievement of social goals. Yet it proved extremely difficult to restrain social expenditure growth, particularly as unemployment began to rise in the early eighties. At the political level, many governments felt that the limits of taxable capacity had been reached so that the longer-run focus shifted from programme expansion to tax relief. The combination of these pressures meant that governments were finding it difficult to close the gap between expenditure and revenue that had opened in the aftermath of the first oil shock in the mid-seventies. Fiscal imbalances characterised by large structural budget deficits become common throughout the OECD, imbalances that were seen to require urgent action to control the growth in government spending in order that levels of debt and taxation could be reduced.

Public expenditure restraint thus became a central element in the broad economic policy framework and that in turn led to the need to restrain the growth in social expenditures. The resulting 'crisis of the welfare state' was seen as being driven by the need to adjust to an economic context characterised by lower economic growth, structural imbalance and higher unemployment. While there was broad acceptance of the need for greater integration of economic and social policies, what that tended to mean in practice was that social policies had to be accommodated within, and be more consistent with, broader economic imperatives. This led to a questioning of the methods and processes of social programmes, as well as of their objectives and achievements. That in itself was no bad thing. Insufficient attention had been paid to these issues in previous decades, in part because economic growth had guaranteed a steady increase in the level of resources available to social programmes. Moreover, high levels of employment meant that social programmes could use those resources to improve the living standards of children, the disabled and the elderly (through services and income support) and for the short-term income protection of the sick and the unemployed. Issues of prioritisation and resource allocation can too easily be put to one side in a context of resource expansion.

This paper will adopt a general approach to some of the underlying issues, particularly those relating to the efficiency and effectiveness of social programmes, and illustrate these with some specific examples. Relevant Australian experience in recent years will also be discussed in order to illustrate some of the general points that emerge from the analysis. But it is useful to begin with a brief overview of expenditure developments in OECD countries over the last decade.

Expenditure developments in the eighties
Despite the excellent work of the OECD in the last decade, comparable data on social expenditures – government spending on education, health, pensions, unemployment benefits and other social welfare benefits and services – are still less readily available and generally of lower quality than data on aggregate government expenditures. Even the latter are more available on the national accounts classification basis than on the kind of programme (or functional) basis that is more useful and insightful for analytical purposes. This deficiency becomes even more severe when it comes to the availability of national social statistics on social outcomes as opposed to social expenditures (although there are some notable exceptions to this). This is mentioned not only to draw attention to the need for improved social statistics, but also because it reflects the broader balance in priorities given to the social as compared with the economic dimensions of well-being and living standards. In Australia, for example, while statistics on unemployment, the balance of payments, GDP and so on are available monthly, household income and expenditure surveys – a major source of data on living standards, poverty and income distribution – are currently conducted every four or five years. The situation in Ireland is, I understand, not dissimilar. This means that much of the data required to explore the efficiency and effectiveness of social programmes, and the links between measures of social well-being and unemployment and other economic developments, are only available irregularly and normally with a time lag of several years. There is no reason to doubt that improved social statistics would make a contribution to improved analysis and policy formulation in the social sphere similar to that which followed the development and production of national accounts data in the economic sphere. There might also be a marked shift in political prioritisation if politicians were required to comment on monthly poverty and other social statistics as well as on balance of payments or unemployment developments! Table 1 summarises what is currently available on developments

in general government and social expenditures in OECD countries since 1975. Although total government expenditures are available in 1989 for most countries, comparative and comprehensive social expenditure data are not available after 1985. This is particularly unfortunate, since it is clear from Table 1 that the main changes in total government expenditure have occurred in the period since 1985. Between 1980 and 1985, government expenditure continued to increase relative to GDP in all countries except Germany and Norway. The growth of government spending over this period was in fact generally *greater* than between 1975 and 1980, reflecting the severe recession of 1981-83 and the rise in unemployment which accompanied it. Between 1985 and 1989, general government expenditure grew at a slower rate than GDP in almost all countries.

Table 1: **General government expenditure and social expenditure in OECD countries since 1975 (Percentages of GDP)**

	Total government expenditure				Social expenditure		
	1975	*1980*	*1985*	*1989*	*1975*	*1980*	*1985*
Australia	33.6	33.8	38.8	33.0	17.6	17.3	18.4
Austria	46.1	48.9	51.7	49.3	23.4	26.0	28.8
Belgium	44.5	50.7	53.7	49.5	28.7	33.9	35.8
Canada	40.1	40.5	47.1	44.5	20.1	19.5	22.6
Denmark	48.2	56.2	59.3	59.9	27.1	35.1	33.9
Finland	36.1	36.6	41.6	38.6	21.9	22.9	22.8
France	43.4	46.1	52.2	49.6	26.3	30.9	34.2
Germany	48.9	48.3	47.5	44.8	27.8	26.6	25.8
Greece	26.7	30.5	43.7	47.2	10.0	12.6	19.5
Ireland	46.5	50.8	55.2	47.9	22.0	23.8	25.6
Italy	43.2	41.7	50.8	51.7	20.6	23.7	26.7
Japan	27.3	32.6	32.7	33.1	13.7	16.1	16.2
Netherlands	52.8	57.5	59.7	56.0	29.3	31.8	30.7
Norway	46.2	48.3	45.6	53.7	23.2	24.2	23.5
Spain	24.7	32.9	42.1	40.9	*	15.6	15.2
Sweden	48.9	61.3	64.3	60.1	27.4	33.2	32.0[c]
Switzerland	28.7[a]	29.3[a]	31.0[a]	30.0[a]	19.0	19.1	20.5[c]
United Kingdom	46.6	44.9	46.2	39.5	19.6	20.0	20.9
United States	34.6	33.7	36.7	36.3	18.7	18.0	18.2
OECD Average[b]	**40.4**	**43.4**	**47.4**	**45.5**	**22.0**	**23.7**	**24.8**

[a] Current disbursements only.

[b] Unweighted average.

[c] 1984.

*Not available.

Sources: OECD, *Economic Outlook 47,* June 1990; OECD, *The Future of Social Protection,* 1988; OECD, Secretariat estimates (for 1989).

Greece and Norway were the only two countries where the 1989 spending ratio exceeded its 1985 value by more than one percentage point, while small increases were experienced in Denmark, Italy and Japan. Everywhere else the ratio fell over the period, and in many cases it fell substantially.

In Australia, Belgium, Ireland, Sweden and the United Kingdom, for example, the ratio fell by more than four percentage points between 1985 and 1989. In two of these countries – Australia and the United Kingdom – and also in Germany, the spending ratio in 1989 was lower than it was in 1975. Another five countries – Austria, Finland, Ireland, Switzerland and the United States – had spending ratios in 1989 that were only slightly above those in 1975. In only two countries – Denmark and Norway – has the government spending ratio increased markedly since 1985. The years since 1985 have thus seen a reduction in the relative size of government in most OECD countries. This development, along with an increase in average revenues relative to GDP of broadly equal size over the period, has contributed to a significant reduction in the budget deficit to GDP ratio in most countries and thus in the OECD area as a whole.

As already explained, changes in the ratio of social expenditure to GDP are available on a comparable basis for most countries until 1985 only. Table 1 indicates that on average the growth of social expenditures relative to GDP between 1980 and 1985 was somewhat slower than between 1975 and 1980. The growth in total government spending relative to GDP shows an opposite outcome. The slowdown in social spending growth relative to GDP during 1980-85 occurred against a general background of more rapidly rising unemployment than occurred between 1975 and 1980. However, the extent of the rise in unemployment after 1980 varied substantially between countries, implying that the effort made to control spending growth is by no means revealed by movements in the expenditure aggregates themselves.

While in general there is a positive relationship across countries between the growth in the social expenditure ratio between 1980 and 1985 and the rise in the unemployment rate, there are also a number of important exceptions to this rule. In Ireland and Spain, for example, the unemployment rate in 1985 exceeded that in 1980 by around 10 percentage points, yet the social expenditure ratio rose only modestly over this period in Ireland and actually declined in Spain. The Netherlands and the United Kingdom both experienced a rise in unemployment of over 5 percentage points yet each experienced a change in the social spending ratio around one percentage point. Such examples illustrate that while it is generally easier to control the growth of social expenditure when unemployment is falling (or at least not increasing rapidly) a number of countries have managed to exert spending control in a context of rapidly rising unemployment.

Excluding the Southern European economies of Greece and Spain (which does not affect the main thrust of the argument), the countries shown in Table 1 can be classified into three groups on the basis of their relative government size in 1980. The first group, characterised by big government spending ratios, contains Belgium, Denmark, Ireland, Netherlands and Sweden. This group had an average total spending ratio of around 55 per cent in 1980, and an average social spending ratio of around 32 per cent. The second group, characterised by medium government spending ratios, contains Austria, Canada, France, Germany, Italy, Norway and the United Kingdom. This group had an average total spending ratio of around 45 per cent in 1980 and an average social spending ratio of around 24 per cent. The third group, characterised by small government spending ratios, contains Australia, Finland, Japan, Switzerland and the United States. This group had an average total spending ratio of around 33 per cent in 1980 and an average social spending ratio of around 17 per cent. Between 1980 and 1985, the average increase in the total spending ratio was very similar for all three groups – 3.1, 3.2 and 3.0 percentage points of GDP, respectively.

Evidence on selected social expenditure developments since 1985 is presented in Table 2. These data have been derived from a range of OECD sources, some of which have used national data to extend the scope of the comparative social expenditure data. For this reason, the data in Table 2 are not as comparable as those in Table 1. Together, the estimates in Tables 1 and 2 indicate that government spending is high primarily because social spending is high, and that social spending is high mainly because spending on social security transfers is high. Table 2 indicates that the social expenditure to GDP ratio was held broadly constant in the two to three years after 1985. In most countries, health and social security transfer spending were held constant relative to GDP, while education spending declined slightly relative to GDP. The only significant increases after 1985 were health and education spending in Norway, and spending on social security transfers in Denmark, Japan and Norway. The most significant declines in social spending relative to GDP were health in Ireland, education in Finland, France and the United States, and social security transfers in Australia, Belgium, Finland and the United Kingdom. Developments in social security transfers after 1985, as shown in Table 2, need to be assessed against a background of gradual decline in the rate of unemployment in the OECD region. Indeed, the only two countries where the unemployment rate rose between 1985 and 1988 were Italy and Norway, and both were countries where transfer spending rose relative to GDP over the period.

Table 3 complements Tables 1 and 2 by presenting data for a range of countries on the structure of general government spending. It needs to be emphasised that some of these estimates have been derived from national sources, so that there are problems of comparability. Nevertheless, the estimates serve to locate the welfare state and associated levels of expenditure within the broader general government sector of modern capitalist economies. In all countries

Table 2: **Selected social expenditure developments since 1985 (Percentages of GDP)**

	Health		Education		Social Security Transfers	
	1985	1987	1985	1987	1985	1988
Australia	5.0	5.1	5.7	5.2	9.6	8.8
Austria	5.4	5.7	4.4	4.5	20.4	20.3
Belgium	5.5	5.5	7.3	*	21.7	20.9
Canada	6.4	6.5	5.9	*	12.2	12.0
Denmark	5.3	5.2	7.2	6.8	16.3	17.6
Finland	5.7	5.8	6.2	5.1(a)	10.8	9.5
France	6.9	6.7	6.1	5.5(b)	22.1	21.7
Germany	6.4	6.3	4.4	4.4	16.2	16.0
Greece	4.0	4.0	3.3	*	14.8	15.3
Ireland	7.1	6.4	6.4	*	16.6	16.8(c)
Italy	5.4	5.4	5.9	*	17.1	17.3
Japan	4.8	5.0	4.3	4.3(a)	11.0	11.8
Netherlands	6.6	6.6	5.6	5.7(a)	26.1	25.7
Norway	6.1	7.4	5.6(d)	6.7(a)	14.8	16.3(c)
Spain	4.3	4.3	2.2	*	16.5	*
Sweden	8.6	8.2	5.9(e)	5.7	18.2	18.6(c)
Switzerland	5.2	5.2	5.5(e)	*	13.7	13.8
United Kingdom	5.2	5.3	5.0	5.1(b)	13.8	13.1(c)
United States	4.5	4.6	5.3	4.5	11.0	10.6
OECD Average	**5.7**	**5.7**	**5.4**	**5.3**	**15.9**	**15.9**

(a) 1988; (b) 1986; (c) 1987; (d) 1980; (e) 1984.
*Not available.
Sources: OECD, *The Future of Social Protection,* Table 3, p. 11. OECD, *Health Care Systems in Transition,* Table 1, p. 10. OECD, *Historical Statistics 1960-1988,* Table 6.3. OECD, Secretariat estimates (for Education in 1987/88).

Social Policies

Table 3: The structure of general government expenditure in the late 1980s (Percentages of GDP)

	Australia (1987)	Austria (1987)	Denmark (1987)	Finland (1988)	France (1986)	Germany (1987)	Norway (1988)	Sweden (1987)	United Kingdom (1986)	United States (1987)
1. The traditional domain	6.7	5.3	8.2	4.6	7.8	7.9	7.2	6.7	8.9	9.7
Defence	2.3	1.1	2.0	1.5	3.1	2.7	3.0	2.6	4.9	6.6
General public services	4.4	4.2	6.2	3.1	4.7	5.2	4.2	4.1	4.0	3.1
2. The welfare state(a)	19.4	30.4	29.2	22.5	37.3	28.6	32.1	31.9	25.3	13.9
Merit goods	12.1	10.1	13.8	10.9	13.4	12.2	16.5	14.7	12.1	6.0
Income maintenance	7.3	20.3	15.4	11.6	23.9	16.4	15.6	17.2	13.2	7.9
3. The mixed economy	9.1	11.1	14.0	7.7	6.5	7.5	13.3	14.2	8.8	10.7
Economic services	5.1	7.2	5.7	6.1	3.6	4.7	9.4	7.7	4.3	5.7
Public debt interest	4.0	3.9	8.3	1.6	2.9	2.8	3.9	6.5	4.5	5.0
4. Balancing item(b)	1.2	6.0	6.2	5.4	0.0	2.9	0.9	6.5	2.5	2.6
5. Total expenditure	36.4	52.8	57.6	40.2	51.6	46.9	53.5	59.3	45.5	36.9

(a) Merit goods include expenditure on housing and community amenities, which is not part of social expenditure as defined in Table 1.
(b) The data coverage for the different items is not entirely consistent, which explains the presence of this item.
Source: OECD, Annual National Accounts, supplemented by estimates prepared by the OECD Secretariat.

85

except Germany, the Netherlands and Sweden, welfare state spending continued to grow relative to GDP after 1979. The size of the welfare state accounts for close to a third of GDP in most countries, and differences in welfare state spending explain much of the difference in the overall size of the general government sector. The estimates in Table 3 also confirm those in Table 2 in highlighting the role of spending on income transfers in explaining differences in the size of the welfare state.

Such comparisons of differences in the level and change in government expenditure aggregates cannot, of course, provide any insight into differences in the difficulties posed by and hence the commitment required to enact the more recent changes. This is particularly true in the social policy area, where many programmes have introduced contingent entitlements which have meant that expenditure is largely determined, in the short run at least, by exogenous factors relating to broader economic and demographic trends. Because the pressures resulting from those trends differ between countries, comparisons of the levels of, and short-term changes in, social expenditures can provide quite misleading indications of the relative severity of policy changes.

It is in this context that the social expenditure decomposition analysis developed and undertaken in a number of OECD studies provides more insight into the relationship between social policies and social expenditures (OECD, 1976; Saunders and Klau, 1985; OECD, 1985; 1988a; 1988b). Such decompositions disaggregate expenditure movements into demographic, coverage (or eligibility) and benefit level changes. They provide a useful framework for analysing social expenditure trends, for projecting future expenditure developments, and for thinking about relevant policy issues in a structured way. But they no more provide an explanation of *why* social expenditures have grown than the national accounts explain economic growth, or than double-entry book keeping explains company profitability. The decompositions are, however, useful as a first step in delving behind the expenditure aggregates in order to focus on the underlying policy and analytical issues. It is on these issues that the remainder of this paper will focus.

The social policy context in the eighties
As noted above, the broad context for social policies throughout the OECD region in the last decade was shaped by economic considerations, specifically by the push to control public expenditure as part of an overall programme of economic re-structuring. Within this context, the improved integration of economic and social policies has required social policies to take a distinct second place to economic

policy considerations. That may be an improvement over complete policy dichotomy, but it is hardly policy integration in the true meaning of the word. Public expenditure restraint has not, however, been the only economic development in the 1980s that has shaped the social policy agenda. There are at least three other economic developments that have also had a significant impact: changes in the labour market, the general change in economic thinking on the role of economic policy, and demographic change.

Changes in the labour market
It has already been noted that the persistence of high levels of unemployment has placed strains on income support programmes and made the task of expenditure control more difficult. The existence of large scale unemployment has also increased the diversity in the circumstances of those who are unemployed and thus expanded the scope of the kinds of intervention required to address the unemployment problem. Social policies for the unemployed have thus had to deal with a more heterogeneous set of issues and, as long-term unemployment has increased, a more serious set of problems. That task is hard enough when sufficient resources are available, but when they are not it becomes close to impossible. The fate of many unemployed people, particularly the long-term unemployed, has inevitably suffered as a consequence, as evidenced by the emergence of a 'new poor' mainly comprising jobless working age families (Room, Lawson and Laczko, 1989).

Two other relevant labour market trends are the increased labour force participation of married women and the increased prevalence of part-time work. The increase in the former has led to new demands for social programmes, particularly in the areas of child care and related services (eg transport) which facilitate labour market involvement. The growth in part-time work has raised issues about how income transfer arrangements can be re-structured in order to offer the combination of part-time work with part-rate benefit receipt that is perceived as a viable income package in a labour surplus economy. This has in turn renewed interest in the need to avoid poverty traps which provide little financial incentive to seek such a combination of benefit and earnings. These developments have each produced new challenges for income support systems in a number of countries and have further complicated the task of expenditure control. While there had been general acceptance of the need for income support arrangements to facilitate labour market involvement, this has proved difficult in practice because of resource limitations and increasing numbers being forced to rely on the income support safety net.

The change in economic thinking

Labour market change has, however, presented less of a challenge to social policies than the change in economic thinking that has taken place in the last decade. If the fifties and sixties were decades of Keynesian consensus and the seventies the decade of supply-side shocks, then the eighties has surely been the decade of the ideology of the market. There has been a resurgence in belief in market-based solutions to both macro-economic and micro-economic problems and that, not surprisingly, has presented a major challenge to the role of government intervention generally, but also more specifically to social intervention. Much of the basis for this revolution in economic thinking has been primarily ideological in nature, having more to do with notions of individual freedom from the 'coercion of taxation' and other forms of government intervention than with the proven superiority of market mechanisms and competition as means of achieving improved allocative and other efficiencies. This highlights the need to distinguish as far as possible between the expression of value positions and issues of a more technical nature, a point which will be further discussed later.

This revolution in economic thinking has presented more of a crisis for the welfare state than that caused by the decline in economic performance which began in the mid-seventies. The message to emerge from that earlier crisis was essentially that social policies needed to be assessed and restructured in order to become more consistent with (and affordable in) a future of lower economic growth and higher unemployment. In contrast, the new economic rationalist lines of thought suggest not that the welfare state needs to be re-structured, but rather that large sections of it should be dismantled entirely. The economic rationalists argue that not only are social programmes (and their financing) in fundamental contradiction with notions of freedom of choice, competition and market provision, but that the perverse incentives caused by social programmes have contributed to, and not alleviated, the social problems that those programmes were initially designed to address (Murray, 1984).

This is not the place to address these latter claims. It is, however, worth pointing to the fact that reviews of the relevant literature have tended not to confirm many of them. That was certainly a general finding to emerge from work undertaken by the OECD (eg Saunders and Klau, 1985). This is not to deny that there may be individual instances where social programmes have produced moral hazard, adverse selection and disincentive effects that warrant action.[1] However, the available evidence certainly does not provide generalised support for the view that social programmes have contributed markedly to the deterioration of economic performance, nor to the increased severity of social problems. Only the most superficial reading of the evidence, combined with considerable naïvety about the merits of the free market in solving social problems can sustain such a position.

But this does not mean that all of the ideas associated with the new economic rationalism should be rejected. Far from it. There is much of value in thinking about how the design of social policies can benefit from such concepts as consumer choice, competition and market allocation. These lines of thinking have opened up new avenues and possibilities in such areas as the organisation and delivery of welfare services, the responsiveness of welfare services to the needs of users, the relationship between public and private forms of provision, the balance between centralisation and decentralisation in welfare programmes, and the structure of incentives built-in to the design of social programmes. Furthermore, in addition to bringing new challenges to the design, means and processes of social policies, developments in economic and social policy thinking in the last decade have led to a re-assessment of the objectives of social policies, an issue that will be explored in greater detail in the following section.

Demographic change
The final development that has had a major impact on social policy in the eighties has been primarily demographic in nature. In this context, the work of the OECD has been of particular value in identifying the underlying issues and canvassing alternative policy strategies. Put simply, the maturing of the welfare state in the fifties and sixties involved the establishment of programmes guaranteeing citizens a number of entitlements which were provided (generally free of charge at the point of use) to those satisfying certain broadly specified contingencies. Public pensions provided income maintenance during retirement; transfer programmes provided income support (or income maintenance) for invalids, the unemployed and sick; education and health benefits were free of charge or were heavily subsidised, and so on. In this sense, the development of the welfare state represented the establishment of certain basic entitlements – to education, health and income support – which together constitute what Marshall (1981) referred to as the social rights of citizenship. It follows that if the establishment of entitlements was the objective of social programmes, then social expenditures would be the outcome of the interaction between those entitlements and changes in the numbers eligible to receive the benefits in each contingency group.

The OECD decomposition analysis referred to earlier shows that the growth in social expenditure up to the early 1980s reflected increases in the size of contingent groups to a greater extent than increased generosity of programme benefits (OECD, 1985; Saunders and Klau, 1985). Such results raised issues of whether these increases in the number of recipients were exogenous to the development of policies or were in fact induced by them as individuals changed their behaviour in order to satisfy contingency definitions and thus become eligible to receive benefits. This had led in turn to pressures to narrow the scope of the contingency categories and to tighten their administration, so that the integrity and hence legitimacy of social programmes could be protected. In practice, however, such moves have been directed to certain recipient groups only (the unemployed and sole parents) where prejudice and misinformation has tended to be more widespread than solid evidence of fraud and/or abuse.

Expenditure projections using the decomposition framework and based on projected population trends point to a sharp rise in social expenditures as a consequence of the ageing of the population in most OECD countries. In a recent OECD report, for example, population ageing between 1985 and 2040 in a range of OECD countries is projected to cause an increase in social expenditure per person of working age ranging from just over 10 per cent (in the United Kingdom), to around 50 per cent (in Japan and the Netherlands) and to almost 60 per cent (in Germany) (OECD, 1988c; Table 6). Such projections have served to highlight the future financing implications of existing social provisions, and thus the need to consider ways in which these can be met most cost efficiently, effectively and equitably. One important lesson to emerge from such exercises has been that policy action is required now if undue future inter-generational conflicts are to be avoided.

Although the social expenditure implications of population ageing appear dramatic, the assumed rate of economic growth over the projection period has a crucial bearing on the financing implications for social programmes. It is generally the case, for example, that even relatively modest rates of economic growth permit the projected future expenditures to be financed without major increases in contribution (or tax) rates. However, that is hardly reassuring to governments committed to reducing levels of taxation. Furthermore, most projections assume that social expenditure benefits remain unchanged in real terms over the forecast period. This seems to be an unduly optimistic assumption. It does not, for example, conform with the historical experience of increasing real benefit levels in most instances, at least up until very recently. Neither is it consistent with the fact that cross-country comparisons show that pension expenditure per aged person varies *positively* with the proportion of the population who are aged 65 or over (Saunders, 1990a). There is thus a real challenge for governments to persuade those who will retire in the early decades of the next century to accept lower real pension levels or coverage rates, in a way which will be politically acceptable to a group which is becoming an increasingly large proportion of the electorate.

The developments reviewed in this section help explain some of the main features of the current and future context for social policy in advanced countries. The pressures for restraint of social expenditure that have been experienced since the late seventies show little sign of easing in the foreseeable future. In this sense, the crisis of the welfare state which began a decade ago is set to be on-going rather than temporary for a number of related economic, demographic and ideological reasons. It is thus legitimate, indeed essential, that issues relating to the efficiency and effectiveness of social programmes deserve the closest scrutiny.

The efficiency and effectiveness of social programmes
It is not surprising that the forces shaping the evolution of social policies and expenditures in the last decade have also influenced the concepts and terminology of social policy discourse. One illustration of this is to be found by comparing the concepts discussed and analysed in the first OECD report devoted to social policy – published in 1981 (OECD, 1981) – with those utilised in more recent OECD social policy reports (OECD, 1985; 1988c). In *The Welfare State in Crisis* (1981) it is difficult to find any reference to the effectiveness of social programmes. There is extensive discussion of efficiency issues, but this is undertaken by and large in the context of the trade-off between efficiency and equality given prominence in the work of Arthur Okun (Okun, 1975). In contrast, in the later reports *Social Expenditure 1960-1990. Problems of Growth and Control* (1985) and *The Future of Social Protection* (1988c), emphasis is given to the concepts of efficiency and effectiveness, with correspondingly less attention devoted to issues of equality (or inequality). The sense in which the concept of efficiency is used in these later reports also differs from the idea of allocative efficiency which has been the main focus of the analysis of Okun and other economists (eg Barr, 1987a; 1987b). The concepts of efficiency and effectiveness are used to refer to aspects internal to the operation of specific programmes, rather than in relation to more general, societal concerns. This increasing focus on individual programmes has been reinforced by the replacement of concerns about equality – issues of relevance in a broad social context

– to the concern with effectiveness, an issue which is again of more immediate relevance to individual social programmes.

In a period of resource constraint, it is no cause for surprise that policy makers should wish to focus at the programme level on the use and effects of resources. That change in focus is one aspect of the 'new managerialism' that has come to dominate much of public and social policy discussion in the last decade. As argued in the OECD report on social expenditure growth, where there is extensive state involvement in the finance and provision of social programmes:

> ... the task of improving effectiveness and efficiency resolves itself into a management issue, and in particular the establishment of criteria by which management is judged to be successful (OECD, 1985, p. 60).

From this perspective, the concepts of efficiency and effectiveness have become part of a new culture of government, along with such budgetary concepts as cash limits and constitutional spending constraints, and such managerial concepts as performance indicators, decision-making devolution and autonomy, and so on. This focus of attention at the programme level is fine as long as sight is not lost of the broader social picture and of the underlying social objectives to which social programmes are directed. Yet a case can be made that this has not occurred, that in focusing on individual programmes and technical managerial issues, policy-making has become divorced from the underlying social realities and problems.

At the programme level, efficiency is concerned with the relationship between programme inputs and programme outputs, while effectiveness refers to the relationship between programme outputs and programme objectives. Clearly, both concepts can thus become of operational value only after outputs and objectives have been specified and quantified. That is no simple matter, but the task of changing the focus of social policy analysis away from inputs towards consideration of output measures and statements of objectives is nonetheless an important one. All the more so when the amount of resources available to social programmes is becoming increasingly scarce. In that situation, it is perfectly legitimate – indeed essential – to question the objectives of social programmes and to assess their achievements against those objectives.

In general, it is possible to distinguish three levels at which the concept of efficiency can be applied in the context of the public sector. The first relates to the efficient use of *society's* resources, the second to the efficient use of *public* resources, and the third to the efficient use of *programme* resources. The focus in the first is primarily on the appropriate overall balance between the public and private sectors, the focus on the second is primarily on the balance between different government programmes, and the focus in the third is on the alternative use of resources within government programmes. Throughout the last decade, the focus of policy has shifted from the first to the second and, increasingly, to the third of these concepts of efficiency. It is similarly possible, conceptually at least, to approach the effectiveness issue at either of these three levels. But so far much of the debate on effectiveness has concentrated at the individual programme level, in part because it naturally lends itself to analysis at that level.

Three general points need to be emphasised about the application of these concepts of efficiency and effectiveness in the social policy context. The first is that both concepts are essentially *technical* in nature, and the limitation of applying such technical concepts to social programmes which embody important social *values* needs to be recognised. Second, there are likely to be conflicts in practical terms between efficient and effective solutions, just as there are in Okun's 'great trade-off' between efficiency and equality. The nature of any trade-off will, of course, be altered, but not the need to confront conflicting objectives and choose solutions which involve compromising some objectives. Third, as noted earlier, both concepts become of operational use only when programme outputs and objectives have been clearly specified and reliably quantified in some way. This opens up the possibility for debate on what these objectives are, and how (or whether) output can be quantified, a debate on which there is unlikely to be consensus particularly when value positions intercede, as indeed they must.

A final point relates to the dangers of restricting the analysis too much to an assessment of programmes considered separately. This approach runs the risk of down-playing important interactions between programmes. Thus, for example, the effectiveness of programme A may be dependent upon the existence of programme B. Changes to programme B designed to improve its efficiency and effectiveness may thus reduce the effectiveness of programme A. Similarly, while the existence of programme A may be *necessary* to achieve a particular social objective, it may well not be *sufficient* to do so. Other policies and programmes may also be required. If this is the case, then the apparent failure of programme A to produce the desired result may not reflect any ineffectiveness in that programme itself, but rather point to the failure to establish the other conditions necessary for its success. In short, while application of efficiency and effectiveness analysis may proceed within individual programmes, it is a mistake to divorce the analysis

93

entirely from the broader structure of economic and social policies and processes. There is something of a paradox here, in that the focus on individual programmes which has accompanied the application of efficiency and effectiveness concepts has taken place at a time when governments have recognised the need for greater integration of social policies in order to respond to the labour market and other changes described earlier.

Turning more specifically to issues relating to the measurement of programme outputs, as well as to the specification of programme objectives, one runs immediately into problems concerning the quality of available data and social statistics. Following the national accounting conventions, social expenditure data refer to expenditure on inputs (in the case of service provisions like education and health) or to expenditure on benefits (in the case of income transfers). Because of the absence of markets for education and health services (in most instances) there are no price data on which to base estimates of the value of output, as occurs in the case of goods and services produced and sold in the private sector. National accounts conventions (with some minor exceptions) thus equate the value of service outputs with the expenditure on service inputs, the implication being that service productivity is constant and equal to one. The national accounts thus by definition provide no basis for estimating the productivity and hence technical efficiency of social service provisions.

The problems associated with specifying the objectives of social programmes are no less daunting. One of the very useful developments that has occurred in the last decade – both within and outside government – has been the increased attention devoted to specifying exactly what *are* the objectives of social programmes. But this has produced disagreement rather than agreement about what those objectives are and how they should be measured. Most agree, for example, that a basic objective of most social programmes is to ensure greater equality through redistribution. But there are many different meanings of the concept of equality as it applies to social programmes (Le Grand, 1982). Furthermore, measurement of the redistributive impact of programmes requires agreement not only on the specific dimension of equality under consideration, but also on the benchmark situation (or counterfactual) against which comparisons are to be made. The problems involved in specifying such a counterfactual are extremely complex and should not be underestimated – many of the debates about the impact of social programmes revolve around disagreement over what is the appropriate counterfactual against which to assess programme performance. Thus, for example, while it may be difficult enough to establish what has happened to trends in poverty over a particular period of time, it is a far more difficult task to estimate with any degree of reliability what would have happened to poverty if a different set of circumstances had prevailed over the period. Yet it is the latter estimate that is needed in order to estimate the effectiveness of the anti-poverty policies in place at the time.

In order to give more substance to the argument and to illustrate the strengths and limitations of the concepts of efficiency and effectiveness, it is useful to consider some concrete examples. In any discussion of the welfare state, it is important to distinguish programmes that provide income support through the payment of cash transfers from programmes which provide education, health and welfare services in non-cash form. The former programmes involve no direct claim on resources, but redistribute income from one group to another. Efficiency and effectiveness in this context thus relate to the processes through which those redistributive transfer mechanisms operate and what their effects are. By contrast, resources of labour and capital are involved in the provision of non-cash community services, so that the conventional economic theory of production and the concept of productive efficiency appear to have more direct relevance.

Income support

The income support systems in all OECD countries share certain basic similarities and a number of important differences. All are contingent schemes, in the sense that benefits are paid to certain eligible groups defined in various ways according to age (the elderly; dependent children), health status (invalids; the sick) or socio-economic status (the unemployed; sole parents). Differences are more likely to arise about the basis on which benefit entitlement is determined than about the contingencies which determine benefit eligibility. At one extreme are income (or means) tested benefits which vary inversely with the current means of those eligible, and at the other extreme are earnings related benefits which vary positively with previous earnings levels. The former are concerned to provide basic levels of *income support,* while the latter are more concerned with *income maintenance* relative to previous income levels. In other words, the schemes have different objectives, and measures of effectiveness must allow for this. In between these two systems are universal benefits which are paid at the same rate to all those eligible and thus do not vary with either past or current income levels. The methods of financing each of these three forms of income transfers vary, as does their relative importance across countries.

In a context of limited resources, combined with the emergence of new groups requiring financial assistance (eg the long-term unemployed), increasing attention has been focused on the need to improve the targeting of cash transfer expenditures, by concentrating them more on those in greatest need. Leaving aside questions relating to the definition of 'need' in this context, the approach suggests that a movement away from universal and earnings-related benefits towards means-tested benefits will result in a system that is more effective and, in a limited sense, more efficient also. These ideas were in fact first applied to the analysis of cash transfer programmes over a decade ago in a number of reports by Wilfred Beckerman (Beckerman 1979a; 1979b; Beckerman and Clark, 1982). They have also been applied to investigate the efficiency and effectiveness of social welfare provisions in Ireland in a very interesting report recently released by The Economic and Social Research Institute (ESRI: Callan *et al.,* 1989).

The framework developed by Beckerman and used in the recent ESRI study is illustrated in Figure 1, where for convenience the terminology follows that used in the ESRI study. In constructing Figure 1, families are ranked according to their incomes, those with lowest incomes on the left. The lines YX and Y*X indicate the levels of family income before and after the receipt of income transfers, respectively. The vertical distance between Y*X and YX thus represents the amount of transfers received, this amount declining as family income increases and becoming equal to zero at the income level corresponding to point X. The income corresponding to the poverty line is shown by the horizontal line PP. (The fact that the poverty line is assumed to be constant for all families means that income should be thought of as measured in equivalent units, ie after adjusting for differences in family needs.) Total expenditure on cash transfers is equal to the area between the pre-transfer income and post-transfer income lines, or the area A_1+A_2+B+C on Figure 1. (Strictly speaking, this is only true if the distribution of household income is uniform over this range of income.) The pre-transfer poverty gap – equal to the total income shortfall below the poverty line of all families in poverty – is equal to the area A_1+A_2+D. The post-transfer poverty gap is equal to the area D. The payment of transfers thus reduces the poverty gap by an amount equal to A_1+A_2.

Using Beckerman and the ESRI study, the following measures can now be defined:

Poverty Reduction Effectiveness $= (A_1+A_2)/(A_1+A_2+D)$
Poverty Reduction Efficiency $= (A_1+A_2)/(A_1+A_2+B+C)$

Figure 1: **Poverty reduction efficiency and effectiveness**

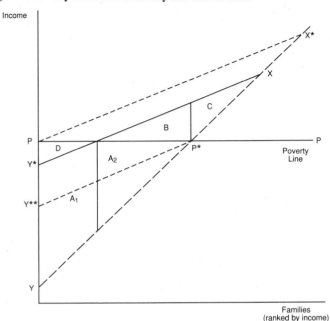

Effectiveness is thus measured by the proportionate reduction in the pre-transfer poverty gap, while efficiency is measured by the proportion of total transfers paid which are received by those families in poverty before the receipt of transfers and which do not 'spill over' by raising them above the poverty line. (These concepts of effectiveness and efficiency broadly correspond to what writers in the personal social services field refer to as horizontal target efficiency and vertical target efficiency, respectively [Knapp, 1988].) For a *given* pre-transfer income distribution (the assumed counterfactual in this situation) and for a *given* total level of spending on transfers, both effectiveness and efficiency would be increased if a greater proportion of transfers were concentrated on those families who would be in poverty in the absence of transfers.

On the face of it, the approach illustrated in Figure 1 provides a useful framework for analysing the effectiveness and efficiency of income support programmes. It is possible to investigate, for example, how changes in the basic benefit level and the withdrawal rate influence effectiveness and efficiency. Consider, for example, changes in the benefit level. If the basic benefit level is increased from YY* to YP then the poverty gap is eliminated so that

97

effectiveness rises to 100 per cent. However, as the new post-transfer poverty line (PX*) in Figure 1 indicates, transfer efficiency declines. Similarly, if the benefit level is reduced from YY* to YY**, transfer effectiveness falls but transfer efficiency rises to 100 per cent. For a given withdrawal rate, there is thus a trade-off between the level of benefits and the effectiveness and efficiency of the benefit system. It is also possible to fix the benefit level and explore the implications for efficiency and effectiveness of changing the (constant) withdrawal rate; in this case, the post-transfer line Y*X would pivot around the point Y* in Figure 1.

The only way in which effectiveness and efficiency can both be made equal to 100 per cent is if the benefit system follows the kinked line PP*X in Figure 1. This is the situation in which the benefit paid is exactly equal to the difference between pre-transfer income and the poverty line. But it is a situation in which the effective marginal tax rate on the pre-transfer poor is equal to 100 per cent. Such an extreme form of the poverty trap is hardly likely to be described as efficient from a broader perspective in which, for example, effects on work incentives are taken into account. What appears to be efficient from a programme perspective may thus be inefficient from a broader social and economic perspective.

The framework shown in Figure 1 underlies recent thinking on reform of the transfer system in a number of countries. In a situation of severe expenditure restraint, considerable attention has been paid to improving the targeting of income support payments by concentrating assistance on those in greatest financial difficulty. In terms of Figure 1, savings made from reducing the 'spillover' payments corresponding to areas B+C, payments which are likely to be very costly if the income distribution is heavily concentrated in this range, can be used to finance increased basic benefits, and thus reduce the size of the post-transfer poverty gap (Area D). Whether such a targeting strategy can work in practice depends upon the relevance of the framework shown in Figure 1 and the applicability of the assumptions which underlie it. One weakness of the framework is that it is essentially static in focus. Movements towards the kinked benefit line PP*X may be frustrated when allowance is made for individual responses to the incentives produced by this move. These include the poverty trap issue noted earlier, but also the incentive for those not in poverty to seek to become eligible for levels of assistance which cause only small declines in their disposable income. Where such behavioural adjustments occur, the problems of specifying the counterfactual once again become considerable.

Another assumption implicit in the framework shown in Figure

1 is that the benefit level is independent of the structure of the benefit system. An alternative view is that the revenue raising potential of the benefit system, and thus the level of benefits that can be paid under that system, depends upon the structure of benefits provided. This view implies that compared with means-tested systems those systems which offer more universal benefits receive greater political support, generate increased revenues and thus enable the payment of higher benefits. Thus while the latter systems may produce less effective targeting of any *given* level of resources, that becomes less of an issue if the level of resources is itself a variable determined by the structure of the system.

The relevance of this point receives support from Beckerman's own cross-country application of the framework (Beckerman, 1979a). His results show that in 1973-74, the Australian transfer system scored high in terms of his efficiency measure, but nonetheless had a relatively high incidence of poverty, while Belgium in the same year had a transfer system which had a low efficiency and yet had virtually eliminated poverty. As Beckerman notes in explaining these findings:

> ... an 'inefficient' pattern of expenditure can still greatly reduce poverty if enough is spent (while) an 'efficient' pattern of expenditure may do little to reduce poverty if very little is spent (Beckerman, 1979a, p. 58).

Some more recent comparative evidence relevant to this issue is contained in Table 4. Analysis is restricted to the elderly, where different income support arrangements can be most easily compared, and where complications arising from variations in economic performance are minimised. The first two columns of Table 4 follow the recent OECD (1988b) classification of pension systems. The next two columns show the elderly as a percentage of the population and pension expenditure as a percentage of GDP. The ratio of these two percentages is shown in column five as a measure of pension generosity, ie pension expenditure per elderly person expressed as a percentage of per capita GDP. The last two columns show the relative poverty rate among the elderly and the effectiveness of transfers in reducing the pre-transfer poverty rate. These poverty estimates have been produced as a part of the Luxembourg Income Study, a project aimed at improving comparative estimates of poverty, inequality and other dimensions of economic well-being (Smeeding, Torrey and Rein, 1988).

Table 4 shows very considerable diversity across this group of eight countries in relation to the structure of pension systems, the incidence of poverty among the elderly and transfer poverty

Table 4: **Public pension systems and poverty among the elderly in selected countries around 1980**

Country	Pension classification in 1985	Pension[a] types	Elderly population percentage in 1980 (%)	Pension expenditure relative to GDP in 1980 (%)	Pension generosity[b] (%)	Relative poverty rate[c] (%)	Transfer poverty effectiveness[d] (%)
Australia	Basic	U&A	9.6	4.9	51.0	15.7	67.9
Canada	Mixed	U&I	9.5	4.4	46.3	17.2	89.8
Germany	Insurance	I	15.5	12.1	78.1	11.1	79.2
Norway	Mixed	U&I	14.8	8.4	56.8	5.6	75.9
Sweden	Mixed	U&I&O	16.3	10.3	63.2	0.8	97.4
Switzerland	Insurance	I&O	13.8	8.1	58.7	11.4	88.9
United Kingdom	Mixed	A&I&C	14.9	6.3	42.3	29.2	49.4
United States	Insurance	I	11.3	6.9	61.1	23.9	68.7

[a] U = universal; A = social assistance; I = social insurance; O = mandatory or quasi-mandatory occupational pensions; C = contracting-out possibilities.

[b] Pension generosity is defined as the ratio of the previous two columns: It is equal to pension expenditure per elderly person as a percentage of per capita GDP.

[c] Using a poverty line of one half of median disposable equivalent income in each country.

[d] Effectiveness is defined as the percentage difference between the pre-transfer/post-tax poverty rate and the post-transfer/ post-tax poverty rate.

Source: OECD, *Reforming Public Pensions*, Chart 1.1 and Annex C. Smeeding, Torrey and Rein (1988), Tables 5.2 and 5.12.

effectiveness. However, they provide little support for the targeting hypothesis based on Figure 1. In fact, the two countries with the greatest reliance on means-tested, social assistance pension provisions (Australia and the United Kingdom) have amongst the *lowest* pension generosity rates, amongst the *highest* incidence of poverty among the elderly and, most significant of all, the two *lowest* transfer effectiveness percentages. Poverty effectiveness is much higher in countries like Canada and Sweden which rely more heavily on universal pension provisions. Comparisons between countries with similarly sized elderly populations reveal a similar picture. Canada's pension system is both more universal and more effective than Australia's. Although, in contrast to Germany, there is a universal element in the Norwegian system, Norway spends relatively less on pensions than Germany, provides less generous pensions, has less poverty amongst the elderly and yet has a system which is no less effective than that in Germany. Finally, although the structure of the UK pension system appears to make it more targeted than that in Switzerland, the United Kingdom in fact has far more poverty among the elderly and its pension system is far less effective in reducing poverty.

In summary, the evidence in Table 4 does not confirm the view that countries with greater targeting of transfer payments for the elderly have less poverty amongst the aged or are even more effective in reducing poverty, than other countries where universal or insurance type pensions exist. As Smeeding, Torrey and Rein note:

> Despite their presumably more effective targeting, countries that rely on means testing seem politically unable or unwilling to raise benefits high enough to be as effective ... as universal and social insurance approaches.
> (Smeeding, Torrey and Rein, 1988, p. 116.)

This evidence should, however, be seen as being suggestive rather than definitive in any fundamental sense. There are clearly issues of cause and effect that need to be unravelled. Nor does it imply that the framework underlying Figure 1 should be rejected entirely as an aid to thinking about effectiveness and efficiency issues in the context of income support. What it does suggest, however, is that there is a need to acknowledge the limitations of applying purely technical analysis to what are extremely complex economic, social *and* political issues.

Yet another assumption that is implicit in the framework of Figure 1 is that families actually receive the benefits to which they are entitled under the transfer system. In fact, of course, there is considerable evidence that the take-up of means-tested benefits is well below 100 per cent. This has been well documented in the United Kingdom (eg Deacon and Bradshaw, 1983) and the available evidence for Australia, while lacking somewhat in reliability, also points to low take-up of the recently introduced family income supplement scheme, an income-tested payment to low-income working families. In the Irish context, the ESRI study referred to earlier estimates that the take-up of the Irish family income supplement lies in the range 13 per cent to 22 per cent (Callan *et al.,* 1989, Table 10.5, p. 149). Such evidence on take-up thus cautions further against undue reliance on transfer targeting as an efficient and effective way of reducing poverty. In the limit, such schemes may assist the poor more in appearance than in reality because of low take-up. And low take-up rates mean that such schemes are less costly than otherwise and may thus be more attractive to governments intent on keeping expenditure to a minimum.

One final point on the limitations of the framework illustrated in Figure 1 is that it considers the issues of effectiveness and efficiency only in relation to how benefits are determined by family income. Targeting is better viewed in a broader context which, rather than focusing just on the determination of benefit entitlement, also addresses issues of eligibility that arise when defining the contingent groups for cash transfer purposes. Thus, a more targeted system may not involve a tighter relation between levels of assistance and private incomes (which inevitably gives rise to efficiency and incentive concerns), but rather a narrower definition of the contingencies which establish the right to assistance in the first place. This second approach has generally been the one pursued, for example, by the current Australian government in attempts to improve the targeting of income support programmes. This contingent-group approach to targeting has the potential to minimise the conflict between effectiveness and efficiency issues, albeit at the cost of introducing new concerns about the erosion of social rights and about the effects of the harsher administrative processes, required to establish eligibility, on stigma and on equity of treatment.

Community and welfare services
Unlike income support programmes which involve a transfer of social resources with relatively low associated direct resource costs, the provision of social services involves a direct claim on society's resources. Furthermore, as Tables 1 and 2 indicate, those claims now absorb a considerable proportion of the national income of most OECD countries. This in turn implies that the potential savings from more efficient use of resources in these areas can be enormous.

As a recent OECD report on financing health care notes, for example, a one-day reduction in the OECD average length of stay in hospital (18 days) would generate cost savings in excess of $17 billion a year (OECD, 1987, p. 98). As noted earlier, the provision of community services like health, education and other personal social services also appear, initially at least, to conform more to traditional models of economic production and thus to be more amenable to analysis in terms of their efficiency and effectiveness (Davies and Knapp, 1988).

However, as already noted, such application is limited by the fact that conventional budgetary and accounting procedures provide no output measures (Levitt and Joyce, 1987). The consequences of this for relative expenditure growth in public sector services generally were drawn out by Baumol (1967) in his model of unbalanced growth. Furthermore, the so-called 'relative price effect' – the tendency for *measured* public sector input cost (and implicit price) increases to outstrip private sector cost (and price) increases – was an important factor contributing to the growth in government expenditure relative to GDP throughout the sixties and seventies (Saunders and Klau, 1985). For governments concerned with expenditure aggregates, there are thus pressures to reduce the growth in input costs rather than to seek to improve the efficiency with which inputs are utilised. Since labour costs represent the largest proportion of input costs, this translates into pressures to reduce the growth in public sector wages relative to private sector wages, and there is evidence that this has occurred in many OECD countries in the last decade or so. It is, however, worth noting that this may result in an 'echo effect' in the next decade, as (relative) public sector wage increases become increasingly essential to stem labour outflow and aid recruitment of suitably qualified personnel. Those pressures have certainly been evident in the Australian public education sector in the last few years, and they are also apparent in a number of other countries.

The limitations of the current treatment of public community and social services in the national accounts could, of course, be overcome if these services were to be provided through private markets on a for-profit basis and priced accordingly. Most of these services are, after all, excludable and thus in principle amendable to market provision, finance and thus allocation mechanisms. But there are other important economic features which suggest that private provision and finance will not result in socially optimal outcomes (Barr, 1987a; 1987b). These include such considerations as adverse selection, moral hazard, imperfect and asymmetric information and externalities, all of which limit the relevance of textbook economic principles to the social services. In addition, there are those important equity principles which saw the public sector playing the dominant role in the provision and finance of social services in the first place. These reflect important underlying social values relating to equality of access, opportunity and outcome and the principle that resources should be allocated on the basis of need rather than willingness to pay. Proposals for large-scale privatisation of the provision and finance of the basic social services often thus make little economic sense and are even less viable when confronted with existing social values and political constraints. Survey evidence, for example, still shows strong public support for public health and education systems and many express a willingness to incur higher taxes in order to improve the quality and quantity of services provided (Taylor-Gooby, 1985).

To argue that large-scale privatisation of social services has little economic merit is not, of course, to argue that selective forms of privatisation may not be a means of achieving increased efficiency and effectiveness. This issue was explored, in his usually provocative way, by Julian Le Grand at the Institute of Public Administration Conference three years ago (Le Grand, 1988). There, Le Grand argued (mainly in the British context) that selective privatisation of the *provision* of welfare had much to recommend it as a strategy, but that privatisation of the *finance* of welfare was both unlikely and undesirable. But Le Grand also argued that the resulting efficiency gains would be achieved only if privatisation moves were accompanied by increased competition and by increased state regulatory intervention aimed at protecting the wider public interest. Such a strategy, while continuing to *subsidise* consumption of welfare services through the public purse, seeks to expand the range of *choices* available to the users of welfare services and thereby to provide the motivation for (private) suppliers to seek efficiency gains. Such a combination of choice and competition would certainly do much to create the climate for improvements in efficiency.

The ideology of freedom of choice is a very powerful force in contemporary economies (both West and East) which the welfare state cannot afford to ignore. Increased levels of affluence, combined with the income elastic nature of health, education and other social services, is generating new demands to which welfare services must respond. Otherwise, there is the risk, emphasised by Le Grand (1988), that the better-off will seek private sector alternatives, the revenue base for public provisions will be undermined, and a dual system of welfare will result in which those on lower incomes and the disadvantaged will be condemned to increasingly inferior quality services. Under that scenario, the goals of the welfare state will be severely compromised and any claims of effectiveness ultimately foregone.

But it is important not to be overly optimistic about what can be achieved by the combination of private welfare provision supported by public finance and controlled by public regulation. There are many examples where such a model has not been overly successful in the past. In Australia, for example, nursing homes have been operated on a model along these lines for around thirty years. Most nursing homes have been run and operated by private entrepreneurs but have received considerable government subsidy and been the subject of extensive government regulation. Yet there is little to substantiate claims of efficiency in the nursing home sector, and there is increasing evidence of poor and demeaning treatment of nursing home clients. Furthermore, Commonwealth (ie federal) government expenditure on nursing homes has grown at a faster rate than expenditure on other programmes where public provision has been more important. Nursing home expenditure grew by close to 18 per cent a year on average between 1972-73 and 1989-90, compared with a growth in total Commonwealth spending of around 13 per cent a year. This, in a context of population ageing and increased demands on long-term care as life expectancy has increased, has led to government initiatives to restrain the growth in nursing home expenditure, to plan and control the number of nursing home beds available, and to greatly expand the funding of community-based care which allows individuals to continue to live in their own homes for longer. The privatisation of nursing home provision has thus led to increased public finance and regulation in order to achieve a better overall balance in the provision of care for the aged, and to improve the *overall* efficiency and effectiveness of the public resources committed to this area. Such examples serve to warn that private welfare provision is no panacea. The public sector does not have a monopoly on inefficient practice and cost blow-outs.

Among the social services, it is in the health sector (defined to include health-related personal social services) that issues of efficiency and effectiveness have received most attention to date. In education, concern among OECD countries in the last decade has focused on the quality of the education process (including curricular issues) rather than on questions of efficiency and effectiveness. The same cannot be said of health systems. Public expenditure on health in OECD countries now accounts on average for approaching 6 per cent of GDP (Table 2), and both the relative level of public health expenditure and its rate of growth exhibit considerable variation across countries. Public provision and finance of health systems in order to ensure equal access to the highest quality health services has been an important component of the post-war welfare state. Yet as a recent OECD report notes:

> Health systems embody the social, economic and cultural imprints of different societies. They embody the often competing, often complementary objectives of numerous public and private organisations and individuals ... Over the past decade the ability of societies to achieve these potentially conflicting objectives has been called into question. Health financing and delivery systems that were initially conceived to provide access to services appeared to be less successful at achieving efficiency. Governments and private purchasers began to question the cost – and health – effectiveness of the additional services they were purchasing. With the achievement of almost universal access in most countries, efficiency and effectiveness issues have moved to the forefront of the policy debate (OECD, 1987, p. 9).

It is appropriate to quote the OECD in this context, because that organisation has played a major role in bringing together comparative health expenditure data, and in analysing of health policy issues. It is worth mentioning some of the major general findings resulting from that comparative work. These include:

— the most important single identified determinant of the level of total health expenditure per capita is the level of per capita national income (Culyer, 1990);

— total health spending tends to be lower relative to GDP the greater is the public sector share of total health spending (OECD, 1987);

— health outcomes measures such as infant mortality rates and life expectancy show improvements over the last three decades (OECD, 1987);

— cross-country evidence indicates significant inverse correlations between total health spending per capita and infant mortality rates, overall death rates and death rates due to diseases of the circulatory system (OECD, 1987); and

— there remain considerable cross-national variations in certain medical care practices (McPherson, 1987). Differences, both across and within countries, in the availability and use of resources in terms of hospital stays and surgical procedures do not appear to be related to health outcomes (OECD, 1987).

Although some of these latter variations suggest that there is the potential for improved efficiency and effectiveness in the use of health resources – a proposition which is very widely shared – the OECD itself is cautious about the practical application of these concepts. Indeed, in discussing the difficulties in health policy formulation the OECD notes simply that:

> Health care outcomes and hence efficiency and effectiveness are not measurable (OECD, 1987, p. 93).

This, however, does not mean that efficiency and effectiveness are not important aspects that need to be addressed. With extensive public sector involvement in the finance and provision of health care systems, there will be a need for improved management policies that seek to re-structure financial rewards and incentives facing both health service users and providers, as well as improvement in service planning and delivery systems. There is also a need for an expanded role for health promotion and prevention initiatives. It seems likely that the recent trend towards increased competition in certain areas of the health sector will continue, but this should proceed *within* a regulatory framework rather than replace it if the important social and equity objectives that underlie the post-war expansion of public health systems are not to be undermined.

Some recent Australian experience

It is not possible in the space available to do justice to the full range of social policy initiatives introduced in Australia in recent years. That task is made even more difficult by the fact that the period since 1983 has been one of considerable change in most areas of social policy. What follows is thus a description of selected policy reforms chosen in the hope that the policies themselves and the issues they raise are of wider interest. The temptation to be overly critical about some aspects of these policies has also been avoided in order that more time can be devoted to a relatively objective and descriptive account of policy reforms, and of some of the more significant issues they have raised. Attention will focus on the period since 1983 when the current government of Prime Minister Hawke was first elected to office. A key feature of economic policy in Australia since 1983 has been the Accord, an incomes policy agreed between the government and the national trade union body, the Australian Council of Trade Unions (ACTU). Under the five successive, re-negotiated versions of the Accord, the ACTU has promised (and delivered) wage restraint by its members in return for government commitments to a more equitable tax system, expanded occupational superannuation coverage and increased 'social wage' provisions in the areas of social security, education, health and housing.

Throughout the period since its first election to office, the government has emphasised the need for structural and micro-economic reforms if Australia's longer-term economic difficulties were to be overcome. These difficulties reflected the traditional reliance on primary products to generate export revenues and a correspondingly under-developed and generally uncompetitive manufacturing sector. Policies to deregulate the external and domestic financial sectors were introduced in the mid-eighties, as were a series of major reforms of the tax system designed to minimise tax-induced distortions in individual and corporate behaviour. Following a worsening of the balance of payments situation in 1985-86, the macro-economic policy stance was tightened, leading to high interest rates and a marked slowdown in domestic demand. The degree of fiscal restraint can be assessed by noting that between 1983-84 and 1989-90, the Commonwealth budget deficit has been reduced by the equivalent of over 6 per cent of GDP, the deficit of 4.1 per cent of GDP in 1983-84 being replaced by a surplus of 2.2 per cent of GDP by 1989-90.

The success of the Accord can be judged at one level by the restraint in wages that it has produced. Thus, between 1982-83 and 1989-90, average weekly earnings *declined* in real terms by 4.8 per cent. However, employment grew very substantially over this period – the total number in employment rising by 1.45 million or more than 23 per cent between June 1983 and June 1989. A consequence of these two changes has been an increase in real per capita household disposable income of some 12.7 per cent over the period, and a decline in the unemployment rate from 10.0 per cent in June 1983 to 5.8 per cent by June 1989. There can be little doubt that the Accord has helped to create the circumstances for extremely favourable employment growth since 1983.

Between 1983 and 1989, for example, the average annual rate of employment growth in Australia was 3.4 per cent, almost three times the OECD average and well in excess of that experienced in any other OECD country. And as noted earlier, the task of social policy is made a lot easier when employment is rising than when unemployment is rising.

Trends in social spending and total government spending in Australia during the eighties are shown in Table 5. An important point to note about the expenditures in Table 5 is the important role played by state and (to a lesser extent) local government in social provisions in Australia. Although social security is the sole responsibility of the Commonwealth (or federal) government, the

Table 5: **Trends in total government expenditure and social expenditure in Australia, 1982-83 to 1989-90 (Percentages of GDP)**

	Education	Health	Social security and welfare	Housing and community amenities	Total social expenditure	Total expenditure
	Commonwealth Government					
1982-83	2.2	2.0	8.3	0.5	13.0	28.9
1983-84	2.1	2.3	8.6	0.6	13.6	29.6
1984-85	2.1	2.8	8.4	0.6	13.9	30.0
1985-86	2.1	2.9	8.1	0.6	13.7	29.6
1986-87	2.0	2.9	7.9	0.6	13.4	28.8
1987-88	1.9	2.8	7.7	0.5	12.9	26.6
1988-89	1.8	3.2	7.1	0.4	12.5	24.3
1989-90	1.8	3.2	7.1	0.4	12.5	23.6
	Total Public Sector					
1982-83	5.7	4.5	8.7	1.7	20.6	41.3
1983-84	5.6	4.8	9.0	1.7	21.1	42.3
1984-85	5.5	5.3	8.8	1.8	21.4	42.4
1985-86	5.4	5.3	8.6	1.7	21.0	42.7
1986-87	5.3	5.4	8.4	1.7	20.8	42.2
1987-88	5.0	5.2	8.2	1.4	19.8	38.8
1988-89	4.8	5.0	7.6	1.1	18.5	36.6
1989-90	*	*	*	*	*	*

* Not available.
Source: Budget Statements 1990-91, Budget Paper No. 1.

states play a major role in expenditures in the area of education, health and housing. However, much of the financing of these (and other) public programmes is raised through Commonwealth taxes which are paid to state governments as tied (specific purpose) and untied (general purpose) grants. Vertical fiscal imbalance is thus a general feature of the Australian public finances. These points aside, Table 5 shows that government spending in Australia – at all levels of government – has fallen markedly relative to GDP since 1983-84. Commonwealth spending fell by 6.4 percentage points of GDP between 1984-85 and 1989-90 and a similar fall is implied for state and local government spending. Commonwealth spending on social programmes has fallen by 1.4 percentage points of GDP since 1984-85 and the decline up to 1988-89 in social expenditure in the public sector as a whole was equivalent to over 2 percentage points of GDP. At the Commonwealth level, the decline in social spending has been of similar relative size in the education, social security and housing areas, while spending on health has risen sharply relative to GDP with the introduction of the universal, government-funded Medicare scheme in 1984. The burden of restraint among state governments has fallen disproportionately heavily in the area of housing and community amenities.

In terms of expenditure restraint, it is thus clear that Australia's record since 1982-83 has been impressive throughout the public sector. The Commonwealth government has been the driving force behind the changes shown in Table 5, and now boasts proudly of a level of government spending relative to GDP which in three years' time is projected to be below that experienced in the 1950s. Yet the Commonwealth government in office since March 1983 has been a Labour government, the trade union movement has been influential in policy formulation (specifically, through the Accord, in the social policy sphere) and both the government and the ACTU have emphasised the significant social justice achievements of the last few years. How can this be? Does it in fact reflect the introduction of more effective and efficient (and less costly) social programmes? It is not possible to give a general answer to this latter question, but the following examples provide at least a partial answer.

Reform of the Australian social security system has been guided since 1986 by the recommendations of the Social Security Review, appointed to report to the Minister for Social Security. These recommendations have seen the expansion in scope and the increase in assistance to low-income families with children; increased integration of the unemployment benefit, sole parent pension and invalid pension systems with education, training and labour market programmes; major changes to income support during retirement, and many other changes too numerous to mention here. Accompanying these changes – many of which have generally been seen as a welcome response to changing economic and demographic pressures – have been a number of changes introduced outside of the Social Security Review process with the specific aim of improving the targeting of the social security system. It needs to be emphasised at this point that the Australian social security system is almost entirely a means-tested system financed from general revenue. There are no insurance elements and, now at least, no universal payments either. All entitlements are determined according to the income and assets of potential recipients, as well as being subject to income tax in most cases.

The Commonwealth government's approach to improving the effectiveness and efficiency of the social security system has recognised the potential conflict between those two objectives, described earlier when discussing Figure 1. In general terms, increased targeting of assistance – which has undoubtedly occurred since 1985 – has *not* been achieved through more stringently applied income tests on entitlement. Indeed, mindful of the harmful effects on incentives of the poverty traps inherent in what is a heavily income-tested system, the government introduced a series of initiatives designed to ease the income test on many working age recipients in 1987. Targeting has thus been increased not so much by increasing the severity of the income test, but by introducing new variables which affect entitlement, by legislation to reduce the scope of eligibility categories, and by far tighter administration of benefit claims and increased scrutiny and review of on-going payments.

The most significant of the changes was the introduction of an assets test on all pensions in March 1985. This measure, subsequently extended to all other payments, had the immediate effect of reducing payments to over 23 thousand pensioners and cancelling payments entirely to a further 34 thousand pensioners. More recently, the government has made a number of changes which have broadened the definition of income for the purposes of the pension income test. These include the decision in the 1990 budget to impute a 10 per cent return on cash and financial balances in excess of $2,000 before application of social security income tests, irrespective of whether or not that return is actually earned.

In relation to the tightening of eligibility, the government has, since 1986, greatly increased the resources devoted to assessing new benefit claims and reviewing the circumstances of existing benefit recipients. Special mobile review teams have been established (and expanded) in order to conduct benefit eligibility interviews in areas identified as having a potential high risk of benefit fraud and/or abuse. The establishment of these teams has been accompanied by increased resourcing of internal departmental administration of benefits. Data published by the Department of Social Security indicates that over the three years to 1988-89 these reviews have led to over 186,000 payment cancellations and 284,000 payment reductions out of a total of almost 2.5 million payment reviews (Saunders, 1991).

The one area where targeting has involved an expansion of the role of income testing is in the family assistance area. In 1986, family allowance payments to families with dependent children, formerly the only universal payment in the system, were made subject to an income test based on family income. This move was accompanied the following year by a significant expansion (in terms of both benefit levels and coverage) in the system of income-tested assistance to low income families with children, when a new family allowance supplement (FAS) scheme replaced the previous family income supplement (FIS) scheme. These changes have increased the effective marginal tax rates on many families with children at both ends of the income distribution. At the lower end, in particular, there are, as noted earlier, concerns that take-up rates of FAS (as with FIS before it) are low, although the evidence on this is admittedly somewhat sketchy.

In terms of the framework of Figure 1, these changes have resulted in a system of family assistance payments that is both more efficient and more effective (in poverty gap reduction terms) than it was five years ago. A far greater proportion of assistance is now directed to low income families, and although head-count estimates show little impact of the changes on child poverty (Saunders, 1990b), application of poverty gap measures reveals that the immediate impact of the new measures was to produce a more effectively targeted system of family assistance (Saunders and Whiteford, 1987; Brownlee and King, 1989). In the longer-run, whether these improvements can be maintained or advanced will depend upon the resourcing of the new scheme (currently guaranteed in real terms by automatic indexation of the new payments) and also by the seriousness of the take-up issue.

The current Australian government has not restricted itself to changes in benefit eligibility and entitlement conditions as a means of improving the efficiency and effectiveness of social programmes. Attention has also focused on the revenue side of the equation, as the following two examples illustrate. The first concerns the financing of income support for sole parent families. The serious financial circumstances of sole parent families has been well documented in Australian poverty research. That research shows that the poverty rate for sole parent families is between five and six times higher than that for couples with children (Saunders, 1990b). Since the vast majority of sole parents were formally in married (or marriage-like) relationships, the impact of family break-up on the financial well-being of custodial parents and their children is clearly evident. The high rates of poverty among sole parents reflected in part the inadequate levels of assistance they received – a situation alleviated (though not removed) by the new FAS scheme. However, there was also evidence that in many cases maintenance orders established by the family court were not being complied with by non-custodial parents.

To rectify this latter situation, the Child Support Act, 1988, established a special section within the Australian Taxation Office to enforce family court maintenance orders through PAYE deductions by the employers of non-custodial parents. The money thus collected is then transferred to the Department of Social Security for payment to the custodial parent. However, under the Act, maintenance income was also made subject to a special, more stringent, income test which meant that the scheme produced some expenditure savings for the government (estimated to be around $38 million in 1988-89). Since the introduction of the Child Support Scheme, receipt of maintenance income by sole parent pensioners has increased substantially and that has meant an improvement in the financial well-being of one of the most disadvantaged groups in the Australian community. There has been an increase from 30 per cent (in 1987) to over 70 per cent (in 1989) in the payment of maintenance orders, and an increase in average payment per child of around 25 per cent (Department of Social Security, 1989). The new scheme is still in its infancy and it is too early to make a thorough assessment of its total impact. It has, however, generated considerable interest in other countries and somewhat similar legislation has recently been foreshadowed by the UK government.

The second example relates to the financing of higher education. In the mid-seventies, the Whitlam government abolished fees for higher education institutions, as a means of encouraging greater equality in higher education participation across different socio-economic classes. Following concerns that the social class profile of tertiary students showed little subsequent change, and after several years of internal dispute about whether or not to re-introduce tertiary fees, the Hawke government introduced a Higher Education Contribution Scheme (HECS) in 1988. Under HECS, students attending higher education institutions are required to re-pay part (equivalent, on average, to about 20 per cent) of the estimated tuition cost of their education, but only after they have entered the workforce and have an independent income that exceeds the level of average earnings. It can thus be seen as a 'graduate tax' on higher income graduates, or as a deferred system of student fees where the fee is determined by an estimate of the realised return from higher education. Furthermore, a proportion of the revenue raised under HECS (around $100 million in 1989-90) has been, and will continue to be, re-directed to higher educational institutions in order to fund an expansion of new places in a sector which has suffered greatly from government expenditure restraint for the last fifteen years.

Both of these examples raise important issues in relation to the balance of responsibilities for funding social programmes. They each involve changes to financial rewards and incentives and over the longer term it will be important to monitor the impact of these changes on individual behaviour. They represent examples of the 'user pays' approach to the privatisation of public welfare. Contrary to the views expressed by Le Grand in 1988 in relation to British experience, these Australian initiatives represent privatisation of the finance and not the provision of social programmes. They have allowed a government committed politically to expenditure restraint and lower taxation to fund increased social provision by tapping into new sources of revenue. In this sense, they have helped to make certain social programmes more effective by providing more resources than would otherwise have been available given the political constraints within which the government was operating. They represent the beginnings of earmarked contributory funding of social programmes in a country which has never embraced the social insurance principles of contributory finance and benefits. Finally, the Australian initiatives illustrate the need for responsive social programmes in a climate of rapidly changing social and economic relationships.

Summary and conclusions
The last decade has been one of on-going crisis in social programmes as governments have struggled to restore financial balance to public finance and to respond to emerging challenges and evolving social, economic and demographic developments. One feature to emerge from that crisis has been a greater questioning of the means and ends of social programmes. In addressing these issues, this paper has been broad in scope, but hopefully that has not affected the effectiveness of the arguments presented, nor the efficiency with which they have been discussed. It has attempted to describe the general context within which social policies have been evolving in the last decade, to assess the relevance of the concepts of efficiency and effectiveness to social programmes, and to illustrate their application both in general and with specific examples.

There is much to be welcomed in a re-assessment of a set of programmes which have been in place for close to half a century and in some cases far longer than that. However, much of that re-assessment has taken place in a narrow confine in which expenditure restraint has been the driving-force behind change, and in an ideological context of freedom, choice and deregulation that strikes at the heart of many of the goals of the post-war welfare state. While the concepts of efficiency and effectiveness have merit, they are essentially technical concepts and should be recognised as such. The social values implicit in all social programmes mean that they will never be completely amenable to purely technical analysis. The limitations implied by this for what can be achieved through application of efficiency and effectiveness concepts to social programmes need to be acknowledged. This involves giving due recognition to such factors as programme interaction and more general concepts of resource usage efficiency and effectiveness, as well as to equity considerations.

There is a need for efficiency and effectiveness concepts to be applied not just at the individual programme level – important though such analysis is – but also for the focus to be broadened in order that more general social issues and problems can also be addressed. What is ultimately required is an analysis of the *social* efficiency and *social* effectiveness of what are, after all, *social* programmes. Development of the debate in this direction has much to recommend it.

The welfare state has not been protected from the rapid economic and social changes that have occurred in the last decade. Nor should it be. If the future of social programmes is to be secure and sustainable, issues of resource efficiency and programme effectiveness must be addressed. The debates those issues have opened up, about the goals of social programmes and the specification of output and outcome measures, are important, as are the improvements in efficiency and effectiveness brought about by changes in policy formulation and implementation. But it would be a mistake to believe that changes guided by the new managerialism will avoid all of the social programme difficulties and disappointments of the last two decades. Policy changes which result in a more efficient and effective use of the resources devoted to social programmes are to be welcomed. The real challenge is to ensure that those changes are introduced within a framework of social institutions, processes and policies which protect the disadvantaged and offer certainty and hope to the vulnerable.

Notes

[1] Moral hazard refers to instances where the existence of insurance encourages risk taking. If a person's possessions are insured against theft then there may be a tendency to be less vigilant about burglary. Similarly if a person's life is insured there may be a tendency to be less careful about health. Adverse selection refers to instances where people in high risk categories purchase more insurance than people in low risk categories. A majority of high risk people in the insurance pool will tend to increase premiums which in turn may discourage some low risk people from buying insurance.

References

Barr, N., *The Economics of the Welfare State,* London: Weidenfield and Nicholson, 1987a.

Barr, N., 'The Welfare State as an Efficiency Device', *Discussion Paper No. 22,* The Welfare State Programme, Suntory Toyota International

Centre for Economics and Related Disciplines, London School of Economics, 1987b.

Baumol, W.J., 'Macroeconomics of Unbalanced Growth: The Anatomy of Urban Crisis', *American Economic Review,* June 1967, pp. 415-426.

Beckerman, W., *Poverty and the Impact of Income Maintenance Programmes in Four Developed Countries,* Geneva: International Labour Office, 1979a.

Beckerman, W., 'The Impact of Income Maintenance Payments on Poverty in Britain in 1975', *Economic Journal,* June 1979b, pp. 261-279.

Beckerman, W. and Clark, S., *Poverty and Social Security in Britain Since 1961,* Oxford: Oxford University Press, 1982.

Brownlee, H. and King, A., 'The Estimated Impact of the Family Package on Child Poverty', in D. Edgar, D. Keane and P. McDonald (eds.), *Child Poverty,* Sydney: Allen and Unwin, 1989, pp. 123-145.

Callan, T., Nolan, B., Whelan, B.J., Hannan, D.F. and Creighton, S., *Poverty, Income and Welfare in Ireland,* Dublin: The Economic and Social Research Institute, 1989.

Culyer, A.J., 'Cost Containment in Europe' in OECD, 1990, pp. 29-40.

Davies, B. and Knapp, M. (eds), *The Production of Welfare Approach: Evidence and Argument from the PSSRU,* special issue of the *British Journal of Social Work,* Vol. 18, 1988, Supplement.

Deacon, A. and Bradshaw, J., *Reserved for the Poor,* Oxford: Martin Robertson, 1983.

Department of Social Security, *Annual Report 1988-89,* Canberra: Australian Government Publishing Service, 1989.

Knapp, M., 'Searching for Efficiency in Long-term Care: Deinstitution-alisation and Privatisation', in B. Davies and M. Knapp (eds.), 1988, pp. 149-171.

Le Grand, J., *The Strategy of Equality. Redistribution and the Social Services,* London: George Allen and Unwin, 1982.

Le Grand, J., 'The Privatisation of Welfare', in M. Mulreany and L. St. J. Devlin (eds.), *Public Expenditure and the Private Sector,* Dublin: Institute of Public Administration, 1988, pp. 75-92.

Levitt, M.S. and Joyce, M.A.S., *The Growth and Efficiency of Public Spending,* Occasional Paper XLI, National Institute of Economic and Social Research, Cambridge: Cambridge University Press, 1987.

Marshall, T.H., *The Right to Welfare and Other Essays,* London: Heinemann Educational Books, 1981.

McPherson, K., 'International Differences in Medical Care Practices', in OECD, 1990, pp. 17-28.

Murray, C., *Losing Ground. American Social Policy 1950-1980,* New York: Basic Books, 1984.

Okun, A., *Equality and Efficiency: The Big Tradeoff,* Washington DC: The Brookings Institute, 1975.

OECD, *Public Expenditure on Income Maintenance Programmes,* Paris: OECD, 1976.

OECD, *The Welfare State in Crisis,* Paris: OECD, 1981.

OECD, *Social Expenditure 1960-1990. Problems of Growth and Control,* Paris: OECD, 1985.

OECD, *Financing and Delivering Health Care. A Comparative Analysis of OECD Countries,* Paris: OECD, 1987.

OECD, *Ageing Populations: The Social Policy Implications,* Paris: OECD, 1988a.

OECD, *Reforming Public Pensions,* Paris: OECD, 1988b.

OECD, *The Future of Social Protection,* Paris: OECD, 1988c.

OECD, *Health Care Systems in Transition. The Search for Efficiency,* Paris: OECD, 1990.

Room, G., Lawson, R. and Laczko, F., ' "New Poverty" in the European Community', *Policy and Politics,* Vol. 17(2), 1989, pp. 165-176.

Saunders, P., 'Population Ageing and Pensions Policy', *Australian Journal on Ageing,* May 1990a, pp. 49-55.

Saunders, P., 'Employment Growth and Poverty: An Analysis of Australian Experience, 1983-1990', *Discussion Paper No. 25,* Social Policy Research Centre, University of New South Wales, 1990b.

Saunders, P., 'Selectivity and Targeting in Income Support: The Australian Experience', *Journal of Social Policy,* forthcoming.

Saunders, P. and Klau, F., *The Role of the Public Sector. Causes and Consequences of the Growth of Government,* OECD Economic Studies No. 4, Spring, 1985.

Saunders, P. and Whiteford, P., *Ending Child Poverty: An Assessment of the Government's Family Package,* Reports and Proceedings No. 69, Social Welfare Research Centre, University of New South Wales, 1987.

Smeeding, T., Torrey, B. and Rein, M., 'Patterns of Income and Poverty: The Economic Status of Children and the Elderly in Eight Countries', in J.L. Palmer, T. Smeeding and B.B. Torrey (eds.), *The Vulnerable,* Washington DC: The Urban Institute, 1988, pp. 89-119.

Taylor-Gooby, P., 'The Politics of Welfare: Public Attitudes and Behaviour', in R. Klein and M. O'Higgins (eds.), *The Future of Welfare,* Oxford: Basil Blackwell, 1985, pp. 72-91.

5

An Efficient Economic Development Policy: The Role of a Regional Development Authority

NORBERT VANHOVE

The stages of a regional economic policy

REGIONAL economic policy has four stages: objectives, strategies, instruments and evaluation.

The objectives of regional policy are largely determined by the prevailing problems. They are also influenced by an amalgam of political, social and economic pressures. Rarely are objectives formulated in quantitative terms; they generally describe existing problems and fields of intervention rather than provide a well-defined formulation of targets. In fact there are real difficulties in adequately defining the strategy to be followed and the instruments to be used.

One can identify an evolution in the formulation of the objectives over the period that regional economic policy has been applied in Europe. Originally, regional policy was a type of rescue operation for certain small problem areas. It was only at the outset of the sixties that a link was made between regional and national policies. At that time interdependence was recognised and the criterion of growth was introduced. There was an emphasis on the rational use of resources. Later a closer link was made between regional policy and physical planning goals. This link was very clear in countries such as France, the Netherlands and the United Kingdom. In recent years regional economic policy has been increasingly incorporated in an overall policy. Policy makers are increasingly concerned that the classical approach to regional policy, which involves attracting projects from abroad or from other regions, is inadequate to organise the national space; there is also a need for action to implement the reorganisation.

The second stage of a regional policy involves the elaboration of a strategy. In the past this stage was very often neglected. Yet the elaboration of strategy is the most important stage of policy for a region. It concerns the path or the paths that should be followed to develop the objectives with the support of the action programmes and instruments. Strategy elaboration is always conducted over the medium or long term. The choice of strategy is difficult but essential. Once a strategy has been defined it should be reasonably permanent though of course there should be some scope for flexibility as the occasion demands.

Regional strategy must incorporate greater variety than a corresponding strategy for firms. The latter very often produces one product or similar products. A region is composed not only of many economic sectors with unequal growth capabilities but also of thousands of firms some of which are large while the majority are small and medium-sized enterprises.

For the formulation of a good strategy, a SWOT analysis can be very helpful. SWOT stands for Strengths, Weaknesses, Opportunities and Threats. The regional policy strategist should ask a variety of questions. What are the strengths of a region? A strategy should be based on the strong points. What are the weaknesses? Improvement of the weak points is necessary but cannot be the starting point for a strategic approach. What are the opportunities for a region? They can be internal but very often they are external factors. Finally, what are the threats? The latter can also be internal and external.

The definition of the instruments of a regional policy is the third stage. Instruments are much more than financial incentives. One can distinguish many categories of instruments such as: (a) infrastructure, which encompasses not only roads, railways, canals, and industrial estates but also knowledge centres, telecommunications and housing; (b) financial incentives such as grants, interest rebates, and tax exemptions; (c) discouragement measures such as industrial development certificates which discourage development in certain areas; (d) decentralisation of government offices; (e) regional allocation of public investment and government contracts; (f) regional development agencies and (g) macro policy instruments. The last named can have indirect effects and also direct effects, for example through the use of regionally discriminating tax and expenditure policies.

Finally each policy should be evaluated. The most common mistakes are to underestimate the size of the problem and to look for swift solutions. There is often a lack of realism about the time horizon of regional development. Regional development is a long term process. 'Stop–go' policy is disastrous for the development of a region. From time to time the policy should be evaluated.

There are several evaluation methods such as cost-benefit analysis, multiple regression analysis and modified shift-share analysis (which applies national growth rates per industry to a region's industry-mix). Each method has its merits and drawbacks, and these should never be forgotten. Evaluation must also take account of the fact that the development of a region is never the result of just one factor, and that it is difficult to isolate the effect of any one instrument.

Topics for the elaboration of an industrial development strategy
The elaboration of a strategy should be based on the results of the SWOT analysis.

Complementary to the SWOT analysis we can both raise a number of questions and indicate possible elements of a strategic approach.

Possible elements of, and questions to be resolved by, a strategy are:
- The resolution of the choice between 'work to workers' or 'workers to work'. It might be a slogan but for some regions the question is pertinent.
- The choice of subregions within the region to be given priority.
- The choice between a concentrated or non-concentrated approach within the problem region. A decision must be made about which centres should receive priority.
- Whether or not to adhere to the growth pole theory. Which form of polarisation do we prefer: technical, income, or geographical polarisation?
- The creation of an enterprise and innovation zone.
- The promotion of research and technological innovation.
- The deconcentration of congested areas.
- To which sectors do we give priority? Do we revitalise key industries within the region or do we give priority to a diversification from the existing base of industries into new areas?
- In certain regions there may be a need to choose between 'industry or tourism or both'.
- Do we attract 'high-tech' activities or do we improve process technology?
- Do we adopt the classical development model of attracting projects either from abroad or from other regions, or do we promote indigenous development?
- Is priority to be attached to small and medium-sized enterprises or to the location of a number of large firms, or both?
- Do we engage in co-operation with other regions and/or market

selection (which involves concentrating on a selected number of export markets)?
– The decentralisation of power to the regions.
– The establishment of a regional development authority.

Many of the strategic options should be backed by action programmes. This can be illustrated by two examples. Firstly, the Regional Government Agency for Development of the Region of Madrid (IMADE) identified the following strategic areas as part of its 1989-92 strategic plan:

Strategic areas	Examples of programmes
1. Development of strategic business infrastructure	– Madrid Technological Park – Coslada Transport Centre
2. Modernising the business mesh	– Technological updating of small and medium-sized companies – Information on and assessment of intercompany co-operation – Sectoral operations
3. Territorial plans	– South and Henares plan in the South-Metropolitan Area
4. Nurturing new technology	– Promotion of technical resources – Technology centres
5. Strategic development of the region	– Economic promotion of Madrid

A second interesting example is the Kent County Council Study 'An Economic Strategy for Kent' (Byles 1989). The strategy has four main elements:

Revitalisation of key industries with growth potential and stimulation of the adaptation of current activities and processes to meet the demands of the future. In particular emphasis is placed on the transfer of technology between companies and industries on a county, national and international basis, within the context of the Single European Market.

Diversification from the existing base of industries and services into new areas, in particular those sectors with good growth and export prospects, in order to promote wealth and job creation for the Kent economy.

Capitalisation upon the current and future opportunities that exist

121

within the county for physical development, to provide a secure
basis for future investment, and continued improvements in the
quality of life for the people of Kent.

Mobilisation of the county's human resources through training
programmes to enable the workforce to be more responsive to
industry's needs, both in the immediate future and longer term.

The Kent economic strategy also contains the necessary action
programmes. In total nine were retained. The 'Key Strategic
Priorities' are listed in the concluding section of each of these
programmes. The action programmes are:

1. Business development

   eg

   Relationships with large firms

   Business advice

   Kent Investments Limited (Venture Capital Fund).

2. Land and buildings

   eg

   Enterprise zones

   A high quality business park

   Revitalisation of the former Chatham Dockyard

   Provision of suitable housing.

3. Tourism and arts development

   eg

   Preparation of a tourism development framework

   Marketing the arts to residents and visitors.

4. Physical infrastructure

   eg

   Dartford Northern bypass.

5. Training

   eg

   The establishment of a Kent Employers and Training
   Database to assist in forecasting employment needs in the
   future.

6. International connections

   eg

   Development of links with the countries of the European
   Community to promote Kent as a location for investment.

7. Channel tunnel

   eg

   Passenger station at Ashford.

8. The Single European Market

   eg

   Establishment of a European Business Information Centre
   for Kent.

9. Promotion and marketing of Kent for business
   eg
   Overseas based mobile investors.

The role of a regional development authority

Each region should possess its own regional development authority. There are two reasons underlying this assertion. First, the people of the region have the best knowledge of the strengths and weaknesses of the region. Second, regional development depends to a large extent on the motivation of the people responsible for development. The region should be involved in the conception and implementation stages. Failing this, regional development remains a dead letter. If the regional development authority is to be successful and motivation nurtured, a high degree of autonomy is a prime condition. At the regional level, the autonomous regional development authority must be flexible.

We look upon a regional development authority not only as an instrument of regional policy but above all as an element of the overall development strategy.

The regional development authority can play a role at five levels: research, strategy, promotion, co-ordination, and implementation.

Research
It seems unthinkable to promote a region without a profound knowledge of such factors as the economic forces at work in, the economic potential of, the socio-economic deficiencies in, and the needs of, the region itself. Moreover this knowledge must be placed in the context of general economic development and the evolution of the different economic sectors and subsectors. A regional development authority should not only have a basic knowledge of a region, but should also be promptly able to provide information on various subjects. Sometimes the agency may be entrusted with market research for a particular sector (eg tourism); to that end it should have a study office or study department.

Strategy
On the basis of all such information, the authority is in a position to develop a strategy for the medium and long term. It must address such questions as which part of the region should be given priority, which centres can be promoted, and which activities should be attracted.

Promotion
Promotion is multi-faceted and makes demands on the ambition

and dynamism of the general manager of any large concern. The daily tasks include:
  - assisting existing firms either in their expansion or in dealing with problems of various kinds (technical, financial, infrastructural etc.);
  - advising the public and private sectors;
  - attracting new projects;
  - stimulating the improvement of general economic infrastructure;
  - promoting subcontracting;
  - providing information to industry, social organisations, schools and the local population, through press, radio, television, conferences, newsletters, guided visits, articles and, possibly, the agency's own review. The information service is extremely important in regional development.

Co-ordination

Quite often many government agencies are involved in the implementation of certain projects and a regional development agency should fulfil the role of co-ordination in order to shorten the procedure period and to increase the chances of a project being implemented.

Moreover, regional growth is strongly inter-related with physical planning, housing, education, and the environment. Co-ordination in these areas is also essential.

For the frontier regions, co-ordination is necessary, not only within the region or between regions, but also with the region(s) on the other side of the international border.

Implementation

This function includes first and foremost the creation of regional infrastructure such as industrial sites, ready built factories, and housing to sustain regional development. A regional agency may be financially responsible (with its own equity capital), and/or work with funds allocated by central government. The agency may participate in investment projects or even create firms both in the competitive and non-competitive sectors.

On account of the inter-relationship between regional development and physical planning, a regional development authority may be given responsibility for the preparation of physical planning documents (detailed plans, master plans, district plans, and regional plans).

This list of functions shows that a dynamic regional development agency plays the role of catalyst in regional development. Without such an agency it is impossible to accomplish maximum growth at the regional level. A regional development agency should not act purely as a public administration body, but rather as an institution for promotion; and it should be run as a business concern.

The reform of the Community's structural funds and a strategy for regional development

In this section I aim to review the origin and the broad principles underlying the reform of the EC's structural funds. The interested reader can refer to the Commission of the EC's document 'Guide to the Reform of the Community's Structural Funds' (1989).

The reform of the structural funds involves a switch from a project-based to a programme-based approach. This new approach should make it possible to give Community action the necessary breadth and depth, while at the same time allowing for greater flexibility. Community operations that are spread over a number of years, with joint action by the structural funds, the European Investment Bank (EIB) and the other financial instruments, will be better able to respond to changing economic and social conditions. Programming should thus facilitate:

some degree of decentralisation of the management of Community assistance;

predictability of Community assistance, which will stimulate investment;

improved assessment of Community assistance;

better processing of applications for assistance.

Programming will also make it possible to take a coherent overall medium-term view of the operations to be mounted in pursuit of each priority objective and to establish a framework for the co-ordination of these operations.

We have already established that strategy is an important stage in policy formation. In the 'Guide to the Reform of the Community's Structural Funds', for the first time the notion of strategy is mentioned in an official EC document on regional development. As far as the operational arrangements are concerned four stages are provided for. The first stage is the preparation of development plans by the national authorities, in partnership with the regional and local authorities. In the plans four matters should be dealt with.

Part 1: an economic and social analysis of the region, area or sector.

Part 2: a development strategy taking account of method and means of implementation, national and regional financing and Community operations already under way.

Part 3: an assessment of development priorities to be financed.

Part 4: an estimate of total funding requested, broken down by structural instrument (structural funds, EIB, other instruments).

Referring to what we emphasised in the sections on elaboration of a strategy and on regional development authorities, two elements are essential:

– partnership with the regional authorities;
– a development strategy along with method and means of implementation.

The development plans are the starting point for negotiations with the Commission of the EC and must culminate in a Community Support Framework. This brings us to the second stage. In the Community Support Frameworks the priorities (strategies) are determined.

The Community Support Frameworks are the Commission's response to the needs defined in the plans. They give the broad guidelines for the measures to be taken jointly by the member states and the Community and provide the reference framework for the applications for assistance submitted to the Commission by the member states.

Each Community Support Framework must include:

1. A statement of priorities for action.
2. An outline of the forms of assistance.
3. An indicative financing plan specifying the financial allocations envisaged for the various forms of assistance and their duration.

The third step is the operational stage which works through infrastructural, sectoral or other operational programmes.

Finally the Community Support Frameworks and the assistance operations are monitored and assessed.

In the case of Ireland – an objective 1 region – the specific priorities (in fact strategies) in the Community Support Framework (Commission of the EC 1989) that should ensure a significant impact are:

Priority 1: Agriculture, fisheries, forestry, tourism and rural development
'The objective of this specific priority is to build on the comparative advantage provided by Ireland's natural resources and its clean environment. Some of the indigenous sectors of the economy still have good development potential and comparative advantages. Assistance from the funds will therefore be concentrated on those activities where development potential clearly exists, in agriculture, horticulture, aquaculture, fisheries, forestry and tourism. Further

development of industries based on natural resources, in particular food processing, will be promoted. In addition to productive investment, applied research, demonstration projects, technical assistance and promotional activities will also be covered under this priority.'

Priority 2: Industry and services
'A noteworthy feature of the expenditure proposed in the Community Support Framework is a continuation of the shift in industrial development resources towards the support of non-capital expenditure items including those in the areas of marketing, technology development and support and training. The focus of support will be on the internationally tradeable sectors, ie trading goods and services sectors subject to international competition. These will be supported by the Community.'

Priority 3: Measures to offset the effects of peripherality
'Problems related to the peripheral location of Ireland are an obvious subject for a specific priority. All types of infrastructure which will facilitate communication between Ireland and the rest of the Community will be considered under this heading. Investments in National Primary Routes fall under this priority as do ports, airports and railways to the extent that they contribute to reducing the effects of peripherality.'

Priority 4: Human resources measures
'The overall employment target, deriving from the approach set out in the Programme for National Recovery, is to boost job creation from the 29,000 recorded in 1988 to 35,000 per annum over the plan period. This is to be achieved through the twin approach of reinforcing the modernisation of the economy while at the same time boosting the employment potential of those traditional sectors such as tourism, demonstrating continuing development potential.

'The appropriate development of human resources is essential to the success of the strategy. Training and employment measures will therefore be targeted on growth sectors and skill areas including management, finance, marketing, production, quality control, technology, business planning and modern languages where deficiencies have been highlighted; and such areas as tourism, financial services, pharmaceuticals, aquaculture, horticulture which have been identified as growth sectors.'

A case study: the example of West Flanders
The Regional Development Authority of West Flanders is responsible for the economic development of the region. A distinction

should be made between five organisations which are working together in the same building, each of which has its own legal status (see Figure 1).

In 1954 on the initiative of the Province of West Flanders, the Westflemish Economic Council (WER) and the Westflemish Study Office (WES) were established. In 1976 the WER was transformed into a Regional Development Authority. The study function is attributed to the WES which is responsible for research. Several economic studies led to the construction of the new European port of Zeebrugge. The recent publication *West Flanders 2000 – A strategy for economic development* (1990), which we will return to below, is the latest research published by the WES.

Figure 1 shows that three other functions (strategy, promotion and co-ordination) are attributed to the Regional Development Authority. The final function or implementation is discharged by three inter-municipal organisations.

Figure 1: **Institutional framework of regional development in West Flanders**

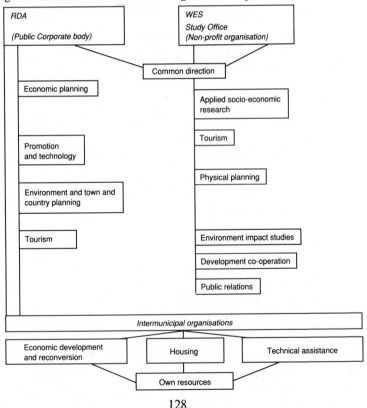

A characteristic of the institutional framework is the personal link. The Regional Development Authority and the WES have a common management. This is also the case for the three inter-municipal organisations. Furthermore the WES and/or Regional Development Authority is represented in the inter-municipal organisations. This guarantees a common policy from research through to implementation for the West Flanders region.

One inter-municipal organisation is responsible for the industrial estates. A second one is involved in housing programmes (purchase of land and equipment). The third inter-municipal organisation provides technical assistance (eg preparation of physical plans, construction of recreation facilities etc.) to the local authorities.

The recently published West Flanders 2000 strategy is based on a SWOT-analysis. The main points of this analysis are:

Strong points:
— the existence of entrepreneurial ability
— a positive work-attitude
— a favourable geo-economic situation
— the port of Zeebrugge
— the existence of 'external economies'
— a conducive living environment
— efficient economic institutions.

Weak points:
— the existence of disparities within the province
— insufficient growth of the industrial structure
— problems of renovation and upgrading of coastal facilities for the development of tourism
— the need for better links between harbours and their hinterlands
— problems with supply, quality and price of water
— insufficient representation of West Flanders in national government, in national organisations and in the national press.

Opportunities:
— the EC internal market
— better co-operation with Northern France
— the channel tunnel and the TGV
— congestion and traffic problems in other areas.

Threats:
— changes in the EC common agricultural policy which will affect farmers specialised in cereal and dairy production
— if insufficient attention is devoted to marketing
— the shortage of industrial sites
— the ageing of the population

— the channel-tunnel
— North Sea ecology, particularly the poor quality of water
— the danger of falling behind in adopting new technologies such as telematics.

The strategy of regional development is based on six pillars. For each pillar an action programme is being prepared.

Strategy

1. Optimisation of the geo-economic location in the EC

2. Integration of West Flanders in the international transport network

3. Indigenous development of industrial and service sectors

Action programme

— marketing of the region
— the development of an international school
— the development of Bruges as headquarter centre
— the development of industrial estates
— the development of telecommunication infrastructure
— the development of the port of Zeebrugge
— the development of the port of Oostende
— the development of the airport of Oostende.
— highway programme
— road programme
— railroad programme
— waterways programme.
— the promotion of subcontracting
— technological renovation
— the creation of an innovative production environment
— the promotion of permanent education
— a better link between education and industry
— the development of business centres
— support for technology management
— support for export management

	— multi-functional service zones.
4. Tourism planning and product improvement	— a plan for development of the coast and hinterland — a marketing plan — product improvement and renovation — a tax contribution by the private sector (tourism sector) for the development of tourism.
5. Development of horticulture and ornamental plant cultivation	— special training programmes — the upgrading of the agricultural sector.
6. Optimisation of the living environment	— the concentration of cultural, social and medical amenities in the medium and small towns — the development of new green areas — the lay-out of green areas around industrial estates — the development of programmes related to the environment.

Conclusion

In the post-war period West Flanders has experienced successful economic development. In terms of industrial employment it was the region with the highest increase of jobs in industry. In periods of growth West Flanders scored better than the other provinces and in periods of decline it contained employment losses to a greater extent than other Belgian provinces.

In the 1950s West Flanders accounted for about 16 per cent of Belgian unemployment. In 1989 the share was reduced to 7 per cent. In terms of income level West Flanders moved from an index figure of 75 in comparison to the national average in the 1950s to an index figure of 95 in 1988.

These indicators show that an efficient economic development policy at a regional level can be successful. Without a regional structure the same performance would not have been achieved. It is the result of a structured approach, good research, a well-considered strategy, good co-operation between the local authorities and the hard work of an enthusiastic staff.

References

Byles, T., *An economic strategy for Kent,* Kent County Council, 1989.

Commission of the European Communities, *Guide to the Reform of the Community's Structural Funds,* Luxembourg, 1989.

Commission of the European Communities, *Community Support Framework 1989-93. Ireland,* Luxembourg, 1989.

IMADE, *Profile, Strategy, Balance Sheet, Memory 88,* 1990.

Vanhove, N. and Klaassen L.H., *Regional Policy: A European Approach,* Aldershot, 1987.

Vanhove, N., Theys, J. and AI., *West-Vlaanderen 2000 – Een Strategie voor Ekonomische Ontwikkeling (West Flanders 2000 – A Strategy for Economic Development),* Bruges, 1990.

6

Efficiency and Effectiveness in Public Investment Appraisal

JOHN BLACKWELL

THIS chapter deals with efficiency and effectiveness in capital project appraisal and is particularly concerned with public projects. We commence with an outline of some of the key principles underlying the evaluation of capital projects. Then some of the main features of the published studies featuring capital appraisal in Ireland are assessed. The main problems that have arisen in these studies are outlined and their implications for future work are indicated.

The justification for attention to this topic hardly needs pleading. Despite real reductions in recent years, the Public Capital Programme in Ireland remains a substantial proportion (currently a third) of total gross fixed investment and amounts to 7.3 per cent of gross national product. Moreover, monetary and exchange rate policy changes, and the limits that apply to the use of fiscal policy in an interdependent Europe, have made clear the limitations that now attach to the use of discretionary fiscal policy in Ireland. This highlights the need – always present, but hitherto often unappreciated – to focus clearly on efficiency in the use of resources in economic policy-making in Ireland.

Private and public evaluation
At the outset, some points of principle can be made about the difference between private and public evaluations of capital projects. There is a long history of project appraisal applied to public projects, with a good deal of work done on water resources and transport projects in the United States from the 1940s onwards. The methods used had an influence on capital project appraisal in Europe, and especially on the appraisal of transport projects. It is a sobering thought that the first paper on the appraisal of transport projects was published by an engineer, Dupuit, in the nineteenth century

133

and languished for many decades before the principles outlined were used in assessments of capital projects. The high-water mark of the programme budgeting approach to the evaluation of public expenditure was reached in the United States in the 1960s. This had an influence on the approach used in Ireland in the 1960s and 1970s. In 1970, a comprehensive budgeting system was adopted in the civil service, with the aims of clarifying the objectives of public expenditure and analysing alternative ways of achieving these objectives. For a time, Public Capital Programme projects were evaluated. In recent years, a thoroughgoing approach of formal investment appraisal has not been used for the Public Capital Programme. However, a welcome advance was made through the publication by the Department of Finance of *Comprehensive Public Expenditure Programmes* (an outline of programmes, their main components, their objectives and the public expenditure associated with them but not unfortunately the tax losses or so-called 'tax expenditures'). Other recent developments are noted below.

Private firms continually assess whether proposed investments are likely to be worthwhile, although it seems that in the private sector in Ireland, there has been little use of formal methods of assessment. This reflects the size distribution of Irish industry, which contains a large proportion of relatively small firms, with limited resources to devote to formal assessment. It also reflects the fact that the large-scale capital projects, typical of those that require project appraisal, have been projects in areas such as fertilisers, gas, and steel which have tended to fall within the ambit of state-sponsored bodies.

The standard techniques of capital investment appraisal are well established. They involve an assessment of the consequences of the project over a defined life, taking account of the outputs which in turn involves assumptions both about the price at which the output is sold and about foreign exchange rates in the case of exports. Account has also to be taken of the costs of the project, including the labour costs for different skills, and the costs of various materials used in the process of production. The additional benefits – in this case the gross revenue in Irish pounds – are compared with the additional costs. Among the various alternatives, the firm should choose the one with the highest net benefit of profits. In assessing net benefits or profits account must be taken on the costs side, of opportunity costs, ie the return on investment that the firm could have obtained elsewhere.

While this procedure wins a good deal of acceptance, it is less clear that this framework is seen as one that can be used to compare various different methods of achieving outcomes. In the case where a firm wishes to increase its capacity, there can be a number of different ways, in principle, that are open to it. For instance, different types of technology can be used, different combinations of capital and labour resources can be deployed and different combinations of output can be produced.

Moreover, this seemingly straightforward account has to be qualified. A feature of capital projects is that the returns to the investment accrue over a period of time. Indeed, the costs will also occur over a period, although much of the capital expenditure is likely to be bunched towards the early years of the planning period. This raises two questions: over what period are the returns and the costs to be projected? And how are the returns and the costs that accrue in different years to be compared with one another? Some projects such as electricity generation and forestry can show a marked stream of returns only over many decades. A firm cannot be expected to put the same value on a pound received today as on a pound received in ten years' time.

This difficulty can be handled by using the property that a pound today is worth more than a pound received in a number of years' time (since today's pound can be invested at the going rate of interest to reap a return per annum). Hence, the income streams occurring in various years can be discounted, using a discount factor which is smaller, the further into the future is the income stream. The classic case of the problems that arise in relation to the time horizon is the case of forestry, where the major part of the returns can take 35-40 years to accrue. If the rate of interest is 5 per cent (relatively low by comparison with the rate actually used in many instances in recent years), then a pound received forty years from now is worth only 14.2 pence today. If a discount rate of 10 per cent is used, the pound received forty years from now is worth only 2.2 pence today!

While precise evidence on the use of evaluation in the private sector in Ireland is lacking, it does seem that in many instances, 'rules of thumb' such as a 'payback' rule (which focuses on the period of years over which the initial investment is recovered) are used, rather than the idealised procedure outlined above. Alternatively, quite short time periods are used, within which the flows of revenue and outgoings are compared. This may be defended as a way of handling increased uncertainty about such matters as product prices (due to exchange rate fluctuations between Ireland and non-EMS trading partners) and interest rates (given the marked rise in real interest rates that has occurrred in recent years). While uncertainty is considered below, at this stage it can be argued that uncertainty can best be handled within the above framework by putting limits, and possibly probabilities, on the various possible outcomes.

Where lie the differences between this type of private investment appraisal and cost-benefit analysis as used by governments? There are three main differences. Firstly, the firm will be interested only in the returns and costs that pertain to itself. By contrast, government may be concerned with the benefits and costs that apply to a much wider group, such as all consumers, and all producers. For instance, there could be adverse consequences for the environment as a result of a project, consequences which can affect a wide group of consumers and producers.

Secondly, the firm will use market prices to value both costs and returns. In the case of government appraisal, market prices might not be used for a number of reasons. It may be that there is no market in the product in question. For instance, clean air may be 'produced', but the question is what price to put on this. Even more difficult issues can arise. The classic one, associated in particular with transport projects, concerns the value to be put on the avoidance of accidents and the saving of life itself. Another reason why market prices may not be a guide arises where the prices that *are* in the market do not represent the true costs or benefits to society. A related question that often arises here, and is very relevant to the Irish case, is what wage rate to use on the cost side of a project (where labour costs consist of employment times the wage) if there is a high rate of unemployment. This is discussed below.

Thirdly, the discount factor used can differ between private and public evaluations. The government may feel that it has to take the welfare of future generations into account, by using a rate of discount that would be lower than that used by a private firm. While there is not the opportunity here to consider the complex and much debated issue of the appropriate discount factor for public projects, it can be noted that, in practice in many instances the government will use a discount rate lower than that used by private firms. This is because a favoured approach is to use as a guide the rate at which borrowing can be undertaken. The rate at which government can borrow will always tend to be below that applying to even the most solid of private firms.

The method of cost-benefit analysis, as outlined above, concentrates on economic efficiency as the key criterion in the evaluation of alternative policies. Implicitly, the aim is to maximise economic efficiency, or to achieve objectives with the least commitment of resources. Reflecting this is the criterion that the project with the highest net benefit (excess of benefits over resource costs) should be chosen.

However, public projects could also have objectives in the sphere of income distribution. Even if there are no specific objectives about income distribution, most projects will provide gains or costs to some groups more than to others. One instance of a proposal that brought out income distribution effects in the starkest terms was that for an oil refinery in Dublin Bay in the 1970s. Among the losers would be the residents of Dublin Bay, the income of whom tends to be above average, and who would lose amenity benefits. However, the amenity benefits of the bay would also be lost by a much larger group of people with a variety of incomes. This shows the difficulties in practice that can apply in allowing for income distribution effects.

If no allowance is made for income distribution, the implicit assumption is that a pound of benefit or cost is the same, no matter who benefits or loses.

In principle, distributional weights could be attached to the estimates of benefits and costs. That is, the population could be divided into income groups with particular weights given to net benefits that accrue to each group. If the aim is to redistribute income towards group A, then this group's net benefit would attract a higher weighting. While this is the principle, there are few instances in the literature on cost-benefit analysis where distributional weights have been used. This reflects, in part at least, the difficulties in arriving at a set of distributional weights. One can say that the weighting is up to the decision-maker rather than the analyst, but this does little to diminish the difficulties of arriving at a set of weights. The weights could come from an analysis of past behaviour: by examining the actual choices made, it might be possible to obtain at least a range of weights. In summary, the advantage of using weights is that it makes explicit the value judgements that otherwise might remain hidden, and helps to ensure consistency between different investment decisions. The argument against the use of weights is that in most cases it asks too much of the administrative and political system of decision-making. In no cases, in fact, have distributional weights been used in Ireland.

There are alternative methods of allowing for income distribution. In line with the requirement that project evaluation needs to use the 'with-without' criterion (or a comparison of outcomes in the presence of the project with outcomes without the project) there could be a report on the distribution of income with and without the project. However, in the Irish case the statistics on income distribution are so inadequate that this approach could hardly be used.

Less ambitiously, there could be a report on how the project affects particular groups in the population. This could have the merit of at least making clear the 'trade-offs' that can be involved in the selection of projects. For instance, one proposal could benefit a group that is felt to be particularly deserving, but at the cost of an efficiency loss, by comparison with an alternative proposal. This method of allowing for income distribution effects has rarely if ever been used in Ireland. It might be argued that neglect in this area does not matter, on the grounds that the government could always redistribute income directly, if it wanted to, by means such as taxes and transfers. This is hardly defensible, especially when it is recognised that the battery of 'direct' methods of income redistribution involve economic costs to society. Moreover, some forms of investment are particularly associated with objectives to redistribute income. Health care and education are two instances of this. If income distribution is left out of account in these areas, an important dimension is missing. In fact these are areas where little has been published in Ireland by way of formal evaluation. This is no small matter, since 'social infrastructure' currently makes up approximately one fifth of the Public Capital Programme in Ireland. On balance, there is a strong case that the impacts of projects on the distribution of income should be assessed and shown, without using distributional weights. In this way, the trade-offs involved can be made clear. Also in this way, proposals can be ranked in order from the point of view of their impacts on income distribution.

Cost-benefit analysis and cost-effectiveness
In some cases, instead of using full-blown cost-benefit analysis to analyse projects, governments may use cost-effectiveness analysis, that is an analysis of the extent to which a programme attains its objectives. This method tends to be used in those cases where the assessment of benefits gives rise to particular difficulties: for instance where the saving of lives is involved. Suppose that there are a number of public health programmes that are expected to result in a reduction in mortality. The costs associated with achieving the objective of reducing mortality under each of the programmes can be estimated. The programme with the least cost can be identified. In one sense, this is a more limited exercise than that of the full cost-benefit analysis. Instead of putting a money value on benefits along many different dimensions, one benefit is focused on. Moreover, a money value is not put on this particular benefit.

In general, it has to be recognised that the benefits side tends to give rise to most of the problems in public project appraisal, for at least two reasons. Firstly, the benefits tend to accrue further ahead than the bulk of the costs – giving rise to greater difficulties of projection over future years than typically arise in the case of costs. Secondly, as indicated above, the placing of a money value on some benefits has often been an especially difficult task. Hence, there are instances where cost-effectiveness analysis can well be justified.

There is also the potentially useful device of mapping out the incremental costs and incremental benefits associated with a project. Put in cost-effectiveness terms and staying with the public health example, the incremental costs associated with incremental reductions in mortality under various methods can be estimated. This is potentially useful, since one suspects that there are cases where along some range of activity, there could be large marginal returns for relatively small incremental outlays. Such cases could be emphasised as a priority for investment. An example of the possibility of such areas of high incremental return is the case of investment in environmental improvement. Starting from a relatively polluted position it is quite likely that large incremental reductions in pollution could be achieved in the early stages of programmes.

Cost-effectiveness analysis is easiest to use in cases where it is possible to concentrate on one objective. If there are a number of different objectives, one is again confronted with many of the problems that arise on the benefit side in cost-benefit analysis and in particular the difficulty of how different types of benefits are to be weighed up. In cost-benefit analysis, the measuring rod is the money price that people would be prepared to pay to obtain benefits. By contrast, in cost effectiveness analysis this measuring rod is not used.

Problems of allowing for a multiplicity of objectives have been notable in the sphere of health care – a sphere of inquiry where there has been a dearth of published studies of an evaluative nature in Ireland. On the output side in health care, there can be a number of different objectives. In the specific instance of care of the elderly, the objectives can include the maintenance of health and independence, social integration, and relief of the burden carried by family and friends in providing long-term care to elderly people (Wright, 1978, p. 47). Despite the difficulties posed by allowing for multiple outcomes in health care, 'modified' cost-effectiveness analysis has been used when comparing alternative ways of caring for people. One study (Wallston *et al.,* cited in Goddard, 1989, pp. 25-26) uses interview data in order to ascertain weights to be applied to the outcomes on different dimensions, thereby leading to a single measure of outcome.

Evaluation of social policies
Relatively little published work is available in Ireland on the
evaluation of social policies. One possible area, mentioned above,
involves the care of the elderly and a particular method deserves
mention, even though we do not have the opportunity to go into
it in detail here. I refer to the 'production of welfare' approach.
In one particular case, it has been used in assessing work on costs
of residential care of the elderly (Knapp, 1981). This approach
distinguishes between the final outputs of a project and the
intermediate outputs. The final outputs consist of the impacts on
people: in the specific case of residential care for the elderly, they
would consist of changes in individual well-being. The final outputs
measure the degree to which objectives such as reduction in
loneliness, and the provision of shelter and nutrition, are met. By
contrast, intermediate outputs measure the services themselves, such
as, in this example, the number of places provided in residential
homes and the services provided within the homes. Much of the
official discussion of care will refer to intermediate outputs, but
a good deal of importance attaches to the final outputs which are
often not estimated or considered. Indeed, the ultimate objectives
relate to the final outputs rather than to the intermediate ones.

In this approach, there are two types of input. Firstly, there
are economic resources that are typically counted in evaluations
of expenditure, that is the labour contributions and the capital
equipment. Secondly, there are the non-resource inputs which would
include the social and caring environment within the home in this
example, and the characteristics of residents themselves. These are
usually not considered in evaluation studies. Whether or not the
provision of resource inputs has beneficial effects on final outputs
can depend on the extent to which the non-resource inputs are
working in the same direction. While there has been little or no
application of this methodology in published studies in Ireland,
it has been used in a number of evaluations in the United Kingdom,
including studies on long-term care of the elderly (Challis and Davies,
1986).

Public investment appraisal in Ireland
While this chapter concentrates on the evaluations done over the
past two decades, assessments of the Public Capital Programme
were also carried out, as indicated above, in the late 1960s and
early 1970s. Published work includes studies by Bristow and Fell
(1971) on Bord na Móna, by O'Donoghue (1968-69) on Aer Lingus,
and by Mulvey (1970-71) on Irish Shipping. One inherent difficulty
that arises in studies such as these is that they were concerned with

relatively global operations of a firm or sector. That immediately leads to problems since the method of cost-benefit is more appropriate to a limited project where one does not have to take account of wider effects on the economic system. If one tries to apply the 'with-without' criterion to an economic sector, there are difficulties with working out the main interconnections between that sector and the economy and society at large.

Since the 1970s, project work has continued within the Department of Finance (especially in the analysis section), in the Institute of Public Administration and in individual state-sponsored bodies, although much of this work has not been disseminated. The lack of dissemination of evaluations is unfortunate, since that means that one of the main ways in which progress is possible – through debate and constructive criticism about alternative approaches – has to a degree been blocked. It also means that any 'outside' view on the state of evaluation will be based on only a part of the total pool of evaluations undertaken.

Much of the published work has been in the sphere of transport and in areas such as drainage – very much reflecting the classic origins of cost-benefit analysis. One example, worth noting for its level of detail and its concern with enumerating a wide range of effects, is by Farrell and Howard (1975). Another notable publication in the same area is a cost-benefit analysis of the River Maigue drainage scheme (OPW, 1978). The 1975 study was concerned with the arterial drainage system. The benefits comprised the increases in landholders' incomes and the savings in terms of discontinued maintenance of earlier schemes; the costs comprised capital and maintenance costs, the investment by landholders, and the loss of income due to factors such as the widening of channels. The study compares a full scheduled scheme with an abridged scheme. However, three aspects of this study can be questioned. Firstly, benefits and costs are grouped into primary and secondary impacts. Ideally, all the impacts should be grouped together. Secondly, employment and training are treated as benefits while the opportunity cost of labour (discussed below) is treated as a cost. Labour costs should be entered on the cost side of the calculation, and should include any adjustment for opportunity costs, as discussed below. The inclusion of training raises at the very least the possibility of double counting. If output and hence income effects are calculated, this should embody the imparting of skills which are a part of the execution of the project. Thirdly, while some effort was made to consider a range of alternative investments, the range considered seems to have been a limited one.

In the mid-1970s cost-benefit analysis was applied to the road programme (Barrett, 1975-76). This study estimated the net benefits from investment in the programme. As tends to be the case in the evaluation of transport investment, the value of time savings accounted for most of the benefits. We have noted above that difficulties can arise when a global programme is assessed. In this particular case, the problem concerned the inter-dependency in the road network. One aspect of this is that if one segment of a road is improved, there can follow congestion elsewhere in an urban area. Another aspect is that a move to a higher level of service on the road system as a whole is not a marginal change, but has wide effects such as changes in aggregate demand and in costs throughout the economy. The study engaged in some testing of the sensitivity of outcomes to different values of time, but there was room for more sensitivity tests of this nature, for example to different values for accident costs, different rates of growth in car numbers and in traffic volumes, and different growth rates in the value of time savings over time.

A more recent study, the case of the Naas motorway by-pass (Barrett and Mooney, 1984), had the advantage of dealing with a more delimited road investment. While it was estimated that there would be savings in accident and fuel costs, the bulk of the benefits consisted of time savings. The estimated rate of return was comfortably above the test rate of discount of 5 per cent in real terms that had been established in 1984 by the Department of Finance. The study tested the sensitivity of outcomes to different values put on the key elements. Among the different variations, the outcomes were most sensitive to variations in the value of time. While a money value was not put on the value of changes in the environment, a broad indication was given of the likely changes in noise, atmospheric pollution, and the physical environment.

In a subsequent paper, Mansergh (1985) queried these calculated returns on a number of counts. Among the questions raised by Mansergh, taking the Naas study as an example of an approach to cost-benefit analysis in general and its application to road investment in particular, are two that are central to evaluation. Firstly, does project evaluation take adequate account of the return to the exchequer: even if there is a high rate of return to investment, could the acceptance of the project actually worsen the state of the public finances? Secondly, what are the employment implications and are there alternative methods which would be more effective in increasing employment in the longer term? These are key questions, concerned with two issues of central concern to economic policy-making in Ireland, the state of the public finances and the degree of unemployment. They are taken up further, below.

One point, though, should be made immediately. If employment impacts are to be taken into account when comparing alternative investments, it should be recognised that there is a limit to the extent to which there can be comparisons of the net returns between projects that differ considerably in their nature. In particular, it is questionable to what extent projects that use market prices to different degrees can be compared: for instance, a traded good and a project in health care. This was recognised by the National Planning Board (1984, Part II.4) in the principles that it laid down for public investment planning. Thus, the best that can be done may be to evaluate projects in such disparate areas, within a given budget for each area.

In recent years the most contentious areas of transport investment have concerned, not the inter-urban road network, but urban road investment. While there are particular difficulties with the evaluation of urban road investment, it is a pity that no evaluations, if any were done, of the main urban plans of recent years have been made available. Among other things, evaluations could have brought out the nature of the implicit values underlying the projects and the extent to which the main difficulties arising in assessing them were faced. Among the main areas of difficulty are the following: (a) the need to consider a range of options, including public transport alternatives; (b) the assessment of environmental impacts – not just on the natural environment but also on the built environment, allowing for the additional difficulty that some of the impacts on the built environment could be irreversible; (c) the social impacts including those on the stability and location of long-standing communities; (d) the likelihood that much urban road investment leads to the generation of more traffic with implications both for congestion elsewhere in the road system and for the extent of likely time savings.

A further area of difficulty in urban transport appraisal raises an important general point. This is the link between pricing policies and the appropriate level of investment. Put at its simplest: urban road users pay below the incremental costs of their road use (see Barrett and Walsh, 1983). Hence decisions on road investment can be distorted and the benefits from urban transport investment (which will reflect the number of people prepared to use the roads at the current set of prices) will be overstated.

A related point came up in one of the classic studies of transport investment, and indeed of cost-benefit analysis as a whole, that of the Victoria Line in the London underground. The initial study was done by Foster and Beesley (1963). The study worked out the rate of return in cost-benefit terms and showed that the discounted present value of the Line was positive at different rates of discount. Several kinds of net benefit were estimated including time savings, savings in outlays such as the operating costs of road users, and the value put on comfort and convenience. In a subsequent study (Beesley and Foster, 1965), the authors considered the implications for the rate of return, of different assumptions about how the investment was to be financed. The authors found that if the investment was to be financed through the traditional fare policy, that is, if London Transport engaged in a flat-rate percentage increase in fares, there would be a serious loss in net benefits. The second study worked out the implications for the rate of return of different pricing policies. This case raises one of the key areas of difficulty, not least in Ireland: the difference between the net return, calculated in the traditional manner using cost-benefit analysis, and the financial return to the government and its agencies. This is taken up further, below.

The largest single project evaluation exercise that is regularly carried out in Ireland is probably that of industrial projects undertaken by the Industrial Development Authority. Currently the expenditure of IDA grants amounts to approximately 8 per cent of the Public Capital Programme, but this understates the relative importance of these projects in terms of the economy. One paper (McKeon, 1979-80) outlines the IDA evaluation procedures, at least at the time the paper was given. The steps involved are as follows: (a) a determination of whether the project is commercially viable; (b) a determination of whether the grant paid, together with the costs of infrastructure to the exchequer, falls below a defined fiscal threshold; (c) a test of whether the contribution to the economy (essentially the net benefit in the classic cost-benefit sense, as outlined above) is at an acceptable level in cases (less than 5 per cent of the total, according to the paper) where projects are above the fiscal threshold. At this stage a few comments can be made on this paper; other issues raised are considered below under general problem areas of project appraisal.

Firstly, there is the oddity that the IDA, when considering projects, estimates likely impacts on the environment, yet in the economic evaluation these impacts on the environment are not taken into account. Secondly, there is the relationship between the discount rate used by the IDA and the discount rate used for public projects in general. The rate of discount used by the IDA is a 10 per cent real rate when assessing the fiscal returns. While it might be said in mitigation that the time period involved is a relatively long one, of 15 years, nonetheless this is a very high real rate. By comparison, the Department of Finance test rate of discount, as mentioned above, is 5 per cent in real terms. The UK treasury, not noted for its laxity, in April 1989 increased the required rate of return for nationalised industries from 5 per cent to 8 per cent (while increasing the required rate from 5 per cent to not less than 6 per cent for the non-trading part of the public sector). Thirdly, there is the question of what is meant by commercial viability since in the IDA assessment in most cases it entails viability in the presence of a grant. Fourthly, there must be some concern over the 95 per cent of projects that are not subjected to a 'cost-benefit' type appraisal, even in the qualified manner employed by the IDA. Among these are likely to be projects that are commercially viable (in whatever sense of the term one uses) but that would show up badly on a full project appraisal.

Before turning to a brief overview of neglected areas of analysis, the guidelines for capital expenditure appraisal, contained in a Department of Finance circular of 1983 (circular 1/83, the appendix to which is reproduced in Dáil Éireann, 1985) should be mentioned. The procedures cover three major areas, namely, all projects costing over £5m; the annual reviews of the five year programmes in telecommunications, roads, sanitary services, health, education and housing; and complex or specialised projects. The procedures require, among other things, that all projects should contain a statement of the objectives of the project or programme, consideration of possible alternative ways in which the objectives of the project or programme could be achieved, a financial assessment covering costs over time in both cash and real (inflation-adjusted) terms and involving exchequer outgoings (both direct and indirect), an assessment of the distribution of the benefits and costs of the project or programme, and consideration of general economic effects on areas such as employment and the balance of payments. These principles are, in general, eminently sound and indeed refer to many of the issues already discussed here. However, the procedures do not highlight the necessity to take account of tax losses, which can be important in particular projects, and curiously only refer to sensitivity analysis when discussing financial flows to the exchequer. The treatment of exchequer effects is taken up below. It would be interesting, to put it at its mildest, to know what the experience of the evaluations has been in the period since this circular was issued.

Finally, in this section, we briefly consider the extent to which particular sectors have been ignored in the evaluation work done to date. Over the past two decades, only a limited number of investment areas have been the focus of published appraisals of capital investment in Ireland. Evaluation work has been notable by its absence in health care, in urban renewal and improvement to the general built environment, in at least some forms of anti-pollution measures and in public training services. Perhaps the greatest deficiency has been the absence of evaluations in the sphere of public expenditure on training. There is a significant amount of public expenditure on this programme; for example, the 'grant for training' to FÁS is currently some £40m and it would lend itself to appraisal. A number of interesting issues would arise in appraisals of such programmes, including the potential to make comparisons by using a control group: a group of people alike in all respects with the group receiving the 'treatment' (in this case training) except that they do not receive the treatment. In addition, the possibility of 'displacement' effects would arise – whereby people on the programme, coming, for example, from the ranks of the unemployed, would, when trained, displace workers who are in employment. There is also the question of whether, at the margin, publicly-financed programmes provide training services in some cases that would otherwise have been undertaken by private firms, thereby incurring unnecessary losses to the exchequer. Not least, there are potential income distribution impacts. Indeed there is always a potential tension between the use of public training programmes to help groups who are in some sense disadvantaged, and the use of such programmes to improve economic efficiency – that is to ensure that training that would boost aggregate demand actually occurs. Among the benefits of training programmes are the flows of increased incomes from the trainees, compared with the outcomes in the absence of the programme (the 'with-without' criterion). This is where the importance of a control group can come in, since the effects of policy need to be separated from what would have happened in any event.

Problem areas

Now the main problem areas that arise in project appraisal, taking account of the experience outlined above, are briefly considered. These are: shadow prices; the treatment of net revenue or net costs to the exchequer arising from projects; how to deal with risk and uncertainty; and the question of irreversibility in some projects.

Firstly, there is the question of 'shadow prices', mentioned at the outset: cases where prices do not reflect the true costs and benefits (at the margin) to the economy. The most important case that arises relates to the relatively high unemployment rate in Ireland. It could be argued that, in such a case, the extra cost to society of hiring an unemployed person is very low, since little or no output is sacrificed or foregone elsewhere in the economy, the person, say, being hired off the unemployment register.

An adjusted wage, called the 'shadow wage', could be used to calculate the wage bill associated with the project so that it reflected the opportunity costs to society of employing the labour required in the project. There is, however, little agreement as to how to arrive at this shadow wage, although because of high unemployment it is generally set below the market wage. In an extreme case it could be argued that if all the workers employed on the project would otherwise be unemployed, no output would be foregone by employing them on the project and hence the shadow wage for these workers would be zero.

Even if this assumption is accepted, it could be argued that account should be taken of the fact that workers employed on the project increase their consumption as a result of the income which they earn while so employed, and that this represents an increase in the output of consumption goods at the cost of investment goods to the community. Thus, even if it were accepted that those working on the project would otherwise be permanently unemployed, the conclusion would not necessarily be that the appropriate shadow wage would be zero. Furthermore, if there is a wage below which people would voluntarily remain unemployed rather than be employed, the shadow wage may need to be higher than indicated by the opportunity cost of labour.

At the other extreme to the view that the shadow wage is zero, is the view that if the workers in question would be readily re-employed elsewhere in the economy at roughly the same wages as must be paid to hire them for the project, the market wage would be the appropriate measure of their true cost to the project.

In assessing where, between these two extremes, lies the appropriate treatment of the shadow wage, it is important to consider the skill levels of the workforce employed in the project, and the workings of the labour market. Does the workforce on the project come from those who are employed elsewhere? In the case where an evaluation is done of a project which needs state subsidy to survive, one would need to estimate whether the employees could be fairly quickly absorbed into employment elsewhere if they lost their jobs. And, if so, would they in turn displace other workers from employment? In cases where there were unskilled workers who would face prolonged unemployment if they lost their jobs, current earnings from employment overstate the costs to the economy of employing these workers. The appropriate way to deal with this would be to recalculate the company's costs using a shadow wage in place of the actual wages of these workers. This shadow wage would be calculated as the market wage *less* whatever allowance would need to be made for the fact that the value of the output which is displaced elsewhere in the economy by employing these workers may be less than their wage.

The implication of the above is that the shadow price of labour should not be regarded as something that is constant over time or something that is the same for all types of labour. One point of concern is that there is no consensus about the appropriate shadow wage and no guarantee of consistency about the shadow prices used across different public sector projects – and this could lead to distortions in the allocation of resources. It does seem that the shadow price of labour used in IDA evaluations has been low or zero in many cases of grant-aided industry (McKeon, 1979-80) and the extent of the undercounting will depend on skill content and conditions in the labour market.

Honohan (1986) has argued that the actual shadow price of labour is much higher than the ratio of the wage rate that is often used. However, one of the planks in his argument has to be questioned. He argues that there is no guarantee that overall employment in a project will increase by as much as direct employment, and that unemployment will not fall in line with any increase in employment, referring to research which suggests that it takes about two new jobs to reduce the level of unemployment by one, even in the short run.

The point about the distinction between the direct increase in employment in a project and the total increase is well-taken; it is another aspect of the points made above about the need to take account of the skill levels and the nature of the labour market. However, the point about the 'slippage' between an increase in employment and a reduction in unemployment does not of itself mean that the shadow wage used has been too high. Among the reasons for this slippage are: (a) people come back from abroad to take up jobs in Ireland, and (b) people who are not counted in the register of the unemployed take up the jobs. In case (a), if the aim is to increase total output and employment in Ireland (rather than output per head), the immigration to Ireland is not of itself an indication that the shadow wage is too high. In case (b), in a number of cases the people involved would be regarded as being in the labour force on a wider definition that would include those who had stopped looking actively for work because of discouragement, *or* had been denied unemployment benefit (for instance, on grounds of means-testing).

One way to approach the problem of the shadow wage is to use sensitivity analysis – testing the implications for the outcomes of different discounts applied to the market wage. This was the approach used in a study of natural gas allocation (in particular that component that went to fertiliser production) that did not employ a full-blown cost-benefit analysis (Blackwell *et al.,* 1983). Rather, this study engaged in an examination of various alternatives at the margin. Having started with commercial outcomes, account was taken of wider economic impacts including indirect employment effects and an allowance for a shadow wage. The sensitivity of outcomes to discounts of 10, 20, 30, 40 and 50 per cent from the actual wage bill were assessed. Two plants were investigated; in the highly capital-intensive plant, as would be expected, the discount used had little effect on the outcome. In the other more labour-intensive plant, there was a higher proportion of unskilled workers which meant that outcomes were more sensitive to the discount in that plant.

We now turn to the second of the four problem areas discussed in this section, namely, the question, already raised, about the treatment of net revenue or net costs to the exchequer arising from projects. This is a most complex area, partly because there is sometimes a lack of clarity about the distinction between gross flows to and from the exchequer, net flows to and from the exchequer, and the 'real' net benefits. Some of the flows to and from the exchequer will not affect the net benefits directly although they will have implications for the distribution of income. Take the example above of an evaluation of public training services. If trainees find employment, they will lose unemployment benefit, and gain a gross wage, out of which they will pay direct taxes (income taxes and social insurance contributions); at the same time, taxpayers will gain to the extent that their direct taxes are lower. While this simplified example does not pick up all of the financial flows, it does bring out the difference between the key net benefits (in this case represented by the additional gross wages of trainees who find jobs) and the gross financial flows.

The net financial flows usually mean that there is a net financial cost to the exchequer to ensure that a project occurs. Take the case of a transport project. Having counted up all the benefits and costs (which can include the government as a direct beneficiary, eg lower transport costs associated with government transport use), the project may need a government subsidy if it is to go ahead. This is a particular case of the point made above in relation to the Victoria Line study: the need to take account of the means used to finance a project. In the case where a net government payment is needed, that will involve additional taxation and, as argued by Honohan (1986), the 'real' costs for the economy of the levying of that taxation should be taken into account. This means that in the case where an increased subsidy needed for a project to occur is exactly balanced by increased tax revenue, there could still be an additional real burden on the economy.

Often the distinction between the income distribution implications of the financial flows and the 'real' economy effects working through the burden of taxation, is not made with sufficient force. While the Department of Finance guidelines refer to income distribution effects, in practice there is need to distinguish between the initial incidence of taxes and benefits and the final one (dealing with the ultimate beneficiaries and bearers of costs). The latter could be quite different from the former.

There are a number of ways of dealing with this problem. One is to work out the financing implications, followed by the taxation implications and then go back to adjust the net benefit calculations. Another way is to put a limit on the government budget – as a result, not all projects with a positive net benefit would be accepted but those showing a certain minimum benefit-cost ratio would be accepted.

The third of the four problem areas concerns the question of how to deal with risk and uncertainty. Stiglitz (1988) has said that the most common mistake made in dealing with uncertainties is to argue that, in the presence of risk, the government should use a higher rate of discount. The key point is to adjust the flow of net benefits to allow for risk, with risky projects involving a risk premium. The present values can then be worked out using the regular discount rate. Here the Department of Finance guidelines are less satisfactory than one would expect, since they say that the rate of return in a high risk project in a new technological area would have to provide a margin of 7 per cent over the cost of funds. Moreover, the guidelines do not advert to the need to take account of the likelihood that the further ahead the projected flow, the higher the likely degree of uncertainty.

A less formal way of handling uncertainty is to employ sensitivity analysis. Here the sensitivity of outcomes to different values for the key elements (eg prices and exchange rates) would be tested.

The final problem area concerns the question, as mentioned above, of irreversibility that can arise in some projects. Instances of this would be cases of 'development' in urban areas involving the destruction of buildings that were irreplaceable, or a project that led to a loss of amenity forever. This issue is likely to be of increasing concern, since as real incomes increase, there tends to be a greater concern with environmental issues, and also there tends to be increased pressure on facilities that are fixed in supply and not replicable (what Hirsch [1977] called 'positional goods'). The problem here involves a lack of symmetry. The option of 'no development' involves the possibility that there could be development at some later stage; while if development occurs, it cannot be reversed. In the context of environmental projects, a method of dealing with this, called the Krutilla-Fisher-Porter approach has been outlined (OECD, 1989). Without going into detail, the net benefits of development in this approach would be the gross benefits of development, less the development costs, less the net benefits of preservation. In turn, the benefits of preservation are likely to increase over time relative to other benefits in the economy, partly because of the points made above about growing demand for goods such as the experience of natural beauty, and the fixity of supply. Such increase in benefits of preservation is allowed for in this approach.

Summary and conclusions
Given the size of the Public Capital Programme and the importance of efficiency in using resources, there is a strong case to be made for the systematic evaluation of capital projects in the public sector. This chapter has identified areas where there has been a notable lack of disseminated evaluations. The lack of dissemination of evaluations, even when they are made, is unfortunate, partly because it is possible to learn from mistakes. Such learning can take place, for example, by comparing the returns from projects after the event with the returns that were predicted in advance.

In some cases, there may not be need for full cost-benefit analyses. Nor will it always be desirable, since evaluation itself uses up resources. More limited investigations, at least at the outset, can often be useful. This can involve cost-effectiveness analysis. In addition, this work can identify, through the use of sensitivity analysis, the key elements on which the net returns from the project can depend. In turn, this can suggest the issues which could be the subject of more detailed investigation.

The importance of considering appropriate alternatives has been a recurrent theme in this chapter. This is where one of the main skills in project analysis lies. The focus here should be on the key alternatives which exist at the margin, and the principal constraints on achieving improvements in efficiency.

Another theme has been that of trying to ensure some kind of consistency in appraising projects throughout the public sector. Two areas in particular where this has arisen are the choice of discount rate and the shadow price of labour.

Finally, there is need to link together the appropriate pricing of resources and the investment decision. This came up in the study of natural gas allocation mentioned above and in transport work. If pricing policies are distorted, the results of investment appraisal can give the wrong signals.

References

Barrett, S.D., 'The Economic Evaluation of Road Investment in the Republic of Ireland', *Journal of the Statistical and Social Inquiry Society of Ireland,* Vol. 23, Part 3, 1975-76, pp. 1-36.

Barrett, S.D. and Mooney, D., 'The Naas Motorway Bypass – A Cost Benefit Analysis', *Quarterly Economic Commentary,* January 1984, pp. 21-34.

Barrett, Seán and Walsh, Brendan, 'The 'User Pays' Principle: Theory and Applications', in John Blackwell and Frank J. Convery, eds., *Promise and Performance: Irish Environmental Policies Analysed,* Dublin: Resource and Environmental Policy Centre, University College, Dublin, 1983.

Beesley, M.E. and Foster, C.D., 'The Victoria Line: Social Benefit and Finances', *Journal of the Royal Statistical Society,* Series A, Vol. 128, 1965, pp. 67-88.

Blackwell, John, Convery, Frank J., Walsh, Brendan M. and Walsh, Michael, *Natural Resource Allocation and State Enterprise: N.E.T. as a Case Study,* Dublin: Resource and Environmental Policy Centre, 1983.

Bristow, J.A. and Fell, C.F., *Bord na Móna: a cost-benefit study,* Dublin: Institute of Public Administration, 1971.

Challis, David and Davies, Bleddyn, *Case Management in Community Care,* Aldershot: Gower, 1986.

Dáil Éireann, *Report of the Committee on Public Expenditure: Control of Capital Projects,* Dublin: Stationery Office, 1985.

Farrell, G.J. and Howard, J., 'Aspects of Cost Benefit Analysis of an Arterial Drainage Scheme', Paper at the Institution of Engineers of Ireland, February 1975.

Foster, C.D. and Beesley, M.E., 'Estimating the Social Benefit of Constructing an Underground Railway in London', *Journal of the Royal Statistical Society,* Series A, Vol. 126, 1964, pp. 46-78.

Goddard, Maria, 'The Role of Economics in the Evaluation of Hospice Care', *Health Policy,* Vol. 13, 1989, pp. 19-34.

Hirsch, F., *Social Limits to Growth,* London: Routledge and Kegan Paul, 1977.

Honohan, Patrick, 'Traps in Appraising Public Projects', *The Irish Banking Review,* Spring, 1986, pp. 28-35.

McKeon, J., 'The Economic Appraisal of Industrial Projects in Ireland', *Journal of the Statistical and Social Inquiry Society of Ireland,* Vol. 24, Part 2, 1979-80, pp. 119-143.

Mansergh, Nicholas, 'The Value of Cost Benefit Analysis of Road Projects', *Quarterly Economic Commentary,* April 1985, pp. 36-47.

Mulvey, C., 'An Application of Cost-Benefit Analysis to the Strategic

Shipping Sector', *Journal of the Statistical and Social Inquiry Society of Ireland,* Vol. 22, Part 3, 1970-71, pp. 38-68.

National Planning Board, Proposals For Plan. 1984-87, 1984.

O'Donoghue, M., 'A Cost-Benefit Evaluation of Irish Airlines', *Journal of the Statistical and Social Inquiry Society of Ireland,* Vol. 22, Part 1, 1968-69, pp. 155-180.

Office of Public Works, *River Maigue Drainage Scheme: Cost-Benefit Analysis,* 1978.

OECD, *Environmental Policy Benefits: Monetary Valuation,* Paris: OECD, 1989.

Stiglitz, Joseph E., *Economics of the Public Sector,* 2nd. ed., New York: Norton, 1988.

Wright, K.G., 'Output Measurement in Practice', in A.J. Culyer and K.G. Wright, eds., *Economic Aspects of Health Services,* London: Martin Robertson, 1978.

7

Performance Measurement in Theory and Practice: Dutch Experiences[1]

ANTHONY G.J. HASELBEKKE and ARIE P. ROS

Introduction

EMPLOYEES in the public sector are often subject to criticism and mockery. In the Netherlands the story is told that civil servants do not look out of the window in the morning, because if they do they have nothing left to do in the afternoon. With this stereotype in mind it is not surprising that a lot of people started to chuckle when they saw the following headline in Dutch newspapers: 'Civil servants to work for 38 hours a week'. This headline referred to the news that the working time of public sector employees had been reduced from 40 to 38 hours a week. Many people suggested that it meant an increase of 38 hours instead of a reduction of 2 hours.

Generally speaking, people believe that the performance of the public sector in terms of productivity, and related concepts like efficiency and effectiveness, is poor. But is this really true? Is there any (quantitative) information about public sector performance? And if there is, what exactly is measured? With what could or should figures on productivity be compared? What standards are to be met? What problems, both in theory and practice, are to be solved? What is actually done with the information generated? These and some related questions are dealt with in this contribution, which consists of four parts.

Firstly, some conceptual remarks are made about performance measurement in the public sector. As will be shown, the ultimate goal of measurement is to get information about productivity, efficiency and effectiveness. Therefore information is needed on the one hand about the performance of the public sector and on the other hand about the impact (the outcomes or the effects) of those performances. Secondly, some of the problems involved in performance measurement are dealt with. Those problems are not new; they have been examined in budget concepts like the Planning-Programming-Budgeting System (PPBS), Zero Base Budgeting (ZBB) and Management by Objectives (MBO).[2] Despite these problems measurement can be undertaken and completed. Thirdly, several examples are given from Dutch experiences with (performance) measurement. In the ideal case, the results of performance measurement have a role to play in policy-making, in day-to-day management, and in policy-evaluation. Finally, we show that at local government level, performance measurement is (to a large degree) incorporated in the budget process. By contrast, at central government level hardly anything is done in the field of measurement.

Avoid talking double Dutch: conceptual remarks

The traditional public sector budget is an input budget. This means that money amounts are allocated to activities that government intends to carry out. Government should, for instance, provide national and local security, education, health care, social security and things like roads, bridges, passports and so on. How the goods and services are produced is often ignored. For a long time, a lot of people used to consider only what entered the public sector and what came out. What happened inside the so-called 'black box' remained unclear. In those times budget approvals by representatives in parliament appeared to be giving a certain amount of money for a 'good' policy without asking concrete services in return. Recently this attitude seems to have changed somewhat. This change is due to the following three factors:

- The relatively diminishing resources for public provisions; the growth rates of the sixties and the early seventies can no longer be reached. Even the public sector has encountered limits to growth. If the government wants to maintain its service level, it must increase its productivity and produce in a cheaper way.
- The necessity to give value for money; citizens have become more critical with regard to government activity than in the past. They want more information about how their money is used and what they get for it in return.
- The availability of new management and information techniques; with these it is possible to handle large streams of information on input and output. This has changed the attitude towards performance measurement and performance management.

In the literature on performance measurement the concepts of productivity, efficiency and effectiveness play a pivotal role. Tons of paper have been used to clarify these concepts.[3] Nevertheless it is still not clear what these concepts exactly mean. Should they for instance relate to quantities or to amounts of money? Should they relate to actual or planned magnitudes? Furthermore, by no means is there consensus about what kind of quantities or money amounts should be involved. Moreover, other terms with sometimes slightly different meanings are used when efficiency or effectiveness is meant. Such a term is *economy*.

In order to clarify concepts it is necessary to go into some definitions. Of course, we do not want to fall into endless hair splitting. Terms and concepts are only means to achieve an end, namely a better understanding of what goes on. Figure 1 is useful for that purpose. It shows that inputs are transformed into outputs (performances) in a production process. An input, for example, is the number of bureaucrats working on a certain job in a certain department. That job could be, for example, judging applications for subsidies. The number of applications under review is an indicator of the throughput. The results of the process, for instance the number of both positive and negative decisions, are indicators of the output. These magnitudes are expressed in physical units; they can also be expressed in value units. In that case one can look at the amount that is spent on a specific category of bureaucrats, the amount related to the applications under discussion, or the costs of decisions taken. In the last case costs are used as a proxy for the value of the output. This value cannot be measured directly, because market prices are not paid for the goods and services provided.

Figure 1

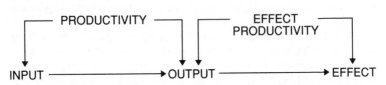

Sometimes output is used as input in the same organisation; in that case one can speak of 'intermediate goods'. On the other hand, when a citizen or a company receives the good or the service, the term *final* good is used. An example is the supply of electricity. Some electricity is used as an input to government organisations and in such cases it is an intermediate good. In other cases it is delivered to houses or factories, and then it is a final good.

Policy objectives are normally expressed – if expressed at all – in terms of activities (throughput) or in terms of output. But what matters in the end are the outcomes or *effects* of outputs, not the outputs themselves. Bradford, Malt and Oates (1969) call these outcomes or effects 'C-output' (things of primary interest to the citizen), in contrast to the output itself which is entitled 'D-output' (services directly produced).[4] The difference between output and effect can be illustrated by the case of police protection: in terms of outputs it is relevant to know how many patrols have taken place, or how many thieves have been caught. But ultimately what matters is by how much the crime rate has decreased, or, to go even further, to what extent safety in the streets has risen. These are the effects.

Absolute magnitudes are of course the building-stones for performance measurement. But they should not be studied in isolation. They become increasingly meaningful when the *relation* between several indicators is considered. This relation is normally expressed in ratios.

The ratio between output and input is *productivity*. Productivity can be measured in physical units, for instance the number of solved crimes per policeman or the number of decisions on applications per bureaucrat. It can also be measured in value units, such as the number of solved crimes per Irish pound or per Dutch guilder. This ratio is often inverted to costs per number of outputs, or *unit cost*. It does not matter which one is used as long as one realises that a decline in the former is equivalent to a rise in the latter and vice versa. When moving towards the right-hand side of the figure, we arrive at the *effect-productivity*. This is the relation between effects and output. It is always expressed in physical units, because effects can only be measured in physical terms, for example, the number of committed crimes in relation to the number of criminal investigations.

Figure 1 describes what actually happens. This can differ from what should happen. In other words there can be a difference between actual and planned inputs, throughputs, outputs and effects. A policy objective could be, for instance, to increase the number of policemen by 10 per cent (input), in order to increase the number of patrols by 15 per cent (output), with the intention of getting the number of committed crimes down by 5 per cent (effect). Actual input can differ from desired input, for instance because of a lack of capacity in police schools or a lack of interest by potential candidates. Therefore the actual input could be raised by less than 10 per cent, say 5 per cent. This does not automatically imply that the desired 15 per cent increase in patrols could not be realised. Maybe the same result could be obtained by a change in the work pattern of the police force: more patrols and less desk work. But even if the number of patrols could be raised by 15 per cent, this does not mean that the intended effect, the 5 per cent reduction in crime, will also be realised. It may turn out that for a decrease of 5 per cent in the number of crimes more than a 15 per cent increase in patrols is needed. To complicate matters further, the decrease in committed crimes does not automatically imply that people in the street feel safer by the same proportion.

From this it can be concluded that it is – at least in a theoretical framework – of crucial importance to make a distinction between actual and desired production. Alongside the actual or realised magnitudes we can therefore distinguish planned input, planned output and planned effect as well as *planned productivity* and *planned effect-productivity*. In Figure 2 plans and realisations are presented together.

Figure 2

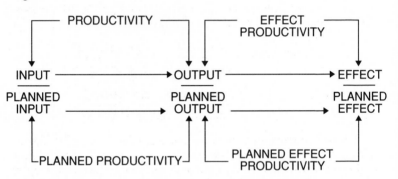

From Figure 2 it is easy to arrive at the concepts of efficiency and effectiveness. In simple terms efficiency means *doing things right*. Accordingly, efficiency has to do with things that have been done, in relation to things that should have been done. In other words, efficiency measures to what extent the actual performance differs from the planned one. This means that efficiency should be defined as follows:

$$\text{Efficiency} = \frac{\text{actual output}/\text{actual input}}{\text{planned output}/\text{planned input}}$$

$$\text{or} \quad \frac{\text{actual productivity}}{\text{planned productivity}}$$

Because productivity can be measured in physical as well as

in value or money units, efficiency can be expressed in both these dimensions. In the case of value or money units it is usual to speak of cost-efficiency. Sticking to the examples given before, an efficiency measure is for instance the realised ratio of solved crimes per policeman over the desired ratio, or the actual unit cost of dispatched applications in relation to the target.

As said before, output is not produced for its own sake, but for specific purposes like safety in the streets. These are the outcomes or the effects, and they occur outside the production unit. Therefore other factors than those related to the production process may also influence actual effects of government policy. That is one of the problems in tracing the relationship between outputs and effects. In common parlance effectiveness means: *doing the right things.* This means that a comparison must be made between actual and planned effects on the one hand, and between what actually has been done and what should have been done on the other. Effectiveness can thus be defined as follows:

$$\text{Effectiveness} = \frac{\text{actual effects}/\text{actual outputs}}{\text{planned effects}/\text{planned outputs}}$$

$$\text{or} \quad \frac{\text{actual effect-productivity}}{\text{planned effect-productivity}}$$

Because effects can only be measured in physical terms, effectiveness is a two-tier ratio of physical quantities. An example is the ratio of actual over desired decline in crimes to the ratio of the actual over the planned increase in the number of solved crimes.

Another term that is sometimes used can be derived from the scheme, namely the term *economy*. Economy is the ratio of actual input and planned input. In our view this ratio is of limited value in judging the performance of an organisation. When actual and planned input differ, this may have consequences for the output. But it does not necessarily change that output. In the example of police patrols given above, it can happen that the planned (increase in) output could be realised with less than the planned (increase in) input, because of changes in the production process. So the term economy can only be used in a meaningful way if there exists an idea about the quantity and quality of the output and of the way in which this output should or could be realised. In that case economy can be seen as a measure of the costs of inputs consistent with a specified quality and quantity of outputs. But then it does not differ from the term *efficiency* as defined above.

Table 1 brings together elements of the terms defined above in a set of 20 different indicators. Cell (3) in Table 1 refers to inputs in value terms, ie the kind of figures almost exclusively contained in government budgets in most Western countries. As we all know, that kind of budget says nothing about activities (throughputs) or outputs, let alone about effects. Table 2 shows which kind of ratios can be derived from these figures.

Different people may be interested in different kinds of information. For politicians it can be important to show the electorate that their policies have been successful. In that case figures on effectiveness (cell 20) would be necessary. If they want to show the electorate or parliament that they used resources economically, they are interested in figures on productivity, effect-productivity and efficiency. In general, interest is growing, on the one hand, in figures on outputs and effects and, on the other hand, in figures on the ratios just mentioned. In other words, cells (9) to (20) are of growing importance.

Table 1

| | Physical units | | Value units | |
	Absolute	Ratio	Absolute	Ratio
Input	(1)	(2)	(3)	(4)
Throughput	(5)	(6)	(7)	(8)
Output	(9)	(10)	(11)	(12)
Effect	(13)	(14)	X	X

Table 2

| | Physical units | | Value units | |
	Absolute	Ratio	Absolute	Ratio
Productivity	X	(15)	X	(16)
Effect-productivity	X	(17)	X	X
Efficiency	X	(18)	X	(19)
Effectiveness	X	(20)	X	X

For all of the possibilities under concern it is necessary that policy goals are clearly stated in quantitative terms. But that is one of the biggest problems. If there are no quantitative policy goals one may be confined to using cells (1) to (8). Although these cells do not tell anything about productivity and the like, nevertheless they can give useful information. Some examples will be given below. Before that a few remarks on problems with measuring public performances are mentioned.

Not just a Dutch disease: measurement problems

In theory it seems easy to construct a set of data on outputs and effects. In practice, however, there are many difficulties. Most of them are well known and often used as an alibi to prevent figures on productivity and the like from playing a role in the political decision-making process. Experiences with PPBS, MBO and ZBB offer a lot of evidence for this view.[5] The problems with measurement of public performances can be technical, administrative, or political in nature.

Technical problems have to do with the nature of public goods. These goods largely consist of intangible services. Services are produced and consumed at the same time and are mostly delivered without a price. In that case it is not easy to identify what exactly is produced. Many services are also related to specific situations or to specific persons. Because of differences in situations or personal circumstances the quality of the services can differ. In other words: the output is often not homogeneous and therefore is difficult to measure in comparable and meaningful units. Moreover, problems arise when costs have to be allocated over products: what kind of costs should be allocated and how should they be divided among different products or groups of products? To be more specific: how do we handle overheads and depreciation? Even if we are able to clear all problems related to the output, similar problems arise with the measurement of the effects. Furthermore, effects occur not only as a result of a production process, but also as a by-product of events outside that process. How can those elements be eliminated? It is not difficult to enlarge this litany of problems of a technical nature.

The administrative and political problems have to do with the fact that performance measurement can be seen as a basis for productivity improvements. Information on productivity and related items can be used to compare departments or organisations with other departments or organisations. Such a comparison can result either in attempts to improve the efficiency in the production of goods and services, or in the elimination of certain activities. Uncertainty about the use of figures on output and productivity can lead to resistance from civil servants. 'What agency could be expected to cheerfully supply information that might result in the loss of jobs, resources and prestige?' Downs and Larkey asked several years ago.[6]

The same goes for politicians. Figures on output and the like can show that policies were not very effective. They can also draw attention to public provisions that are of particular interest to pressure groups or to the suppliers themselves. In the literature these provisions are called privilege goods.[7] Because of these considerations politicians often hesitate to express policy goals in clear-cut terms. They prefer to be vague in order to escape control. Nevertheless, in practice there has been some progress in measuring and comparing performances. This is shown in the next section.

Performance measurement: the Dutch treat
Considering the problems involved in public sector performance measurement, one could easily get the impression that the prospects for success in practice are very poor. Even when there is agreement on the usefulness or the necessity of performance measurement, the ultimate conclusion could be that it is a hopeless task. This conclusion would however be premature. Measurement of public sector performance can be done and in fact is being done. This will be illustrated by a number of examples from Dutch practice. Of course they cannot give a complete picture of what is going on in the Netherlands in this field. They just give an impression of the present state of the art.

The most important studies in this field are those by a quasi-autonomous research organisation with a somewhat confusing name. It is called the Social and Cultural Planning Office (SCP). It does not make plans, however, and neither does it confine itself to social or cultural issues. It carries out studies and provides information on a wide range of topics from benefit incidence to holiday plans, and from the effects of copyright to public sector performance. With its performance studies, the SCP has built up quite a reputation in the Netherlands. A number of examples of these studies will be given.

The first two examples are taken from an SCP study by Goudriaan *et al.*, published in 1987[8]. We start with a simple comparison of the volume of two types of employment at the level of Dutch central government: employment in overhead and final production. Overhead, or intermediate production, is concerned with goods and services that are used in the organisation itself. It covers a wide range of activities, such as policy advice, management, control, cleaning, catering, and internal mail. Final production on the other hand is used outside the organisation. Those involved in it are people such as policemen, doctors, judges and tax collectors.

The aim of this part of the study was to see whether or not there has been a disproportionate growth in overhead employment compared to employment in final production. An affirmative answer would imply that the traditional image of bureaucracy still applies: more and more resources are used for bureaucratic purposes. In that case, both politicians and bureaucratic managers would have one or two things to explain. A less than proportionate overhead growth, on the other hand, would change this image. It would indicate a good performance, to say the least. In Table 3 the growth in both types of employment between 1975 and 1983 is given for a number of departments. The figures are expressed as index numbers.

Table 3: **Manpower employed by intermediate producers in Dutch central government and relevant final producers in 1983 (index: 1975 = 100)**

Department	Intermediate producers (1)	Final producers (2)	(1/2) × 100
Justice	122	124	99
Home Affairs	164	114	145
Education and Science	136	111	123
Finance	136	117	117
Housing	135	127	107
Transportation	123	101	122
Economic affairs	140	94	149
Agriculture	119	91	130
Social Affairs and Employment	141	95	149
Social Welfare, Health and Culture	120	117	103
All departments	129	102	127

Source: Goudriaan *et al.* (1987), p. 202.

Clearly, overhead or intermediate employment has risen in every department by some 20 per cent or more. The clear leader is the Home Office with a growth of no less than 64 per cent. On average, central government overhead employment grew by almost 30 per cent over nine years. This increase is disproportionate if it is stronger than the employment growth in final production. The second column clearly shows that this indeed was the case. Only in the Department of Justice did final production experience a slightly stronger growth in employment than intermediate production. In all other departments overhead grew faster. In three cases final production even showed a *decrease* in employment, thus rapidly worsening the balance with overhead employment. This balance is shown in the third column, where the first two figures are expressed as a ratio. A ratio exceeding 100 means that overhead employment grew faster than final production employment.

This example shows that it is possible to yield interesting information on public sector performance by using nothing more than figures on inputs alone. Moreover, only quantities are considered here. In terms of Table 1, only indicators 1 and 2 are present here. Yet it cannot be concluded from this example that public sector performance has been bad. For that, information is also needed on the output that has been produced. What the figures can do, however, is to give some kind of an alarm signal. Was it really necessary to employ so many more people in intermediate production? What has been happening at the Home Office? Why has final production employment in three departments declined? These and other questions become more than just a shot in the dark because they are based on measurement, on quantitative information. And that is one of the prime tasks of performance measurement, even in this rudimentary stage: to supply the necessary information on the basis of which testing questions can be asked, further studies can be done, and appropriate measures can be taken.

The second example is an attempt to give a bird's eye view of productivity developments in the Dutch public sector between 1975 and 1983. Six large sub-sectors are distinguished: health care, education, social and cultural services, police and justice, public transport and the executive branches of the tax and social security administration. These sub-sectors cover the vast majority of Dutch public sector activities. For each sub-sector a number of output indicators is chosen, such as in-patient days or treatments, the number of pupils or solved crimes, and the amount of passenger miles, tax assessments or benefit payments. The study is noteworthy in at least two respects. First, it attempts to say something about the changes in performance over a number of years, while many other studies confine themselves to a cross-section analysis within a particular year. Second, the study tries to sketch in outline the performance of the Dutch public sector as a whole, instead of looking at a single activity in detail.

For each of the six sub-sectors just mentioned the study presents figures on inputs, outputs, and labour productivity. Table 4 shows figures for output and labour productivity expressed by means of index numbers.

Looking at the first column, it appears that the output of the public sector clearly has risen in the nine years under consideration. In each sub-sector an output growth of at least 10 per cent has been realised. However, if we look at the second column, it appears that in most cases the increased output has been realised by a more than proportionate rise in labour input. Only the tax and social security administration has shown an increase in labour productivity. Not surprisingly, this result for the tax and social security administration is mainly due to large-scale computerisation projects. In all other sectors productivity has gone down, resulting in a fall in labour

Table 4: **Trends in output and real labour cost per unit of output, 1975-1983 (index: 1975 = 100)**

	Output	*Labour productivity*
Health care	110	90
Education	110	99
Social and cultural services	112	93
Public transport	110	98
Police and justice	123	99
Tax and social security administration	142	115
Total	112	95

Source: Goudriaan *et al.* (1987), p. 198.

productivity of the Dutch public sector as a whole by some 5 per cent. This is even worse than the often heard contention that the productivity of the public sector has a slow growth or no growth at all.

The politicians and civil servants who work in these sectors are perhaps the first to claim that the methods used in this performance measurement are too crude to warrant absolute conclusions, that the indicators do not reflect the actual output they produce and so forth. Politicians and civil servants have their ways of dealing with uncomfortable facts. But then again, it can hardly be a coincidence that in five out of six sectors productivity seems to be problematic. The least one could say is that a denial of the bad news shifts the burden of the proof to those who deny.

Undeterred, the Social and Cultural Planning Office went on with performance measurement studies. A third example is taken from a recently published study on the performance of four specific government activities, namely police protection, homes for the aged, public libraries and secondary education.[9] This study is an extensive piece of work, containing almost 300 pages of analysis. This study does not pretend to say anything about public sector productivity in general, but analyses the four activities in depth.

Figure 3 presents productivity developments since 1969 in the area of homes for the aged. The figures are shown as index numbers. Both labour and total productivity are shown.

The trend is clear: a marked decline in productivity for more than ten years in succession. Part of this decline is due to a more than proportionate growth in the numbers of old-aged people suffering both mental and physical disability. These people of course

Figure 3: **Homes for the aged: productivity, 1969-1984 (index: 1969 = 100)**

need a more than average amount of care. But according to the authors of the study, this can only explain a small fraction of the productivity decline. It is to be feared that 'genuine' loss in productivity was occurring here. This is supported by recent developments. In the early eighties productivity suddenly started to improve. This coincides with the implementation of severe budget cuts which began to hit the homes for the aged. The authors conclude that these cuts must have reduced the slack that had been built up in the previous decade. This observation provides an excellent illustration of the fact that a smaller budget does not necessarily mean a lower service level. Efficiency improvement is an alternative outcome.

Figure 4 illustrates a happier story, at least as far as performance is concerned. It shows productivity developments in public libraries, expressed in index numbers. The output indicator here is the number of books lent out.

Bearing in mind that we are still dealing with a public sector activity, an almost incredible increase in productivity is shown. Especially after 1965 we see an improvement of both labour and total productivity to about 2.5 times the original level. Which private sector company would not desire something even remotely close

Figure 4: **Public libraries: productivity, 1954-1984 (index: 1954 = 100)**

to this? Several factors together explain this success story. Not surprisingly, large-scale automation has increased productivity. Furthermore, there has been a substantial increase in scale by some forty per cent. Econometric analysis has shown that public libraries indeed experience economies of scale. A third explanation – related to the former – no doubt is the tremendous increase in the actual output of the libraries. Over thirty years the number of books lent out rose by 1,400 per cent! In the fifties and sixties there must have been a considerable amount of excess capacity. While growing in output, this excess gradually has evaporated, thus adding to the productivity increase.

A final example taken from the 1989 SCP study shows that the results for a government activity as a whole may be quite different from those for the component parts. It shows productivity developments for the Dutch police. On average police productivity has slightly risen for some decades. The Dutch police service however is organised in two strictly separated entities. The state police is confined to smaller villages and operates under the responsibility of the Minister of Justice. In fact it is a decentralised agency of central government. The municipal police service, on the other hand, is confined to towns and cities. It is a local government organisation under the authority of the mayor (burgomaster). In Figure 5 productivity developments for these two different police forces are shown, again expressed in index numbers.

Considering the fact that the two organisations have the same tasks, there is a remarkable difference in performance: a small decrease in state police productivity and a strong increase in the case of the municipal police. Some have argued that part of this difference is due to the longer average distance the state police must travel to an accident or a crime. After all, they have to do their job in the countryside. But this can hardly explain any difference in productivity growth, since these greater distances also were present at the beginning of the period. So what is the real reason? The SCP study does not tell, and personally we think it does not want to tell. Widespread gossip in the Netherlands is that bureaucracy and the accompanying inefficiency are typical state police characteristics. It is rumoured that their representatives in the advisory committee of this SCP study have done their utmost to prevent figures from being published at the necessary level of detail. Again we have here a good reason for asking testing questions. After all, the police service is quite different from the homes for the aged inasmuch as the former can benefit to a far greater extent

Figure 5: **Police: productivity, 1955-1986 (index: 1955 = 100)**

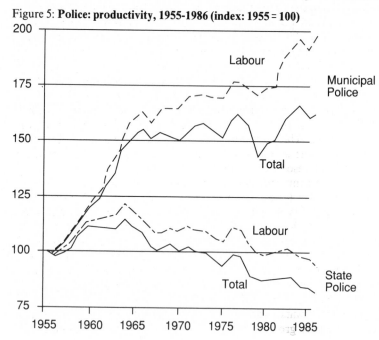

than the latter from technical innovations such as computerisation, better means of transportation and so forth. Therefore productivity developments in the municipal police service seem to be the normal case, while the state police appear to be the odd one out. Most probably the state police would not have been against a limited publication of the figures for the police as a whole. The overall figures would show a modest productivity development and disturbing facts would not have to be explained.

The political use of performance measurement: Dutch gold or not?
So much for the performance studies. Let us now turn for a moment to the political use of performance measurement. Here also there is good as well as bad news. To begin with the bad news: central government in the Netherlands has a poor reputation as far as performance measurement is concerned. Since 1978 there has been an opportunity for every department to employ performance budgeting. Success in this field, however, has been virtually absent. There is no actual obligation to use a performance budget, and if one is constructed it is merely considered as a gadget for a few productivity fanatics. The attention of most politicians and bureaucrats is still almost exclusively devoted to the traditional input budget. Up to the present the debates on the budget are concentrated both on broad policy measures and on the required amounts of money. Political interest in other types of performance measurement, such as the ones just mentioned, is lacking.

At the level of local government things are developing more favourably. It is always nice to conclude a story with a happy ending; that is why we have placed local governments at the end.

In financial terms local governments in the Netherlands have had the hardest time of all public sector organisations in the past two decades. They are subject to severe restrictions on deficit financing, while at the same time their capacity to mobilise their own current resources is limited. Not more than 10 per cent of local government's current receipts come from taxes, fees, charges and the like. The bulk of their income comes from central government grants. And it is here that major reductions have occurred. One can safely say that most of the budget cuts that were initiated by central government subsequently were passed on to local governments. This has been one of the major reasons why many local governments have started to apply serious performance measurement systems. They argued that every guilder saved because of productivity gains offsets a guilder lost in cuts in central government grants. And of course they were right. The result has been a steadily growing stream of local budgets and management systems that depend on performance measurement. In many cases also the policy goals are explicitly stated in output terms. This year, one city for the first time even presented a budget constructed entirely in output terms. Some local governments even formulate desired effects. Thus it becomes possible to apply the concepts of efficiency and effectiveness. Often this is accompanied by some form of contract management.

All in all, performance measurement at the local level in the Netherlands is on firm ground at the moment. Expectations are that it can only gain in importance in the near future. As far as central government is concerned, one can only hope that things will improve. There are good reasons to believe that this hope will not be in vain. First, knowledge of, and skills in, performance measurement are growing. Freshly educated professionals have come across performance measurement in their studies and when they become politicians or public sector managers one may expect them to remember something of it. Second, a tighter financial situation, inconvenient as it is, may have the beneficial side-effect of a more receptive attitude towards performance measurement. While the escape-routes of higher taxes and deficits are more and more cut off, attention has to be turned towards savings in expenditures. Voters and/or customers become increasingly aware of the need for efficiency and effectiveness in this field. Finally, the increasing use of performance measurement may be self-reinforcing. It should become increasingly clear that it has proven to be a valuable instrument for improvements in efficiency and effectiveness and that it is not just the latest fashion. Therefore, acceptance by opponents and those who are indifferent or still in doubt will also come closer.

Notes

[1] The authors wish to thank Peter A. Cornelisse for his comments on an earlier draft of this paper.

[2] *Planning-Programming-Budgeting System (PPBS)*. A programme budget allocates costs to particular activities. PPBS is a type of programme budget which attempts to establish objectives, to set priorities for the attainment of these objectives and to examine possible alternative programmes. In order to determine the efficiency of each programme the total costs and total benefits are compared. The most efficient and effective programmes are then selected to become part of an overall integrated programme.

Zero Base Budgeting (ZBB) is a type of programme budget which, like PPBS, attempts to establish objectives for the main areas of an organisation's activities. Budgets formulated under ZBB require activities to be justified as if they were being started for the first time. ZBB is a 'bottom up' process which works upward from the lowest tier of an organisation, in contrast to PPBS which works from the top down. ZBB requires those with responsibility throughout an organisation to rank the importance of their activities. As the process works through successive tiers, the overall priorities of the organisation are established. *Management by Objectives (MBO)* in an organisation works through setting targets which become the basis for improving efficiency and for increasing managerial motivation. MBO identifies obstacles to the achievement of objectives and identifies corrective action. Results are evaluated periodically and, where necessary, new targets are set.

[3] See for instance Hanusch (1984), Downs and Larkey (1986) and Hepworth (1991).
[4] Bradford, Malt and Oates (1969), p. 186.
[5] See for example Harper (1969), Wildavsky (1975), Brady (1973), Ross and Burkhead (1974), Mark (1981) and Downs and Larkey (1986).
[6] Downs and Larkey (1986), p. 163.
[7] See for instance Wolfson (1979), p. 14.
[8] Goudriaan *et al.* (1987).
[9] Goudriaan *et al.* (1989).

References

Bradford, D.F., Malt R.A. and Oates, W.E., 'The rising cost of local public services: some evidence and reflections', *National Tax Journal,* Vol. XXII, No. 2, June 1969, pp. 185-202.

Brady, R.H., 'MBO goes to work in the public sector', *Harvard Business Review,* March-April 1973; reprinted in F.J. Lyden and E.G. Miller (eds.), *Public Budgeting,* Englewood Cliffs, 1982, pp. 169-183.

Downs, G.W. and Larkey, P.D., *The search for government efficiency,* New York, 1986.

Goudriaan, R., de Groot, H. and van Tulder, F., 'Public sector productivity: recent empirical findings and policy application', in H.M. van de Kar and B.L. Wolfe (eds.), *The relevance of public finance for policy-making,* Proceedings of the 41st Congress of the International Institute of Public Finance (Madrid 1985), Detroit, 1987.

Goudriaan, R., van Tulder, F., Blank, J., van der Torre, A. and Kuhry, B., *Doelmatig dienstverlenen* (Efficiently producing services), Rijswijk, 1989.

Hanusch, H. (ed.), *Public Finance and the Quest for Efficiency,* proceedings of the 38th Congress of the International Institute of Public Finance (Copenhagen, 1982), Detroit Michigan, 1984.

Harper, E.L., 'Implementation and use of PPB in sixteen federal agencies', *Public Administration Review,* Nov/Dec 1969, pp. 623-632.

Hepworth, N., *Performance measurement in public sector management,* proceedings of the second Public Sector Conference of the Fédération des Expertes Comptables Europèens (FEE) (Rottach Egern, 1990), London, 1991 (forthcoming).

Mark, J.A., 'Measuring productivity in government, federal, state and local', *Public Productivity Review,* Vol. V, No. 1, March 1981, pp. 21-44.

Ross, J.P. and Burkhead, J., *Productivity in the local government sector,* Lexington (Mass.), 1974.

Wildavsky, A., *Budgeting, a comparative theory of budgetary processes,* Boston, 1975.

Wolfson, D.J., *Public finance and development strategy,* Baltimore, 1979.

8

The 'Next Steps' Project: Efficiency and Effectiveness in the UK Civil Service

E.P. KEMP

I AM going to limit the scope of this paper to a part of the civil service in the United Kingdom: the part that actually delivers services. This means that I am ignoring the great mass of the public service domain including health, education, local authorities, the railways, coal, and the majority of the armed services, although we do touch on parts of these. I am left with about half a million people delivering services costing something like £15 billion a year. This may not sound much out of a total public expenditure of nearly £200 billion, but £15 billion is substantial. The old rule of thumb used to be that each billion saved would mean a penny off income tax, so on that admittedly crude basis, if you got rid of the United Kingdom civil service you could cut income tax by something like 15 per cent.

The origins of 'Next Steps'
I would like to dispel a myth, perpetuated by programmes like 'Yes, Minister', that the UK civil service consists of elderly, white gentlemen working on policy matters in London. In fact, civil servants come from all ethnic groups, many are young, the majority are female and only 20 per cent work in London. About 95 per cent of the work we do is concerned with delivering services and it is upon this that 'Next Steps' concentrates.

The basis of 'Next Steps' is a mercifully thin little book called *Improving Management in Government: The Next Steps* (1988), and generally known as the Ibbs Report because it was produced by the Government Efficiency Unit when Robin Ibbs was at its head. Ibbs himself was not an economist, public sector specialist or administrator – he was a senior director from ICI and is now also deputy chairman of Lloyds Bank. The then Prime Minister, perhaps, noticed that the civil service was one of the estates of

172

the realm which had not been sufficiently addressed by the various revolutions of the previous few years and asked the Efficiency Unit to look to see if there were changes that could be made.

The report concluded that, although there had already been important improvements in the way the civil service was operating, there was scope for more to be done. Also, the Efficiency Unit found that civil service managers would like to see further change and, in particular, wished to be given more room and flexibility for the exercise of personal responsibility. The main finding of the Ibbs Report was that, to the greatest extent possible, the executive functions of government – the 95 per cent of the work concerned with delivering services to which I referred earlier – as opposed to policy advice, should be carried out by units within departments described as agencies. These units would be headed by a chief executive, appointed by and accountable to, the minister from whom he or she is delegated responsibility for day-to-day matters. Ibbs also recommended that a progressive programme be implemented to achieve the aim of transferring executive functions to units, that staff be properly trained to better enable them to deliver and manage services and finally, that a project manager be appointed to try to make it work.

There is nothing new about the idea that the executive functions of government should be carried out by units called agencies: Fulton (1968) proposed this twenty years ago but he talked in terms of units of accountable management, whereas Ibbs talks of agencies. They are making the same point: that the half a million civil servants in the UK do not form a uniform service with one employer. In fact, we have hundreds of small businesses of different kinds, as is evident from Tables 1 and 2, and Ibbs concluded that it was not practicable to try to run this diverse service as one organisation with uniform management tools, financial regimes and pay. As the report noted: systems existed that were approximate to everyone and suited no one.

In February 1988 the Prime Minister issued a statement that to the greatest possible extent the Ibbs recommendations should be implemented. There was nothing in the statement about doing it only if it makes things better, or if it is easier to do it that way. There was an implicit act of faith that this approach would bring about greater efficiency and effectiveness in government.

I was appointed Project Manager and I would like to say something about our approach to 'Next Steps', which may be considered as unintellectual. The project has not arisen, as many things did in the old civil service, from a prolonged period of navel examination followed by numbers of working parties producing

Table 1

Executive agencies established	Staff*
Building Research Establishment	680
Central Office of Information	740
Central Veterinary Laboratory	560
Civil Service College	200
Companies House	1,100
Driver and Vehicle Licensing Agency	5,300
Driving Standards Agency	2,100
Employment Service	33,800
Historic Royal Palaces	330
HMSO	3,200
Hydrographic Office**	890
Information Technology Services Agency	2,900
Insolvency Service	1,400
Intervention Board	860
Laboratory of the Government Chemist	320
Land Registry	10,800
Meteorological Office	2,250
National Engineering Laboratory	520
National Physical Laboratory	830
National Weights and Measures Laboratory	50
Natural Resources Institute	330
Occupational Health Service	100
Ordnance Survey	2,550
Patent Office	1,150
QE11 Conference Centre	60
Radiocommunications Agency	460
Registers of Scotland	1,000
Resettlement Agency	530
Royal Mint	970
Training & Employment Agency (NICS)***	1,700
Vehicle Certification Agency	70
Vehicle Inspectorate	1,600
Veterinary Medicines Directorate	70
Warren Spring Laboratory	300
Total	79,720

*Figures based on staff in post as at 1 April 1990.
**Defence Support Agency. Figure does not include service personnel.
***(NICS) – Agency from the Northern Ireland Civil Service.

very wise reports. That approach may, eventually, have resulted in a pretty good civil service. However, there is the possibility of delay and that absolutely nothing might happen. We have approached 'Next Steps' in a bottom-up, pragmatic way, going

Table 2

Executive agency candidates announced	Staff**
Cadw	220
Central Science Laboratory	400
Central Statistical Office	1,000
Chessington Computer Centre	430
Child Support Agency	not yet known
Civil Service Commission	340
Defence Accounts Organisation*	2,100
Defence Research Agency	11,700
Farm and Countryside Service	2,550
Fisheries Protection Service	170
Forensic Science Service	580
Fuel Suppliers Branch	30
Historic Buildings and Monuments	570
Military Survey*	850
NHS Estates	130
Passport Office	1,200
Planning Inspectorate	550
Pollution Inspectorate	210
Property Holdings	1,600
RAF Training*	2,500
Royal Parks	570
Service Children's Schools*	1,000
Social Security Benefits	68,200
Social Security Contributions	6,200
Valuation Office	5,700
Youth Treatment Service	220
Rating Division (NICS)***	270
Social Security Operations (NICS)*** 28 in number	5,000
Customs & Excise**	26,900
Inland Revenue ** (excl. Valuation Office)	60,400
Total	201,590

*Defence Support Agency. Figure does not include service personnel.
**Moving towards operating fully on Next Steps lines, as set out in the Chancellor of the Exchequer's statement of 25 July 1990.
***(NICS) — Agency candidate from the Northern Ireland Civil Service. Many other areas of government are under consideration including Prisons and other parts of the Ministry of Defence.

straight for it and trying to solve problems as we have come to them. I am rather fond of the quotation from Machiavelli which I feel is absolutely true. He wrote that nothing is more difficult to arrange, more doubtful of success or more dangerous to carry through than to bring about a new order of things. Of course,

Machiavelli only had to deal with a lot of ambitious, scheming, murderous Italian princelings whereas we ... well perhaps I had better leave that!

We have approached the project with no particular prior view, especially on one aspect: the merits of public versus private services. Personally, I am totally agnostic on this: I am not one of those people who seem to think that the public sector has a special dimension which makes it different from the private sector. I don't think that a bit. There are differences, but I think you can exaggerate those differences. For example, people say that there is something very special about the public service and its ethics but I don't actually think that is true. I think that the public sector has ethics and the private sector has ethics too. The notion that there is something particularly special about the public sector can be exaggerated. What we are trying to do with 'Next Steps' is to pick up the best of both the public and the private ways. I think that it is a job to be done and one to be done properly and well and I think that is what we are trying to achieve.

The public versus the private sector
What constitutes the difference between the public and private sectors is an important question. I think the basic difference between the public and private sectors is that the public sector does not choose what it does. The present UK government takes the view that the public sector should not do anything that the private sector can do for it and that it should not do anything that does not actually have to be done. This means that the public sector does not have the options open to it that the private sector does. I will illustrate this by an example I often give: Lloyds Bank. If Lloyds Bank decides that it is not worth its while to provide banking services in Scotland it does not have to and no one can make it do so. However, the public sector cannot decide not to collect taxes in Scotland or to stop delivering social security benefits there. In this respect we lack the ability to choose and, generally speaking, we work in areas where people have no alternative choice and where they do not have to pay for the service. In this way the public sector differs from the private sector, where there are always options.

The civil service, like all areas of the public sector, has been subject to the movement to limit resources and keep public expenditure down in order to facilitate tax cuts and similar desirable measures. Coupled with this there is a world-wide desire for improved public services and better value for money: for which we in the UK do not have a marvellous reputation. This brings me back to

176

my main theme because improvements to public services and giving better value for money are at the heart of the 'Next Steps' programme.

The aim of 'Next Steps'

The aim of 'Next Steps' is to deliver government services more efficiently and effectively, within available resources, to the benefit of taxpayer, customer and staff. However, 'Next Steps' did not start out with that aim – this is one that I developed after the programme had been running for some while. I mentioned earlier that Ibbs recommended a progressive programme and this is a usefully ambiguous phrase because it means both that agencies will be introduced increasingly into the civil service and, also, that the concept of agencies is not static and will develop progressively as they are created. To start with, each agency has an individually tailored framework document which, so to speak, guides them. This framework document is a mixture of memorandum, articles of association, informal contract and mission statement, and sorting these out is not easy. It is quite hard work teasing out the minute details of each prospective agency's business but we are learning how to do this and agencies are being set up and coming along well.

However, I must emphasise, as I always do when discussing 'Next Steps', that setting up agencies is just the means to the end: only a start. It might be tempting to put a label on an activity and say, 'This is an agency ... Well done, Kemp!' but that is not the approach nor can it be the approach. What matters is the improved management we are getting and the consequent dividends to the taxpayers, customers and staff. And results are really starting to show through. The first annual review of 'Next Steps' (1990) gives details of all the agencies we have so far – all 34 of them. It shows the nature of their business and the work they do, gives the names and addresses of the chief executives so that anyone may contact them, and, most important, it publicly sets out their performance targets. Each agency has different performance targets which are tailored to the nature of its business.

For example, the review shows that, over the period 1991-94, the Land Registry has a target to achieve, or better, a 6 per cent improvement in reducing unit costs and increasing output per post per year. It should also aim to increase by 1 per cent, over the same period, the number of pre-completion applications handled in four days and to reduce from seven weeks to five weeks the average handling time for post-completion applications. Companies House already meets its operating costs of £37m from receipts and for the two years to April 1991 its targets include the achievement of a 10 per cent reduction in the proportion of companies which have not filed all the accounts and annual returns required by the Companies Act, a 20 per cent reduction in the time taken to process documents and a 7 per cent decrease in unit costs in real terms.

Many of these targets are tied to giving, and improving, service to the customer, which as I mentioned earlier is an important aspect of 'Next Steps'. When he was chief secretary to the treasury, John Major memorably said that 'Shoddy public services should not be an option. Nor should they be tolerated.' Margaret Thatcher, as Prime Minister, identified improvement to public services as one of the great tasks of the nineties. These sentiments are striking chords because in the past management reforms in the UK civil service have tended to be driven by the treasury in a 'screw them down and see if they die' sort of approach. Now we are trying to look at the subject, and tackle it, in a more positive way.

This raises some interesting questions about what a 'customer' is and what a 'service' is. You might like to ponder for a moment who the customer of the prison service is and you will probably come up with a number of answers. For all agencies there is a customer/contractor relationship and underlying the 'Next Steps' approach is the notion that there is a customer of some kind, represented by the minister, and a contractor, which is the agency.

In many of the targets given to agencies there is a trade-off between money and services. In the example from Companies House which I gave earlier, a 10 per cent reduction in the proportion of companies not filing returns is a desirable aim and would signify an improvement for the corporate sector. But it does not sit easily with the other target of a 7 per cent decrease in unit costs in real terms and one can ask how these targets are traded off. A more difficult, though perhaps more obvious, example is the delivery of social security benefits. For example, it would be possible to improve the quality of social security delivery in terms of reducing queues, reducing the error rate and so forth, if the government of the day was prepared to spend more taxpayers' money on a better service. However, it seems to me that in a democracy an important reason why we keep governments is for them to make judgements about how far the taxpayer should have to pay for improved benefits to the general population. What 'Next Steps' tries to do is to make clear that there can be simultaneous benefits to taxpayers and customers.

A highly significant element of 'Next Steps' is openness – all targets are published and all agencies will produce annual reports and accounts which will, I hope, be examined by the appropriate parliamentary select committees. As noted above the annual review gives addresses of all the agencies and the names of the chief executives so that anyone who wants to may ask questions or even visit the agencies. Chief executives will answer questions about their agencies – questioners will not be referred to the parent departments.

It is becoming more the rule that chief executive posts are being advertised outside the civil service. Interestingly and encouragingly, quite a number of sitting civil servants get the jobs. I think this gives them a legitimacy which they might not have if they had merely been appointed and it also gives them a special interest in the post.

The 'Next Steps' programme is trying to take the lid off the public sector to show what people are really doing. Personally, I think that it is the private sector which is secretive and hidden and, in some ways, this is a disgrace. Anyone who has witnessed a Public Accounts committee meeting or something of that sort will know that the questioning has very little in common with the rather stately progress of the annual meeting of a private company where there is little or no questioning.

There is considerable public interest in 'Next Steps' and I don't quite know why. A cynic might say that the general standard of public services is not very good and, therefore, any changes can only be for the better and must be worth doing. But I think there is more to it than that: I think that it is a new approach to management which strikes a chord regardless of whether it is in the public or the private sector. Many forces are at work. Firstly, young people coming into management tend to have a different outlook – they prefer to manage, or be managed, by contract, you might say, rather than by command. They are less prepared to have people tell them what to do and how to do it – they are more independent. Secondly, there is information technology, the impact of which is, I think, greatly underrated. Why, if you have a machine on your desk that gives you information in thirty seconds, do you have to wait two weeks for your boss to tell you whether you can use it. There was a phrase back in the 1960s, 'small is beautiful', and I think we are cashing in on the notion that smaller organisations can work better than large ones.

The future of the civil service
There are a number of issues already arising out of 'Next Steps'. An obvious one is the future of the civil service. Contrary to what some of the unions are saying, 'Next Steps' is not deliberately aimed at breaking up the civil service but it is patently clear that it does have tendencies in that direction. There is a centrifugal force which works on these agencies as they are set up and get more freedom and as the chief executives become more important and better known

as individuals. The tendency is for the agencies to move away from their parent departments and I think that all of us interested in the totality of the civil service need to keep our eyes on this. People are starting to ask, 'What is the glue that holds the civil service together?' The opposite side of this is, 'Will the departments take their hands off and allow agencies freedom to breathe?' This is one of the most difficult issues.

On the whole, contrary to popular belief, the people who have fun under the 'Next Steps' regime are those in the agencies. The ones having a hard time are those back in the departments because they have got to learn new ways; but, sometimes for very good reasons, they are slow to do this. Rightly or wrongly, they may not think they can trust the agencies and they may feel that their jobs are being taken over by people in the agencies.

Another important issue is the question of accountability to parliament. These agencies are still within the civil service – the legislation has not been changed – they are not nationalised industries, they are not quangos and they are not in the private sector. Therefore, their ministers are still answerable to parliament. This leaves us with the problem of sorting out how we give the chief executives sufficient power to get on with the job while retaining the necessary degree of parliamentary accountability. These are just some of the issues which are being discussed at present.

Efficiency, effectiveness and economy
Some may argue that there are three 'Es' – efficiency, effectiveness and equity. I agree that there are three but I'm afraid that I don't include equity. I think the one that is not usually discussed, but which should not be overlooked, is economy – that is to say, actually spending less money. Many economies nowadays, including Ireland and the UK, have policies for reducing public debt and containing public borrowing. We may not always succeed in doing it as much as we would like but that is what we are trying to do. The sheer size of the public sector is an important element in such policies.

In my opinion, the other two 'Es', efficiency and effectiveness, can be addressed fairly simply as either more for the same or the same for less. At slightly greater length you can say that if there is a given set of resources available, the task of the efficient and effective manager is to get as much as he or she can from them or, if a given job of work is required by ministers, to do that job at least resource cost. I remember a very fraught discussion with very senior people in the treasury about the meaning of the words efficient and effective and eventually it was resolved by a homely example of two permanent secretaries who decided to commit suicide. The one from a spending department was rather lavish and put a gold bullet in his gun while the one from the treasury, naturally rather more economical, put an ordinary bullet in his gun. Now, they were both pretty effective in what they achieved but you may wish to consider who was the more efficient.

There are elements of the 'Next Steps' programme which promote efficiency and effectiveness. I think it is important to have units of manageable size and the average size of our agencies, if you leave aside the very big ones (which, I admit, is cheating slightly), is 1,100. These are organisations of manageable size. Once we have the unit we can think about setting its targets and that involves asking questions like: what is the organisation there for? what do we want it for? why do we have it at all? Once we have the answers to these questions and are clear who is the tasker and who is the tasked, who is the contractor and who is the customer, the sorts of targets to be set become clear and in them we have the tools to create efficiency and effectiveness. Other tools include breaking down the uniform pay and personnel regimes in the civil service so that we have systems which are suited to the individual operation in question. Also, so far as one can within a system which requires overall control of public expenditure, financial regimes tailored to the individual needs of agencies will be introduced. For example, in 1990 the Government Trading Fund Act was passed and this will enable appropriate agencies to operate as trading funds.

The government is also encouraging the relocation of civil servants away from London. Relocation and agency status are not automatically connected but there is an important point to be made about relocation. It may be a wild generalisation to say so but I think that organisations which are further from their head office can be more efficient and effective than organisations which are close to head office. An important consideration is that since the head office tends to be in London, relocated agencies are rather cheaper to run. For this and other reasons I think that if an agency does relocate away from the parent department, this can be of help.

Before concluding I would like to say a little about performance motivators. I think you can overrate pay as a motivator – which is just as well, given our pay rates – but I think agencies can provide other motivators. They can create an atmosphere of commitment where, for example, instead of being a member of the Department of Transport, you can be a member of the Vehicle Inspectorate and can respond more closely in what you are doing. You can give a commitment to the organisation and feel that your career and your loyalties are centred upwards rather than sideways. I think that all these things are releasing the energies and imaginations of the staff and making for greater efficiency and effectiveness.

I conclude with a story which illustrates the point that while the civil service, and perhaps all bureaucracies, do have virtues, that simplicity of mind is not necessarily one of them. Bureaucratic organisations have an incredible ability to complicate the simple and I think the following story illustrates this point. There was an Indian prince who had a most beautiful wife whom he adored. She died and he was absolutely heartbroken. He mourned over her little black coffin and he could not bear to let it out of his sight, so he decided to house this little black coffin in the most beautiful building in the world. He sent far and wide for materials and spent his great riches on making the building more and more magnificent. He visited it each day and admired it, sending for more materials and spending even more money on it. Then one day he visited it, looked around and felt that something was not quite right. He did not quite know what it was and he looked around again and frowned. Then he saw the little black coffin, decided it was not quite right and said, 'Take that thing away.' This, it seems to me, is what happens if you take your eye off the ball. You may get the Taj Mahal but you do not get efficiency and effectiveness.

References

Efficiency Unit, *Improving Management in Government: The Next Steps* (the 'Ibbs Report'), HMSO, 1988.

Fulton, Lord John (Chairman), *The Civil Service, Report of the Committee,* HMSO, 1968.

Improving Management in Government. The Next Steps Agency Review 1990, HMSO, 1990.

9

Efficiency and Effectiveness: The Case of American Fiscal Federalism[1]

THOMAS SWARTZ

Introduction

HISTORICALLY, the US has assumed that the provision of basic social goods is a responsibility shared between individuals in society and the three levels of government that comprise the US system of federalism – federal or national government, state governments and local governments (countries, townships, cities, school districts and special districts[2]). Over time the distribution of the responsibility for basic social goods has changed markedly.

In the earliest days of the Union, 1789 to 1929, US federalism has been categorised as 'Constitutional Federalism'.[3] In that period self-reliance and a strict interpretation of the constitutional constraints on the federal government were evident. Of particular note in this period is the fact that state governments were pre-eminent. Federal governmental activities were limited to those powers which were explicitly delineated in the constitution. All other governmental powers were reserved for the states which in turn could delegate some power to their local governments.

The collapse of the American and world economies in 1929, the Second World War and the Korean conflict forced the US courts and congress to reconsider the role of government in the modern world. A limited national government was simply incapable of handling these unprecedented problems. Thus from 1929 to 1953 US federalism entered into its 'crisis' phase. However, the introduction of a highly productive personal and corporate income tax allowed the national government to swell in size and influence. Yet state and local governments were not left to wither on the vine. Although their relative importance declined, these governmental units continued to grow in absolute terms. More importantly, they retained their control over the provision of basic public goods and services: education, public health, welfare programmes (except for the newly created social security system), public order, streets and highways, park lands, and so forth.

As the period of 'crisis federalism' drew to a close in the early 1950s, the relative calm provided national policy-makers with an opportunity to take stock of the consequences of a federal system which charged lower levels of government with the responsibility to provide basic public goods and services. This relative calm also provided them with a highly income elastic revenue system which was not tied to an explicit set of public expenditures. In brief, the national government had what was to become known as a 'fiscal dividend' (the product of an unindexed income based tax system) which it could use on new expenditure programmes now that the crises of the 1930s, 1940s and early 1950s had abated.

In the early days of the 'fiscal federation' period (1953 to present) policy-makers found great unevenness in the provision of basic public goods and services. Those states and local governments that were fiscally secure provided high quality public goods and services. Unfortunately, those states with a low fiscal capacity (ie low ability to generate revenue from a given tax base and tax rate) were forced to provide poor education, inadequate public health services, welfare supports that left many below the poverty line, streets and highways that were not capable of handling the ever expanding traffic levels, questionable public safety standards and so forth. In recognition of this unevenness, congress began to level the playing field for those living in the Old South, in urban areas, and in other distinguishable 'pockets of poverty', such as the rural poverty endemic to the Appalachian range – an area that stretches across thirteen mid-Atlantic states.

However, this process of levelling-up had to recognise the restrictions imposed on the federal government by the US Constitution. The federal government could not simply assume the expenditure responsibility for education, welfare, highways and so forth. Power to spend in these areas was constitutionally reserved for state governments. What the federal government could do was to initiate programmes of grants-in-aid to state and local governments. Funds were generated by the very productive federal tax system and transferred to lower levels of government.

Since the early 1950s, state and local governments were, as a consequence, the beneficiaries of an ever growing level of federal grants-in-aid. However, the growth of this source of revenue was abruptly halted in 1978. First under President Carter, then under President Reagan and now under President Bush, states and their local governments are increasingly expected to pay their own way.

The US federal government in the foreseeable future will no longer attempt to aggressively reduce vertical and horizontal fiscal imbalances among state and local governments. In brief, the old system of 'levelling the playing field' for state and local governments has been replaced with a new system of 'competitive federalism' where the smaller units of government are expected to finance their own activities.

The issue in brief
This sudden change in national policy forced state governments to reconsider their state tax/expenditure policies. The federal government was no longer there to bail them out if they encountered financial trouble. They would have to economise, to compete, and to increase fiscal efficiency and effectiveness.

The policies introduced by state governments provide many lessons for national governments. In the US national leaders have called for the implementation of policies that have long characterised state governments: constitutional/statutorial balanced budget and debt limits, line-item veto power, indexing, and other tax and expenditure limitations.[4] These policy actions are the subject of this paper.

Reshaping the role of government in the US

The tax and expenditure revolt of 1978
The year 1978 will serve as a focal point in this analysis. This year has not been chosen by chance. It was the year of Proposition 13 which initiated a 'tax revolt' that swept across the states. This amendment to the California state constitution passed by voters in a general referendum represents the single most significant piece of control legislation ever enacted by a state government. In one bold stroke it rolled back the local property tax levy by 57 per cent, it limited future increases in that levy to a mere 2 per cent per year, and it dictated that state tax increases must pass both houses of the California state legislature with a two-thirds majority. In brief, its architects intended dramatically and permanently to reshape the role played by the public sector in California. They were successful.

Prior to the passage of Proposition 13, California consistently employed one of the most aggressive tax and expenditure systems in the US. From 1970 to 1978, for example, California experienced a 29.1 per cent increase in state tax revenue per $100 of personal income. This was the fourth biggest increase among the fifty states. In the years that followed this voter initiative the pattern changed

185

Efficiency and Effectiveness in the Public Domain

Table 1: **Tax and/or expenditure limits adopted by state governments from 1976 to the present**

States with limits	*Revenue or expenditure*	*Approximate limits*[1]
Alaska	Expenditure	Appropriations shall not exceed $2.5 billion by more than the cumulative percentage change in population and inflation.
Arizona	Expenditure	Appropriations of state tax revenues shall not exceed 7 per cent of state personal income.
California	Expenditure	Yearly growth in appropriations limit shall not exceed percentage increase in population and inflation.
Colorado	Expenditure	Yearly growth of state general fund appropriations.
Delaware	Expenditure	98 per cent of estimated general fund revenue and prior year's unencumbered funds.
Hawaii	Revenue	Growth of appropriations limited to rate of growth of state economy.
Idaho	Expenditure	Appropriations shall not exceed 5.33 per cent of state personal income.
Louisiana	Revenue	Tax revenue shall not exceed: fiscal year 78-79 tax revenue/1977 state personal income.
Massachusetts	Revenue	The average growth of wages and salaries of the previous 3 years.
Michigan	Revenue	Revenue shall not exceed: fiscal year 78-79 state revenue/1977 state personal income X the greater of state personal income in prior calendar year or average state personal income over previous 3 calendar years.
Missouri	Rev. & Exp.	Revenue shall not exceed: fiscal year 80-81 state revenue/1979 state personal income X the greater of state personal income in prior calendar year or average state personal income over previous calendar years.
Montana	Expenditure	State biennial appropriations shall not exceed state appropriations for the preceding biennium plus the product of preceding biennial appropriations and the growth percentage.
Nevada	Expenditure	Proposed biennial expenditures authorised for the 1975/76 biennium X [1 + percentage population change since 7.1.1974] X [1 + percentage inflation].
New Jersey	Expenditure	Fiscal year appropriations shall not exceed: fiscal year state per capita income, prior

186

Table 1: **(Continued)**

States with limits	Revenue or expenditure	Approximate limits[1]
		state per capita income multiplied by appropriations in prior fiscal year.
Oklahoma	Expenditure	(1) 12 per cent yearly increase (adjusted for inflation). (2) 95 per cent of certified revenue.
Oregon	Expenditure	The rate of growth of appropriations in each biennium shall not exceed rate of growth of state personal income in 2 preceding calendar years.
Rhode Island	Expenditure	Yearly growth in governor's general fund appropriations request shall not exceed 6 per cent.
South Carolina	Expenditure	Yearly growth in state appropriations shall not exceed average growth of personal income over 3 preceding years or 9.5 per cent of total state personal income, whichever is greatest.
Tennessee	Expenditure	Growth in state appropriations shall not exceed growth in state personal income.
Texas	Expenditure	Growth of biennial appropriations shall not exceed rate of growth of state personal income.
Utah[2]	Expenditure	Growth in appropriations may not exceed 85 per cent of the increase in state personal income.
Washington	Revenue	Growth of tax revenues shall not exceed average rate of growth of state personal income over 3 years.

States without limits

Alabama	Iowa	Nebraska	Pennsylvania
Arkansas	Kansas	New Hampshire	South Dakota
Connecticut	Kentucky	New Mexico	Vermont
Florida	Maine	New York	Virginia
Georgia	Maryland	North Carolina	West Virginia
Illinois	Minnesota	North Dakota	Wisconsin
Indiana	Mississippi	Ohio	Wyoming

[1] These limits have been abbreviated and may not fully reflect the exact character of the tax/expenditure controls.

[2] Never implemented.

Source: Significant Features of Fiscal Federalism 1990, Vol. 1 (Washington, DC: Advisory Commission on Intergovernmental Relations, January 1990) Table 5.

dramatically. From 1978 to 1987 the percentage change in state taxes per $100 of personal income fell by 2.2 per cent.[5]

The impact of Proposition 13 did not end there. Within five months of its passage in the summer of 1978, nearly one-third of our states rushed forward with similar voter initiatives for the November 1978 general elections. Not all were successful, but enough were successful to evidence a sea change. The tide of big government as an economic force was running out. State and local governments would play a reduced role in the economic processes of their respective communities.

Table 1 evidences this shift in voter preferences. Between 1976 and 1986, twenty-two states introduced new controls on public enterprise. The large majority of these tax and/or expenditure limitations – fourteen of the twenty-two – were adopted within three years of the California referendum. Some controls tied state appropriations to changes in population or personal income. Others indexed their tax system to protect against the ravages of inflation. All of these controls were designed to halt the growth of the public sector and to force the state governments to be more efficient and less wasteful of scarce resources.

Federal and state intergovernmental revenue reductions
Local governments were not immune to the change that washed across the country. These governments are dependent upon grants-in-aid from their states and the federal government. Prior to 1978, these intergovernmental revenues represented an ever larger portion of their general revenue. As Table 2 suggests, the events of the post-1978 period resulted in local governments being twice affected.

First they were affected by federal cut-backs. President Carter's last budget and certainly the budgets of President Reagan explicitly reduced the role played by the federal government in the affairs of state and local governments. Measured in terms of state/local general revenue, federal grants rose from 17.3 per cent in 1964 to a high of 32.1 per cent in 1978. As a percentage of state/local outlays, federal grants rose from 11.7 per cent in 1958 to 26.5 per cent in 1978. After 1978, these grants steadily fell. Indeed, if the projections of the Advisory Commission on Intergovernmental Relations are accurate, federal support of state/local governments will return to the 1958 level by the year 1998.[6]

Reductions in federal grants to states, coupled with the tax and expenditure controls that states imposed on themselves, meant that fewer dollars were available to share with their local governments. After a short lag, state grants as a percent of local own revenue

Table 2: **Federal and state grants-in-aid, 1958 to 1998 estimate**

	Federal grants in constant 1982 dollars (billions)	Federal grants as a percentage of state/local outlays	Federal grants as a percentage of state/local general revenue	State grants as a percentage of local own revenue
1958	17.6	11.7	NA	NA
1964	33.6	15.4	17.3	42.9
1969	54.8	17.8	20.4	54.0
1974	84.6	22.3	25.8	59.4
1978	109.7	26.5	32.1	59.4
1979	106.7	25.8	31.8	63.5
1980	105.9	25.8	30.4	63.6
1981	100.7	24.7	28.4	62.7
1982	88.2	21.6	23.3	59.4
1983	88.8	21.3	22.3	55.6
1984	90.2	20.9	22.2	54.3
1985	94.0	20.9	21.8	55.3
1986	97.0	20.5	21.9	55.6
1987	90.7	18.3	20.1	53.8
1988	92.5	18.2	NA	NA
1989 est.	94.7	17.1	NA	NA
1990 est.	91.1	NA	NA	NA
1991 est.	89.5	NA	NA	NA
1993 est.	NA	14.0	NA	NA
1998 est.	NA	11.0	NA	NA

Source: Significant Features of Fiscal Federalism, 1988 Edition Vol. II (Washington, DC: ACIR, July 1988) Tables 74.75; 1989 Ed, Vol. I (Washington, DC: ACIR, January 1989) Table 11; 1989 Ed, Vol. II (Washington, DC: ACIR, August 1989) Tables 8, 30, 38; Robert Gleason, 'Federalism 1986-87: Signals of a New Era', *Intergovernmental Perspectives,* Vol. 14, No. 1 (Winter 1989), p. 13.

also fell. There was a steady increase until 1980, but after that year the importance of these grants drifted downward.

The implications of these events should be clear. The changing character of the US system of fiscal federalism means that as the revenue available to both state and local governments begins to disappear these governments must look for ways to eliminate waste and improve efficiency.

Other policies to improve state/local government accountability
In the face of fiscal retrenchment which characterised the 1978-81 period, states introduced a number of other statutorial limitations on the budgeting and appropriation procedure. These currently serve as models for federal action. Most notable are the provisions for

Table 3: **Per capita state/local government debt and its relationship to state balanced budget limitations and constitutional debt limits, 1988**

State	Rank	State/local per capita debt and state rankings			Balanced budget limitations			Constitutional limits on general obligation debt[1]
		Per capita debt	Long term debt rank	Short term debt rank	Governor must submit a balanced budget	Legislature must pass a balanced budget	Governor must sign a balanced budget	
Alaska[2]	1	$20,850	1	4	NA	NA	NA	NA
Delaware	2	5,680	2	8	C	C	C	NP
Utah	3	5,499	3	44	S	C	NP	AV
Arizona	4	5,359	4	6	S	S	S	$350,000
Wyoming	5	4,588	5	45	YR	YR	YR	AV
Louisiana	6	4,504	6	16	YR	YR	YR	(5)
New York	7	4,488	8	1	C	NP	C	V
Washington	8	4,368	7	17	S	NP	NP	T
Minnesota	9	4,134	9	12	C,S	C,S	C,S	NP
New Jersey	10	3,901	12	9	S	C	S	(7)
Nebraska	11	3,848	10	30	C	C	S	$100,000
Oregon	12	3,790	11	25	C,S	C,S	C,S	$50,000
Nevada	13	3,635	14	31	S	C	NP	AV
Colorado	14	3,628	13	40	S	C	—	YR
Rhode Island	15	3,566	17	10	C,S	C,S	C,S	V
Massachusetts	16	3,531	21	2	C,S	NP	NP	NP
Texas	17	3,522	16	32	C	C	C	$200,000
Florida	18	3,507	15	47	S	C	NP	NP
New Mexico	19	3,475	19	42	NP	NP	YP	AV
Kentucky	20	3,468	18	49	C	C	C	$500,000

Table 3: (Continued)

State	Rank	State/local per capita debt and state rankings			Balanced budget limitations			
		Per capita debt	Long term debt rank	Short term debt rank	Governor must submit a balanced budget	Legislature must pass a balanced budget	Governor must sign a balanced budget	Constitutional limits on general obligation debt[1]
Connecticut	21	3,438	20	9	YR	YP	YP	NP
Pennsylvania	22	3,285	22	13	C	C	C	YR
Hawaii	23	3,770	23	11	C,S	NP	C,S	[4]
New Hampshire	24	3,183	24	29	S	NP	YP	NP
Maryland	25	3,122	25	19	C	C	NP	NP
West Virginia[2]	26	2,893	26	48	NA	NA	NA	NA
Montana	27	2,843	27	23	C	C	NP	NP
Kansas	28	2,842	29	14	S	S	NP	$1,000,000
South Dakota	29	2,789	28	50	C	C	C	£100,000
California	30	2,703	30	21	YR	NP	YR	£300,000
South Carolina	31	2,563	31	39	C	C	C	[9]
Oklahoma	32	2,470	32	35	S	NP	NP	V
Georgia	33	2,460	34	22	YR	YR	YR	[3]
North Dakota	34	2,448	33	36	YR	YR	YR	NP
Illinois	35	2,361	35	15	C	C	NP	NP
Vermont	36	2,324	36	24	NP	NP	NP	NP
Tennessee	37	2,258	38	18	C	C	C	NP
Maine	38	2,232	37	37	YR	NP	NP	$2,000,000
Alabama	39	2,183	39	34	C,S	YR	NP	YR
North Carolina	40	2,162	40	20	C	C	C	YR
Michigan	41	2,122	41	27	C	C	C	0

191

Table 3: (Continued)

State	Rank	State/local per capita debt and state rankings			Balanced budget limitations			
		Per capita debt	Long term debt rank	Short term debt rank	Governor must submit a balanced budget	Legislature must pass a balanced budget	Governor must sign a balanced budget	Constitutional limits on general obligation debt[1]
Wisconsin	42	2,100	42	7	NP	NP	NP	AV
Virginia	43	1,997	43	38	S	NP	NP	C,T
Ohio	44	1,874	47	5	YR	YR	YR	[8]
Arkansas	45	1,822	44	41	S	NP	NP	NP
Mississippi	46	1,806	45	43	S	NP	NP	[6]
Missouri	47	1,783	46	46	C	C	C	0
Iowa	48	1,659	48	28	C	C	NP	$250,000
Indiana	49	1,455	49	26	C	C	C	0
Idaho	50	1,204	50	33	C	C	NP	$2,000,000

AV = Percentage of property value   C = Constitutional provision   YR = Yes/restrictions apply   V = Popular vote required for
T = Percentage of taxes   NP = No provision   S = Statutory provision   any debt
     NA = Not available

[1] Different provisions may apply to other long- and short-term debts.
[2] Information not available.
[3] Not more than 10% of prior year's net general revenues.
[4] Not to exceed 20% of average General Fund revenues for 3 fiscal years preceding: may not be exceeded by popular vote.
[5] Limited to 10% of 3-year average of Bond Security and Redemption Fund.
[6] 5% of General Fund.
[7] 5% of General Fund.
[8] Highway, $500 million: coal, $100 million.
[9] Limited to 5% of last completed fiscal year revenue for capital improvement bonds.

Sources: Government Finances in 1987-1988, GF-88-5 (Washington, DC: US Department of Commerce, Bureau of the Census, January 1990) Table 34; *Significant Features of Fiscal Federalism 1990*, Vol. 1 (Washington, DC: ACIR, January 1990) Table 3.

gubernatorial line-item veto power and constitutional/statutorial debt limitations.

Forty states provide for gubernatorial veto authority for major budget items (see Table 6 below) and all states with the exception of Vermont impose some form of a balanced budget or public debt limitation (see Table 3). The efficiency of these fiscal disciplinary procedures along with the impact of direct expenditure and/or tax limitations will be analysed in the remainder of this paper in which an attempt will be made to determine whether or not these constitutional/legislative practices have had a significant impact upon the 'efficiency and effectiveness of the public domain'.

Efficiency and effectiveness: some first approximations
Scholars have long wrestled with the problem of measuring economic efficiency and effectiveness in the public domain. The difficulties are many and varied. The most obvious and fundamental problem is the fact that there are few market prices for the researcher to analyse. Even if these prices were readily available, the problems inherent in assessing the efficiency of an industry which is primarily a service industry must be faced. This in turn forces the researcher to specify the elusive unit of analysis for activities such as police protection, education and health care.

Since a number of policies explicitly designed to improve economic efficiency and effectiveness were introduced in the late 1970s and early 1980s it must be assumed that policy-makers had objectives that they wished to achieve. If these can be identified, a first step can be taken toward developing a research methodology. For some the intent of these policies was to eliminate or at least minimise public debt so that private sector investment initiatives would not be 'crowded-out'. The intent of other policies appears to be more far reaching, namely, a reduction in the size of the public sector or at least a reduction in the rate of growth of this sector so that the totality of the private sector would not be 'crowded-out'. In still other cases the intent is more explicit: to eliminate the waste or what is popularly known as the 'fat' in public enterprise. If it is assumed that these objectives accurately reflect the intent of policy-makers, we can begin to assess the success of their policy instruments.

Balanced budget and debt limitations
At first glance, reasonably unambiguous answers are obtained from an examination of balanced budget and debt limitations. Either a state has been successful in limiting its debt or it has not. Since all states with the exception of Vermont impose some form of

controls and since the restrictiveness of these controls varies from one state to another, success rates are readily determined.

The impact of debt and budget controls are considered in Table 3. States are ranked according to the extent of their per capita debt in various categories. The type of controls is also noted. Some budget controls are relatively non-intrusive such as requiring the governor to submit a balanced budget. More binding controls require the state legislature to pass a balanced budget or force the governor to sign only balanced budgets. Debt accumulations in some cases are limited to a fixed percentage of assessed valuation, in other cases to a fixed percentage of taxes, or in a few cases allowed only after a popular referendum is held.

Curious results are obtained from an examination of balanced budget limitations. Those states with the most restrictive controls are more likely to be heavy per capita debt states. For example, of the fifteen states with the heaviest per capita debt, twelve states require the governor to sign a balanced budget, and a slightly different set of twelve states require the state legislature to pass a balanced budget. At the other end of the spectrum, in the fifteen states with the lowest level of per capita debt, ten have no provision for the governor to sign a balanced budget, and six of the fifteen have no provisions for the state legislature to pass a balanced budget.

At a minimum this casts some doubt on the effectiveness of these controls. The presence of strong budgetary controls does not seem to be highly correlated with limited per capita debt. Two explanations can be offered. Firstly, those states with the highest debt burden may have imposed their controls after per capita debt reached some critical level. Conversely, those state legislatures that have a tradition of fiscal constraint may feel no need to constitutionally or statutorily mandate this constraint. Secondly, these restrictions are intended to contain state debt. They do not necessarily apply to the debt of local governments. Total state/ local per capita debt could rise because local governments incur debt while the state government balances its budgets. If this is the case, the practice reveals a basic inconsistency in allowing local officials of Bean Blossom, New York and Two Trees, Georgia to engage in debt financing while state legislators in Albany and Atlanta are constitutionally or statutorily prohibited from incurring debt.

Table 3 also suggests that explicit constitutional limits on general obligation debt are uncorrelated with per capita debt. Thirteen of the fifteen states with the highest per capita debt have constitutional limitations and eleven of the fifteen lowest per capita debt states similarly limit general obligation debt. Thus both sets of states seem to employ similar strategies to contain debt, and no clear pattern emerges. The only exception to this generalisation is that three states in the low debt group – Michigan, Missouri and Indiana – constitutionally mandate a zero level of general obligation debt.

The lesson to be learned from Table 3 should be clear: there is no easy route to debt limitation. Fiduciary responsibility is more a state of mind than it is a state of law. Low debt correlates with geographic location more than it does with constitutional or statutorial provisions. Only one of the high debt states – Louisiana – is from the Great Lakes or Southeast region, while fourteen of the fifteen low debt states are from these two regions. This suggests that balancing budgets will be hard to legislate in cases where the tradition is not present.

Although debt limitations may not explicitly contain the growth of public debt, these limitations may help to contain the growth of the public sector. A measure of this is found in Table 4. Here the pre/post 1978 changes in tax effort (ie the ratio of tax revenue to the tax base), direct general expenditures and interest expenditures are calculated for those states with a strong mandate to balance their state budgets and compared to those states which do not have this strong mandate.

It might be assumed that the attempts to limit public debt would be translated into reduced tax efforts, general expenditures and interest expenditures. However, when these variables were analysed in Table 4, perverse results emerged. Those states with strong mandates to balance budgets are more likely to experience an increase in tax effort and interest expenditures and a smaller fall in general expenditures than those states that have not mandated balanced budgets. For example, tax effort has increased by 3.2 percentage points for the balanced budget states and by only 1.5 for the non-balanced budget states. Direct general expenditure as a percent of state personal income has fallen by 1.5 percentage points for those states with mandates and by 2.1 percentage points for the non-mandated states. Finally, interest payments as a percent of general public expenditures rise by 3.2 percentage points for the former group of states and by 2.1 percentage points for the latter group.

Although the table has not been reproduced for this paper, an analysis of constitutional limitations on public debt generates results comparable to the balanced budget limitation analysis. Those states which place an explicit limit on general obligation debt experience a sharp increase in tax effort. From 1977 to 1986 tax effort in these states increased by 4.4 percentage points while non-limit states experienced a 1.8 percentage point decrease. At the same time the change in direct general expenditures and interest expenditures in debt limited states is not significantly different from those states

Table 4: **Balanced budget limitations and their effects on tax effort, direct general expenditures as a percentage of personal income and interest expenditures as a percentage of general expenditures: pre and post the 1978 public policy shift**

States where legislatures must pass or governor must sign a balanced budget	Tax effort			Direct general expenditures as a percentage of state personal income			Interest expenditures as a percentage of general expenditures		
	1977	1986	Percentage change 1977-1986	1975	1986	Percentage change 1975-1986	1977-78	1987-88	Percentage change 1977-78 to 1987-88
Alabama	79	86	7	20.2	20.1	-0.1	3.5	5.8	2.3
Arizona	110	99	-11	21.9	20.7	-1.2	2.4	7.7	5.4
California	117	95	-22	22.1	18.0	-4.1	1.9	4.7	2.8
Colorado	95	83	-12	21.5	17.5	-4.0	2.2	7.1	5.0
Connecticut	103	94	-9	15.8	14.4	-1.4	6.0	7.1	1.0
Delaware	80	81	1	20.5	20.1	-0.4	6.1	12.4	6.3
Florida	73	77	4	18.0	15.9	-2.1	3.5	8.1	4.6
Georgia	89	89	0	19.3	17.9	-1.4	3.0	3.7	0.6
Hawaii	115	105	-10	27.6	19.7	-7.9	5.9	7.7	1.9
Idaho	89	90	1	21.6	17.8	-3.8	1.3	3.4	2.1
Illinois	96	106	10	17.5	16.0	-1.5	3.9	6.1	2.2
Indiana	83	94	11	16.0	16.1	0.1	2.5	4.0	1.5
Iowa	90	113	23	18.9	19.1	0.2	1.6	4.2	2.6
Kansas	89	96	7	18.4	17.4	-1.0	3.5	7.5	4.0
Kentucky	84	89	5	19.4	17.8	-1.6	5.1	8.4	3.3
Louisiana	79	91	12	23.0	21.6	-1.4	4.7	11.5	6.8
Maryland	105	99	-6	21.0	16.5	-4.5	4.6	6.4	1.8
Michigan	109	118	9	21.1	20.5	-0.5	3.3	3.9	0.6
Minnesota	112	108	-4	23.7	21.8	-1.9	3.8	7.6	3.8
Missouri	80	82	2	16.5	14.6	-1.9	2.8	5.6	2.7

Table 4: (Continued)

States where legislatures must pass or governor must sign a balanced budget	Tax effort			Direct general expenditures as a percentage of state personal income			Interest expenditures as a percentage of general expenditures		
	1977	1986	Percentage change 1977-1986	1975	1986	Percentage change 1975-1986	1977-78	1987-88	Percentage change 1977-78 to 1987-88
Montana	94	103	9	23.4	25.2	1.8	2.4	7.6	5.2
Nebraska	98	96	-2	17.5	17.9	0.4	2.4	4.9	2.5
New Hampshire	73	62	-11	19.7	13.9	-5.8	4.1	8.5	4.4
New Jersey	113	103	-10	17.9	16.4	-1.5	5.1	8.5	3.4
New Mexico	77	88	11	23.8	25.2	1.4	2.2	8.0	5.7
New York	168	152	-16	26.4	22.5	-3.9	8.1	6.4	-1.7
North Carolina	87	92	5	18.8	16.7	-2.1	2.1	3.9	1.8
North Dakota	88	89	1	20.8	22.3	1.5	2.8	5.6	2.9
Ohio	78	103	25	17.6	17.3	-0.3	3.3	4.9	1.5
Oregon	92	98	6	23.9	21.3	-2.6	5.1	8.5	3.4
Pennsylvania	94	101	7	18.8	16.3	-2.5	5.4	8.0	2.6
Rhode Island	114	111	-3	20.6	19.3	-1.2	4.2	8.1	3.9
South Carolina	86	94	8	21.1	18.8	-2.3	2.3	4.5	2.3
South Dakota	87	95	8	23.1	20.2	-2.9	2.4	8.5	5.1
Tennessee	82	84	2	19.2	17.2	-2.0	3.9	5.7	1.7
Texas	68	79	11	17.4	16.7	-0.7	3.9	8.2	4.3
Utah	91	107	16	23.1	24.0	0.8	1.8	6.1	4.3
Wyoming	82	117	35	27.6	33.7	6.1	3.5	8.0	4.5
Average of states with balanced budget mandate:	93.3	96.5	9.2	20.6	19.1	-1.5	3.5	6.7	3.2

Table 4: **(Continued)**

States without mandates to balance the budget	Tax effort			Direct general expenditures as a percentage of state personal income			Interest expenditures as a percentage of general expenditures		
	1977	1986	Percentage change 1977-1986	1975	1986	Percentage change 1975-1986	1977-78	1987-88	Percentage change 1977-78 to 1987-88
Arkansas	78	91	13	18.6	17.7	-0.9	2.4	5.5	3.1
Maine	100	99	-1	21.4	19.5	-1.8	4.0	5.8	1.8
Massachusetts	133	103	-30	20.6	16.6	-4.0	5.3	6.1	0.8
Mississippi	94	97	3	23.8	21.4	-2.4	3.2	5.4	2.2
Nevada	62	65	3	22.1	18.9	-3.1	3.0	9.0	6.0
Oklahoma	72	85	13	18.5	18.2	-0.2	3.2	5.7	2.4
Vermont	104	91	-13	25.4	21.4	-4.1	4.7	5.6	0.9
Virginia	88	85	-3	17.9	15.4	-2.5	3.1	4.7	1.6
Washington	94	103	9	19.8	18.7	-1.1	4.2	4.5	0.3
Wisconsin	113	134	21	21.8	20.7	-1.1	3.0	4.9	2.0
Average of states without balanced budget mandate:	93.8	95.3	1.5	20.9	18.8	-2.1	3.6	5.7	2.1
US average:	93.5	96.3	2.8	20.7	19.1	-1.6	3.6	6.5	2.9

Source: Significant Features of Fiscal Federalism 1990, Vol. I (Washington, DC: ACIR, January 1990) Table 3; *Government Finances in 1987-1988*, GF-88-5 (Washington, DC: US Department of Commerce, Bureau of the Census, January 1990) Tables 29, 64, 71; *Government Finances in 1977-1978*, GF-78-5 (Washington, DC: US Department of Commerce, Bureau of the Census, February 1980) Table 29.

that do not explicitly limit public debt. This suggests that debt limitations force states to increase taxes rather than decrease expenditures. Thus if the purpose of debt limitation is to contain the growth of the public sector, it does not appear to be an effective policy instrument to achieve that end.

Tax and expenditure control legislation of the 1970s and 1980s
As noted previously, 1978 marks a turning point in the US system of fiscal federalism. Shortly before and after this year twenty-two states imposed new tax and/or expenditure controls. These controls are detailed in Table 1 and summarised again in Table 4. If it is assumed that the intent of these controls was to reduce the size of the public sector – or to at least slow its rate of growth – and to induce a higher level of labour productivity in the public sector then the impact of these controls should begin to appear by the end of the 1980s.

Several measures of the impact of these controls have been constructed. As was the case in Table 4, each of these measurements is flawed and no single measure can capture the full impact of the new control legislation. Taken as a group, however, they suggest a pattern. The measurements are: (i) change in tax effort; (ii) change in direct general expenditures as a percent of state personal income; (iii) change in public payroll as a percent of state personal income; and (iv) change in administrative expenditures as a percent of general expenditures. Each of these variables is reported before and after the 1978 policy shift and each variable is averaged for those states that introduced new controls and for those states that did not introduce new controls.

The results of this admittedly crude analysis are reported in Table 5. Tax/expenditure controls appear to work and in terms of some measures, they work quite well. This is partially true of the tax effort and public payroll variables. The US average tax effort increased from 93.9 in 1977 to 97.8 in 1986 which represents a 3.9 percentage point increase, but in those states with controls the rise of 1.9 percentage points is substantially less than it is in the non-control states which rose by 5.3 percentage points. Comparable results are obtained by examining the public payroll variable. In the 1978-86 period, on average, public payrolls as a percent of states personal income fell by about one percentage point. Those states that imposed controls experienced a 1.2 percentage point reduction in the payroll variable, while the non-control states experienced a somewhat lower reduction of 0.8 percentage points.

The impact of control legislation is less obvious for the other two variables – changes in direct general expenditures and changes

Table 5: **The impact of tax and/or expenditure controls on tax effort, direct expenditures as a percentage of state personal income, and administrative expenditures as a percentage of state personal income: 1975 to 1986**

	Tax effort			Direct general expenditures as a percentage of state personal income			Estimated state/local payrolls as a percentage of state personal income			Administrative expenses as a percentage of general expenditures		
			Percentage change			Percentage change			Percentage change			Percentage change 1977/78 to
	1977	1986	1977-86	1976	1986	1976-86	1975	1986	1975-1986	1977/78	1987/88	1987/88
States with limits(1):												
Alaska	130	168	38	35.4	53.2	17.8	13.9	16.5	2.6	8.9	7.7	-1.21
Arizona	110	99	-11	21.9	20.7	-1.3	11.4	9.0	-2.4	6.1	5.9	-0.22
California	117	95	-22	22.1	18.0	-4.1	10.9	8.1	-2.8	5.7	5.9	0.15
Colorado	95	83	-12	21.5	17.5	-4.0	10.3	8.5	-1.8	6.0	6.8	0.80
Delaware	80	81	1	20.5	20.1	-0.4	8.2	7.8	-0.4	6.7	6.9	0.22
Hawaii	115	105	-10	27.6	19.7	-7.9	9.7	7.4	-2.3	5.2	7.9	2.66
Idaho	89	90	1	21.6	17.8	-3.8	9.3	8.3	-1.0	5.3	5.2	-0.11
Louisiana	79	91	12	20.6	21.6	1.6	9.3	8.7	-0.6	4.8	4.9	0.11
Massachusetts	133	103	-30	20.6	16.6	-4.0	8.9	6.5	2.4	4.5	6.0	1.49
Michigan	109	118	9	21.1	20.5	-0.5	9.7	8.8	-0.9	5.0	4.8	-0.14
Missouri	80	82	2	16.5	14.6	-1.9	8.1	6.6	-1.5	3.9	4.9	0.96
Montana	94	103	9	23.4	25.2	1.7	10.5	9.4	-1.1	6.0	5.4	-0.54
Nevada	62	65	3	22.1	18.9	-3.1	9.8	7.8	2.0	8.1	8.0	-0.07
New Jersey	113	103	-10	17.9	16.4	-1.5	8.3	6.9	-1.4	5.9	5.8	-0.04
Oklahoma	72	85	13	18.5	18.2	-0.2	8.1	8.1	0.0	4.4	5.1	0.63
Oregon	92	98	6	23.9	21.3	-2.6	10.8	8.8	2.0	6.3	6.4	0.09
Rhode Island	114	111	-3	20.6	19.3	-1.2	8.9	7.5	-1.4	4.9	5.8	0.95
South Carolina	86	94	8	21.1	18.0	-2.9	8.9	8.8	-0.1	4.3	4.5	0.13

Table 5: (Continued)

	Tax effort			Direct general expenditures as a percentage of state personal income			Estimated state/local payrolls as a percentage of state personal income			Administrative expenses as a percentage of general expenditures		
	1977	1986	Percentage change 1977-86	1976	1986	Percentage change 1976-86	1975	1986	Percentage change 1975-1986	1977/78	1987/88	Percentage change 1977/78 to 1987/88
Tennessee	82	84	2	19.2	17.2	-2.0	8.5	7.5	-1.0	4.6	4.2	-0.45
Texas	68	79	11	17.4	16.7	-0.7	8.4	7.7	-0.7	4.4	4.7	0.32
Utah(2)	91	107	16	23.1	24.0	0.8	9.8	9.1	-0.7	4.5	6.1	1.52
Washington	94	103	9	19.8	18.7	-1.1	10.1	8.3	1.8	4.4	5.0	0.53
Average for states with limits:	95.7	97.6	1.9	21.8	19.7	-1.1	9.4	8.2	-1.2	5.4	5.8	0.40
States without limits:												
Alabama	79	86	7	20.2	20.1	-0.1	8.8	8.5	0.3	3.3	5.0	1.71
Arkansas	78	91	13	18.6	17.7	-0.9	7.6	7.4	-0.2	4.1	4.4	0.31
Connecticut	103	94	-9	15.8	14.4	-1.4	7.1	6.1	-1.0	4.4	5.7	1.28
Florida	73	77	4	18.0	15.9	-2.1	9.0	6.8	-2.2	6.0	5.9	-0.02
Georgia	89	89	0	19.3	17.9	-1.4	9.2	7.8	-1.4	5.0	5.3	0.38
Illinois	96	106	10	17.5	16.0	-1.5	8.6	7.2	-1.4	4.9	5.3	0.37
Indiana	83	94	11	16.0	16.1	0.1	7.5	7.3	-0.2	4.5	4.8	0.27
Iowa	90	119	29	18.9	19.1	0.3	8.6	8.3	-0.3	4.9	4.6	-0.31
Kansas	89	96	7	18.4	17.4	-1.1	8.2	7.6	-0.6	4.7	6.4	1.70
Kentucky	84	89	5	19.4	17.8	-1.7	7.8	7.5	-0.3	5.5	4.7	-0.73
Maine	100	99	-1	21.4	19.5	-1.8	8.5	7.2	-1.3	4.1	4.7	0.59
Maryland	105	99	-6	21.0	16.5	-4.5	9.4	7.4	-2.0	5.1	5.5	0.43
Minnesota	112	108	-4	23.7	21.8	-1.9	10.1	8.6	-1.5	4.8	4.9	0.16
Mississippi	94	97	3	23.8	21.4	-2.4	9.2	8.7	-0.5	3.8	4.4	0.67

Table 5: (Continued)

	Tax effort			Direct general expenditures as a percentage of state personal income			Estimated state/local payrolls as a percentage of state personal income			Administrative expenses as a percentage of general expenditures		
	1977	1986	Percentage change 1977-86	1976	1986	Percentage change 1976-86	1975	1986	Percentage change 1975-1986	1977/78	1987/88	Percentage change 1977/78 to 1987/88
Nebraska	98	96	-2	17.5	17.9	0.4	8.8	8.5	-0.3	5.2	4.5	0.71
New Hampshire	73	62	-11	19.7	13.9	-5.0	7.8	5.7	-2.1	4.0	5.9	1.85
New Mexico	77	88	11	23.8	25.2	1.4	11.4	9.9	-1.5	5.9	5.7	-0.29
New York	168	152	-16	26.4	22.5	-3.9	11.1	9.5	-1.6	4.8	4.9	0.09
North Carolina	87	92	5	18.8	16.7	-2.1	8.5	8.0	-0.5	4.6	4.9	0.30
North Dakota	88	89	1	20.8	22.3	1.5	8.0	9.5	1.5	3.5	4.3	0.85
Ohio	78	103	25	17.6	17.3	-0.3	7.7	7.3	-0.4	4.9	5.1	0.15
Pennsylvania	94	101	7	18.8	16.3	-2.5	7.8	6.2	-1.6	4.8	5.0	0.21
South Dakota	87	95	8	23.1	20.2	-2.9	9.1	7.7	-1.4	5.6	5.4	-0.23
Vermont	104	91	-13	25.5	21.4	-4.1	9.0	7.2	-2.6	4.7	6.3	1.56
Virginia	88	85	-3	17.9	19.4	2.5	8.6	7.1	-1.5	5.8	6.2	0.47
West Virginia	80	98	18	21.5	21.0	0.5	8.4	9.0	0.6	4.4	5.3	0.90
Wisconsin	113	134	21	21.8	20.7	-1.1	9.6	8.6	-1.0	4.3	4.5	0.21
Wyoming	82	117	35	27.8	19.7	-6.1	10.5	12.5	2.0	5.3	5.2	-0.10
Average for states without limits:	92.6	97.9	5.3	20.4	19.1	-1.3	8.2	7.4	-0.8	4.8	5.2	0.40
US average	93.9	97.8	3.9	20.8	19.6	-1.2	8.8	7.8	-1.0	5.0	5.4	0.40

(1) These limits have been abbreviated.   (2) Never implemented.
Source: *Significant Features of Fiscal Federalism 1970*, Vol. 1 (Washington DC: ACIR, January 1990), Table 5; *Government Finances in 1987-1988*, GF-88-5 (Washington DC, US Department of Commerce, Bureau of the Census, January 1990) Tables 29, 64, 67, 71; *Government Finances in 1977-1978*, GF-78-5 (Washington DC, Department of Commerce, Bureau of the Census, February 1980) Table 29.

in administrative expenses. In part the impact of the controls is obscured by the presence of two strong 'out-liers' (Alaska for the direct general expenditures and Hawaii for the administrative expenses). With the inclusion of these out-liers, there is no measurable positive or negative impact of the controls. When the two out-liers are excluded, the impact of the controls on the remaining forty-eight states is clear. Those states that imposed controls experienced a 2.0 percentage point decline in direct general expenditures taken as a percent of state personal income. This compares quite favourably with the 1.3 percentage point decline for the non-control states. Furthermore, the percentage point change in the administrative costs of the control states is a positive 0.25 compared to a 0.40 increase for the non-control states.

Line-item gubernatorial veto authority

One of the most sensible recommendations designed to induce efficiency in the public sector is the line-item veto. The proponents of this executive authority argue that it will eliminate wasteful 'pork-barrel' spending. If the presence of the line-item veto is effective, this should then be reflected in the magnitude of direct general expenditures, in state/local governmental payrolls, and in tax effort. That is, if the 'veto' is successful in containing the growth of unnecessary government spending, states that utilise it should experience a decline in all three of these variables compared to states that do not provide their governors with this executive privilege.

Forty states currently provide gubernatorial veto authority to their executives. The ten states that do not allow their governors to veto individual budget items are geographically diverse and surprisingly representative of the country as a whole. Since these ten states are from all regions of the country except the Plain States and the Rocky Mountain States, there is no reason to expect a political bias in the non-adopting states. Yet as Table 6 indicates, the ten states that do not employ line-item vetoes are more likely than their counterparts to have a slower growth rate in direct general expenditures, public payrolls, and tax effort.

The differences between adopting and non-adopting states is not inconsequential. From 1975 to 1986, direct general expenditure as a percent of state personal income fell by 2.12 percentage points in the non-adopting states compared to a fall of 0.98 in those states that allow line-item veto authority. State/local payrolls as a percent of state personal income follow the same pattern; between 1975 and 1986 public payrolls fell by 1.39 percentage points in the non-adopting states and by only 0.89 percentage points in the veto states.

Table 6: **The impact of line-item gubernatorial veto authority on tax effort, direct general expenditures as a percentage of personal income, and estimated state/local payrolls as a percentage of state personal income, 1975 to 1986**

States with line-item vetos	Tax effort			Direct general expenditures as a percentage of state personal income			Estimated state/local payrolls as a percentage of state personal income		
	1977	1986	Percentage change 1977-1986	1975	1986	Percentage change 1975-1986	1975	1986	Percentage change 1975-1986
Alaska	130	168	38	35.4	53.2	17.8	13.9	16.5	2.6
Arizona	110	99	-11	21.9	20.7	-1.3	11.4	9.0	-2.4
Arkansas	78	91	13	18.6	17.7	-0.9	7.6	7.4	-0.2
California	117	95	-22	22.1	18.0	-4.1	10.9	8.1	-2.8
Colorado	95	83	-12	21.5	17.5	-4.0	10.3	8.5	-1.8
Connecticut	103	94	-9	15.9	14.4	-1.4	7.1	6.1	-1.0
Delaware	80	81	1	20.5	20.1	-0.4	8.2	7.8	-0.4
Florida	73	77	4	18.0	15.9	-2.1	9.0	6.8	-2.2
Georgia	89	89	0	19.3	17.9	-1.4	9.2	7.8	-1.4
Hawaii	115	105	-10	27.6	19.7	-7.9	9.7	7.4	-2.3
Idaho	89	90	1	21.6	17.8	-3.8	9.3	8.3	-1.0
Illinois	96	106	10	17.5	16.0	-1.5	8.6	7.2	-1.4
Iowa	90	113	23	18.9	19.1	0.3	8.6	8.3	-0.3
Kansas	89	96	7	18.4	17.4	-1.1	8.2	7.6	-0.6
Kentucky	84	89	5	19.4	17.8	-1.7	7.8	7.5	-0.3
Louisiana	79	91	12	23.0	21.6	-1.4	9.3	8.7	-0.6
Massachusetts	133	103	-30	20.6	16.6	-4.0	8.9	6.5	-2.4
Michigan	109	118	9	21.1	20.5	-0.5	9.7	8.8	-0.9
Minnesota	112	108	-4	23.7	21.8	-1.9	10.1	8.6	-1.5
Mississippi	94	97	3	23.8	21.4	-2.4	9.2	8.7	-0.5
Missouri	80	82	2	16.5	14.6	-1.9	8.1	6.6	-1.5

Table 6: (Continued)

States with line-item vetos	Tax effort			Direct general expenditures as a percentage of state personal income			Estimated state/local payrolls as a percentage of state personal income		
	1977	1986	Percentage change 1977-1986	1975	1986	Percentage change 1975-1986	1975	1986	Percentage change 1975-1986
Montana	94	103	9	23.4	25.2	1.7	10.5	9.4	-1.1
Nebraska	98	96	-2	17.5	17.9	0.4	8.8	8.5	-0.3
New Jersey	113	103	-10	17.9	16.4	-1.5	8.3	6.9	-1.4
New York	168	152	-16	26.4	22.5	-3.9	11.1	9.5	-1.6
North Dakota	88	89	1	20.8	22.3	1.5	8.0	9.5	1.5
Ohio	78	103	25	17.6	17.3	-0.3	7.7	7.3	-0.4
Oklahoma	72	85	13	18.5	18.2	-0.2	8.1	8.1	0.0
Oregon	92	98	6	23.9	21.3	-2.6	10.8	8.8	-2.0
Pennsylvania	94	101	7	18.8	16.3	-2.5	7.8	6.2	-1.6
South Carolina	86	94	8	21.1	18.8	-2.3	8.9	8.8	-0.1
South Dakota	87	95	8	23.1	20.2	-2.9	9.1	7.7	-1.4
Tennessee	82	84	2	19.2	17.2	-2.0	8.5	7.5	-1.0
Texas	68	79	11	17.4	16.7	-0.7	8.4	7.7	-0.7
Utah	91	107	16	23.1	24.0	0.8	9.8	9.1	-0.7
Virginia	88	85	-3	17.9	15.4	-2.5	8.6	7.1	-1.5
Washington	94	103	9	19.8	18.7	-1.1	10.1	8.3	-1.8
West Virginia	80	98	18	21.5	21.0	-0.5	8.4	9.0	0.6
Wisconsin	113	134	21	21.8	20.7	-1.1	9.6	8.6	-1.0
Wyoming	82	117	35	27.6	33.7	6.1	10.5	12.5	2.0
Average of states with line-item veto:	96	100.7	4.7	21.05	20.08	-0.98	9.20	8.32	-0.89

Table 6: (Continued)

States without line-item veto	Tax effort			Direct general expenditures as a percentage of state personal income			Estimated state/local payrolls as a percentage of state personal income		
	1977	1986	Percentage change 1977-1986	1975	1986	Percentage change 1975-1986	1975	1986	Percentage change 1975-1986
Alabama	79	86	7	20.2	20.1	-0.1	8.8	8.5	-0.3
Indiana	83	94	11	16.0	16.1	0.1	7.5	7.3	-0.2
Maine	100	99	-1	21.4	19.5	-1.8	8.5	7.2	-1.3
Maryland*	105	99	-6	21.0	16.5	-4.5	9.4	7.4	-2.0
Nevada	62	65	3	22.1	18.9	-3.1	9.8	7.8	-2.0
New Hampshire	73	62	-11	19.7	13.9	-5.8	7.8	5.7	-2.1
New Mexico	77	88	11	23.8	25.2	1.4	11.4	9.9	-1.5
North Carolina	87	92	5	18.8	16.7	-2.1	8.5	8.0	-0.5
Rhode Island	114	111	-3	20.6	19.3	-1.2	8.9	7.5	-1.4
Vermont	104	91	-13	25.4	21.4	-4.1	9.8	7.2	-2.6
Average of states without line-item veto:	88.4	88.70	0.30	19.30	17.18	-2.12	9.04	7.65	-1.39
US average:	93.9	97.72	3.82	18.77	17.56	-1.21	9.20	8.20	-1.00

*Maryland has a strong executive budget.
Source: *Significant Features of Fiscal Federalism 1990*, Vol. 1 (Washington, DC: ACIR, January 1990) Table 5; *Government Finances in 1987-1988*, GF-88-5 (Washington, DC: US Department of Commerce, Bureau of Census, January 1990) Tables 64, 67, 71.

Data concerning tax effort are the most startling. From 1977 to 1986 those states that grant gubernatorial veto authority experienced a 4.7 percentage point increase in their tax effort. During the same period, the remaining states experienced only a 0.3 percentage point increase in their tax effort.

Conclusions
There is no sure way to ensure an increasing level of fiscal efficiency and effectiveness in the public domain. Although many recommendations have been offered, few hold promise of success if we are to generalise from the experiences of state governments.

The three major proposals examined in this paper to induce a higher level of efficiency and effectiveness are 'balanced budget and debt limitation', 'tax and/or expenditure control legislation' and 'line-item veto authority'. Only tax/expenditure controls are likely to affect public enterprise in any meaningful way. The effectiveness of this policy instrument compared to the others that were examined in this paper, is probably due to the 'directness' of the policy. If the objective of these policy prescriptions is either to contain the size of the public sector so that it does not crowd out private sector activity or to force the public sector to explicitly prioritise its spending initiatives, then these policy initiatives go directly at the problem. They limit spending or they limit taxes, which in turn limit spending. Since the spending options available to these governments are reduced, the public sector is forced to set priorities.

But even where a policy instrument is effective in limiting government spending, this is only the first step toward increasing efficiency and effectiveness. Because we may know how to limit the size of the public sector does not mean that we know how to make it spend its limited resources wisely. We must be conscious of any assumption we make that 'belt tightening' will yield this desired result.

Notes
[1] I am much indebted to Bradley Grabs who assembled many of the tables in this paper, to James Robinson who brought clarity to many of my thoughts, and Tasha Gutting who made sense out of my handwriting.

[2] Unlike Ireland, which in 1987 generated 97.6 per cent of its total governmental tax receipts at the national level and only 2.4 per cent at the local level, in the US subnational units of government generate substantial revenue with their own taxes. Additionally, they receive grants-in-aid to supplement their 'own tax' receipts. In 1987 the US federal government generated 69.2 per cent of all governmental taxes in the US, while the

remainder was collected by the fifty state governments (18.8 per cent) and the thousands of local governments (12.0 per cent). See: *Significant Features of Fiscal Federalism, 1990,* Vol. 2 (Washington DC: Advisory Commission of Intergovernmental Relations, August 1990) Table 2.

[3] John Shannon, the former Executive Director of the Advisory Commission on Intergovernmental Relations, created this categorisation for the 1789-1929 period and the categorisations for the other two periods discussed in this paper. However, the interpretation of what occurred in these three periods differs somewhat from those offered by Shannon. See: John Shannon, 'The Deregulation of the American Federal System,' in *The Changing Face of Fiscal Federalism,* Thomas R. Swartz and John E. Peck, eds. (Armonk: M.E. Sharpe, Inc., 1990) pp. 17-34.

[4] A line-item budget lists costs in terms of expenditure items such as salaries, materials and so forth.

[5] Steven D. Gold and Judy A. Zelio, *State-Local Fiscal Indicators* (Denver: National Conference of State Legislatures, January 1990) Table G5.

[6] Robert Gleason, 'Federalism 1986-87: Signals of a New Era', *Intergovernmental Perspectives,* Vol. 14, No. 1 (Winter 1988) p. 13.

References

Fisk, D.M., 'Measuring Productivity in State and Local Governments', *Monthly Labor Review,* June 1984.

Fisk, D.M., 'Productivity Trends in the Federal Government', *Monthly Labor Review,* October 1983.

Gleason, R., 'Federalism 1986-87: Signals of a New Era', *Intergovernmental Perspectives,* Vol. 14, No. 1, Winter 1988.

Gold, S.D. and Zelio, J.A., *State-Local Fiscal Indicators,* Denver: National Conference of State Legislatures, January 1990.

Government Finances, Washington, DC: US Department of Commerce, Bureau of the Census, various years.

Shannon, J., 'The Deregulation of the American Federal System', in T.R. Swartz and J.E. Peck (eds), *The Changing Face of Fiscal Federalism,* M.E. Sharpe Inc., 1990.

Significant Features of Fiscal Federalism, Washington D.C.: Advisory Commission on Intergovernmental Relations, various years.

10

Efficiency and Effectiveness: An Irish Perspective[1]

DERMOT McALEESE

THIS paper studies the efficiency and effectiveness of Irish fiscal policy, with emphasis on the recent past. Unlike other contributors in this volume, I focus on macro-efficiency rather than on micro-economic issues. An Irish reader will readily anticipate the justification: policy shortcomings during most of the last fifteen years have been most conspicuous in the area of fiscal policy. This is not to imply that other aspects of macro policy – still less of Irish micro-economic policy – should be or are being neglected.[2]

The analysis is divided into four sections: fiscal developments to the mid-eighties, fiscal recovery 1987-90, the durability of the recovery and what next after fiscal stability?

Fiscal developments to mid-1980s

The origins of Ireland's fiscal problem have been traced to the deliberate acceptance in 1972 of a current budget deficit as a counter-cyclical tool. Prior to that time, the Department of Finance tradition had been to attempt to balance the current budget year-by-year. The decision in principle to resort to borrowing for current budgetary purposes is described by Whitaker (1983) as one of the two 'tragic policy errors' of the seventies which 'enormously aggravated' Ireland's development problem (p. 13). The second policy error was the excessive optimism which underlay the resumption of economic planning in 1977. A third policy error, which has become apparent since publication of Whitaker's analysis, is the delayed adjustment to Ireland's deteriorating fiscal policy in the first half of the 1980s (McAleese and McCarthy 1989).

During the 1970s, as public expenditure increased, numerous official and unofficial reports were written about the dangers of budgetary imbalance.

The National Economic and Social Council produced a series

of studies documenting the rise in public sector expenditure, analysing its relation to Ireland's growing population and warning of its consequences for financial stability (NESC 1976). Notwithstanding an abundance of sound advice, the public expenditure/ GDP ratio continued to increase and higher taxation followed in its wake. Because of inflation there was considerable tax buoyancy without any need for explicit changes in tax rates. The taxation burden increased by stealth. Matters began to deteriorate at an alarming rate after 1978, with marked increases in all four indicators of government activity: public expenditure, taxation, borrowing, and debt (Table 1). The systematic neglect of the NESC's well-researched warnings is an aspect of recent economic history deserving of a study all to itself.

Table 1: **Public sector in the economy**

	Expenditure/GDP	*Receipts/GDP*	*Debt/GNP*
1973	36.8	32.2	54.5
1980	50.4	37.7	87.6
1986	53.5	42.4	135.1

Source: European Economy, November 1989; Budget 1990; Kennedy *et al.,* p. 89.

Many of Ireland's current fiscal difficulties can be traced to unrealistic expectations about the potency of macro-economic fiscal policy as a tool of stabilisation. Ireland's worsening fiscal position was initially owed to an exaggerated view of what a policy of fiscal expansion could achieve for the economy. Even the Whitaker era's belief that increases in capital expenditure were appropriate for expansionary purposes is by no means above criticism. The 1978 budget raised the projected current deficit from 4 per cent to 6 per cent of GNP as part of a deliberate strategy of propelling the economy on to a higher growth trajectory. Net borrowing by general government (using the European Commission definition) which had been systematically reduced from its peak of 12.5 per cent of GNP in the depth of the 1973-75 recession began to rise again and by 1980 had already exceeded the 1975 level. The strategy of induced growth via expansionary fiscal policy failed for reasons which, in hindsight, seem all too predictable. Instead the policy led to mounting debt and a spate of inflationary wage demands.

By the same token, efforts to repair the damage were delayed by exaggerated fears about the deflationary consequences of reducing the deficit via expenditure cuts. Standard econometric models had much to say about the unhappy implications for employment and growth of any strong contraction of government expenditure. Increased taxation was seen as the less deflationary alternative if corrective action had to be taken. A series of unstable governments and the world recession of 1979 to 1982 made it doubly difficult to appreciate the benefits which might follow from spending cuts.

Professor Lee has aptly summarised the situation in those years as: 'A grim tale of financial irresponsibility as the Irish insisted on living in dreamland' (Lee 1989, p. 489). While a significant reduction had been achieved in the PSBR/GNP ratio by 1986, public debt continued to increase and the overall fiscal position continued to deteriorate. The NESC Report *Strategy for Development 1986-1990* published in November, 1986 reached the conclusion that the economic and social problems confronting the country were 'extremely grave', and that, without a dramatic change in economic policy, 'the medium-term prospects offer no relief' (NESC 1986, p. 303). In the period 1973-86, the national debt/GNP ratio increased from 54.5 per cent to 142.2 per cent. Thus, within a brief span of thirteen years, more debt was accumulated relative to income than in the entire previous history of the state (Kennedy *et al.,* 1988).

The worsening fiscal situation had been anticipated and was the subject of a continuous barrage of criticism by economists. These criticisms centred around a number of themes:

- Because of high import leakages, Irish fiscal multipliers were very low. Budget deficits increased output and employment ... but in Japan and Germany, not Ireland!
- The burden of debt-service and its implications for future taxation was much stressed.
- The expansion of government expenditure because of public sector pay increases undermined the competitiveness of the traded sector of the economy. It was an uphill task initially to convince those in the private traded sector that government expenditure, historically regarded as the solution to their problems, was in this instance the source of them.
- The high level of provision of social services in Ireland relative to other countries with similar levels of income per head placed heavy burdens on the budget. By far the biggest component of the increase in social expenditure up to 1981 consisted of the increase in average real state expenditure per recipient (Maguire 1984, OECD 1987).
- Some simple correlation studies demonstrated a negative link between public expenditure and economic growth, but there was little follow-through of this in the Irish economic literature.
- There were numerous warnings about the fickleness of foreign

lenders and the government was advised that continuation of past policy would lead to a withdrawal of foreign loans and/or domestic capital outflow. The supply of foreign lending did not, as it transpired, run out and Ireland's credit rating survived its awesome debt figures much better than expected (McAleese 1984). Domestic capital outflow did occur but much of it was related to the exchange rate rather than the high debt ratio.

• The micro-economic aspects of the public sector (industrial policy, transport deregulation, income distribution effects of expenditure) were subjected to intense scrutiny as part of the search for a constructive solution to the fiscal problem.

Scepticism about effects of budgetary deficits on the macro-economy was further reinforced with the publication of Bradley *et al*'s (1985) finding that Irish government intervention was generally pro-cyclical rather than counter-cyclical. (The first criticism above, however, somewhat negates the practical significance of such a tendency.)

Looking over the period since 1970, Irish experience in fiscal matters conforms in certain broad respects to that of other EC (9) countries. General government expenditure relative to GDP rose from 37 per cent in 1970 to 53 per cent in 1986. The EC (9) average in the same period increased from 37 per cent to 49 per cent. The tax revenue/GDP ratio also increased, from 33 per cent to 42 per cent for Ireland and from 37 per cent to 45 per cent for the EC (9). The major contrast between Ireland and the EC average lay in the magnitude of the gap between spending and revenue. Irish borrowing ratios were consistently higher than the EC average. Failure to deal effectively with the budget deficits led to cumulative inefficiencies in the Irish economy, many deriving from high taxation, and more important to a sense of deep frustration and failure at a national level. Theories of the ungovernability of Ireland due to the quirks of PR and the unyielding influences of pressure groups were much in vogue at that time.

Back from the brink (1987-90)
The Irish economy has experienced a dramatic change for the better in its public finances in recent years. Comparison with other OECD countries shows Ireland at the top of the league of successful fiscal adjusters, next to Denmark and Sweden (Table 2). Government borrowing relative to GNP has fallen from 13 per cent in 1986 to 2 per cent in 1990 (Table 3). The debt position, which threatened to engulf the economy in the mid-eighties, has started to improve. What is really remarkable is that all this has been achieved without

any deflationary collapse of domestic demand and without the social and political trauma which fiscal adjustment on this scale would lead one to expect (McAleese 1990).

Table 2: **Fiscal adjustment in the 1980s**

	Maximum Deficit (% GDP)	Minimum Deficit (% GDP)	Cumulative Improvement (Percentage Points)
Denmark	9.1 (1982)	+3.5 (1986)	12.6
Sweden	7.0 (1982)	+5.1 (1989)	12.1
Ireland	13.8 (1982)	2.1 (1989)	11.7
New Zealand	8.3 (1984)	1.0 (1987)	7.3
Belgium	12.6 (1981)	6.0 (1989)	6.6
Portugal	12.0 (1984)	6.0 (1989)	6.0
UK	3.9 (1984)	+1.5 (1989)	5.4
Spain	7.0 (1985)	2.6 (1989)	4.4
Germany	3.7 (1981)	0.0 (1989)	3.7
Netherlands	7.1 (1982)	4.4 (1989)	2.7
Italy	12.5 (1985)	10.3 (1989)	2.2
France	3.2 (1983)	1.2 (1989)	2.0
Greece	19.9 (1989)	—	none
EUR12	5.2 (1982)	2.9 (1989)	2.3

Source: McAleese (1990) – updated figures in the case of Sweden.

Table 3: **Back from the brink**

	1986	1987	1988	1989	1990
Fiscal adjustment current budget deficit (% GNP)	8.3	6.5	1.7	1.3	1.2
Exchequer borrowing (% GNP)	12.8	9.9	3.3	2.4	2.1
National debt (% GNP)	135.1	135.3	137.9	129.6	120.2* (115)

* Central Bank figures. The Department of Finance figure for 1990 is 115%. To add to the statistical confusion the European Commission figure is lower still (105% for 1989).
Source: McAleese (1990).

The main features of the post-1986 economic recovery and the reasons for its success have only begun to attract serious research. It is a topic which merits, and no doubt will in time receive, careful analysis. At this stage, some preliminary conclusions can be drawn.

Recovery did not occur in a vacuum. The Coalition government (1982-87) had steered the economy to lower inflation, down from

20 per cent in 1981 to 4 per cent in 1986, through maintaining a moderately strong position within the ERM. The DM/IR£ rate fell from 3.64 in 1981 to 2.91 in 1986, a depreciation of 20 per cent – a far cry from a fixed DM link! The IR£ strengthened against the dollar and sterling which led to a sharp lowering in the rate of increase of traded goods prices. The 8 per cent downward realignment of the Irish pound in August 1986, though much criticised at the time, was in fact a sensible response to weakness in sterling and, as subsequent experience demonstrated, helped to avoid loss of competitiveness without jeopardising the low inflation rate. An objective appraisal would also have to include reference to deregulatory measures taken in 1986 in the case of airfares which bore fruit in subsequent years. Also the Coalition government's persistent reference to the need for fiscal discipline (which regrettably it was itself unable to enforce) at least provided a psychological conditioning of the public which subsequent governments were able to exploit. Finally, the balance of payments deficit had improved markedly from a peak of 15 per cent in 1981 to 3 per cent in 1986.

Four features of the recovery merit special attention. Firstly, strong government control on public expenditure was a key factor. State capital spending was sharply cut in absolute terms. Current expenditure of the main spending departments was curbed. Both the EBR and current budget deficit fell (Table 3). At the same time, social welfare payments were increased by more than the inflation rate, thereby protecting the more vulnerable (Table 4).

Secondly, the Programme for National Recovery, hammered out in 1987 on the basis of consensus between the trade unions, employers and government, held nominal pay rises to a level comparable to those in low-inflation countries in Europe. This helped both the public sector (lower pay bill) and the private sector (improved competitiveness with major trading partners).

Thirdly, a buoyant world economy offered opportunities to exploit Ireland's competitiveness and contributed to rapid export growth. The British market, in particular, provided rich pickings for many Irish exporters. Low oil prices and favourable exchange rate developments (stronger sterling, weaker dollar) also helped.

Fourthly, the government's programme was buttressed in its early years by an unusually constructive opposition. Mr Alan Dukes, the leader of the major opposition party, promised support for the government, on condition that it adhered to sound economic policies. This self-imposed restraint created a welcome atmosphere of stability and set a context in which the new stabilisation policies could work.

And work they did. The long stagnant economy started to grow. First exports, then consumption and finally private investment took

Table 4: **Whose adjustment burden?**

	1986	*1987*	*1988*	*1989*	*1990*
Profits, professional earnings and other income					
% increase in real terms	4.1	5.3	6.6	13.8	8.5
Income from agriculture					
% change in real terms	–8.8	17.2	15.0	1.0	–8.2
Manufacturing output					
% increase in volume	2.9	11.5	12.5	12.7	7.0
Average weekly earnings in manufacturing					
% in real terms	4.7	3.2	3.7	0.1	0.5
Social welfare (% increase p.a. July-June)					
General rates	4.0	3.0	3.0	3.0	5.0
Long-term unemployed	5.0	3.0	11.0	12.0	11.0
Employment (% increase p.a.)	0.2	0.0	1.0	1.2	1.0
Unemployment (%)	17.6	17.1	16.2	15.2	14.0
Consumer Price Index	3.8	3.1	2.1	4.1	3.0

Source: McAleese (1990).

off. Tax revenues increased, despite (or as it could well be argued because of) a lowering of tax rates. A tax amnesty proved to be enormously successful. As the fiscal position improved, Irish interest rates fell which, for a heavily-indebted exchequer, meant even further fiscal relief. The process that Myrdal described as 'circular and cumulative causation' began to operate with a vengeance – this time in the government's favour. Employment started to rise and the unemployment rate (on the Labour Force Survey definition) fell from approximately 18 per cent in 1986 to 14 per cent in 1990.

A striking development was the behaviour of take-home pay. During the period 1980 to 1987, real after-tax pay for the average industrial worker had declined. Yet, since 1987, real increases of 8 per cent for single workers and 5 per cent for married workers have been recorded (Table 5). Significantly, these increases have not been associated with any loss in international competitiveness. On the contrary, hourly earnings, measured in a common currency, which had risen between 1980 and 1987 by 14 per cent fell slightly between 1987 and 1990. Given unemployed labour, improvement in Irish competitiveness was equivalent to more efficient utilisation of international trade. For the first time in more than a decade

Irish labour began to start pricing itself into jobs instead of out of them.

Table 5: **Average industrial earnings 1980-90**

| | Cumulative after-tax % change | |
	Single	*Married*
1980-87	–7.0	–8.2
1988-90	+8.2	+5.0

Source: NESC (1990).

The state of Ireland's labour market is still desperately unsatisfactory. In addition to the high unemployment rate, account must be taken of the high emigration levels during the years of adjustment. Of course, adjustment did not cause emigration. Indeed, had fiscal adjustment been further postponed, emigration rates would most likely have risen even further. What the conjunction of emigration and unemployment data implies is that Ireland's labour market has functioned very inefficiently during the 1980s and continues to do so. In my view Irish policy has focussed excessively on the symptoms of the problem rather than its causes. How else can one explain the serious contemplation of proposals for a national minimum wage, the extension of PRSI to part-time workers and the failure to address the problem of Ireland's high replacement ratios?[3]

How durable a recovery?
The economy is back from the brink. The question is how far back? This can be answered by considering external and internal factors. Table 6 provides a summary of these factors.

Table 6: **Constraints on fiscal policy in the 1990s**

External constraints
Capital mobility
EMS
Business sentiment (foreign)
1992 tax reductions

Internal constraints
Debt/GNP twice EC average
Business sentiment (domestic – expansionary fiscal contraction)
Existing rates of income taxation high relative to EC
Consensus on macro-economic stability (NESC 1990)

First, external factors will exert more control on domestic policy than before. The virtual abolition of exchange controls means that any return to the lax fiscal practices of the late seventies and early eighties will be penalised by an outflow of capital and a prompt rise in interest rates. This may prove a more effective reminder of the virtues of fiscal balance than the censure of economists!

Membership of the EMS will impose another type of discipline. Since 1987, the Irish pound has stayed within the narrow EMS band and the Irish people have enjoyed an extended period of low inflation. Any weakening of this link would be highly unpopular.

Business sentiment will also play a role. Both domestic and foreign investors would react unfavourably to any worsening of the government's finances – for just the same reasons as they responded favourably to the improvement in them. Significant crowding-out would occur. Some economists in Ireland have applied the theory of expansionary fiscal contraction to this process: fiscal contraction can lead to expansion of domestic expenditure because of its effects on business confidence.

Post-1992 approximation of taxes will be another external force to contend with, the implication being that curbs on public expenditure will be needed to make room for reductions in DIRT and falls in VAT and excise duties (de Buitléir 1990; Cromien 1990). With movement to EMU, these constraints are likely to become more binding; and the debate will move on to questions of fiscal federalism.

The accumulated weight of the above factors will be to impart a tendency towards less government expenditure and less borrowing. Exactly how the mechanisms work is something which only time will reveal. The fiscal experience of some US states and cities suggests that, even in a federal system, a mess can be made of local finances. In Canada, each province has its own credit rating (Ryan, 1990). The threat of a downgrading must act as a strong long-run constraint, but gives only moderate protection in the short- to medium-term.

The second set of considerations is less clear-cut in its implications. Is there a domestic consensus in favour of fiscal stability? Or is the experience of the last few years seen simply as an exotic interlude before the nation resumes its past behaviour? Is structural change deeply embedded in the public sector and in the public perception of what that sector can and should provide – or has there been no more than a postponement of demand?

The internal constraints binding the government towards continued adjustment are:

- A high debt/GNP ratio which leaves the economy vulnerable to interest rate increases. The cost of servicing debt absorbs over 70 per cent of income tax revenue.
- Increased awareness of the limitations of government

expenditure as a generator of economic growth. If allowed grow too fast, the public sector requires more taxation and higher tax rates to finance it. This weakens incentives for business investment and undermines the private sector. Domestic interest rates increase. In conditions of uncertainty, a Keynesian expansion adversely affects the aggregate supply curve.

- Income tax and VAT are high relative to the UK and other EC countries and there is strong *domestic* pressure for lower taxation. Lower taxation is also the most effective method of dealing with Ireland's pervasive poverty traps, caused in part by comparatively higher tax incidence at low income levels. Ireland is simply following a worldwide trend towards lower taxation levels. This factor will limit expansion of government expenditure and also, though less directly, of government borrowing.
- A consensus has developed on the need for macro-economic stability.

Employees have no wish to return to the demoralising process of wages chasing prices in ever-increasing spirals which leave nothing in their wake except fewer jobs. The painful disinflation of the early 1980s has warned employers of the dangers of conceding high wage claims and has warned unions of the dangers of demanding them.

The NESC (1990) has lent its considerable weight to the cause of fiscal stability. Recognising the potentially serious consequences of departure from the principles of consistency, continuity and credibility which have been a feature of recent policy, it recommends that 'the current budget deficit and EBR should be maintained in a sustained downward path *each year* between now and 1993' (p. 4.26). It points out explicitly that this will require a 'tough budget' in 1991 *(ibid)*.

These domestic constraints should act as a powerful deterrent to an explicit and obvious abandonment of the adjustment process. Whether they will be sufficient to guard against a relaxation by stealth, where the rhetoric of fiscal adjustment combines with a *de facto* resignation to higher borrowing remains to be seen. The escalation of debt, it will be remembered, was the outcome of incremental policies and occurred in conjunction with continuous affirmation of government intentions to put the nation's fiscal affairs in order.

There are four separate areas of concern. Firstly, there were difficulties in framing the 1991 budget. Because of large carry-over costs of public pay from 1990 and lower GNP growth, the EBR is projected to decline only slightly and the current budget deficit is projected to rise.

Secondly, EC structural funds could, if we are not careful, lead to the same explosion of expectations generated by EMS money a decade ago. There is a psychological problem to contend with here: how to cope with a comparative abundance of capital expenditure while at the same time keeping a tight rein on current expenditure.

Thirdly, the belief that the public finance problem has already been overcome – that the battle is over and now the time for spending has returned – makes it difficult to sustain the momentum of expenditure control. The public spending lobbies are still extremely strong.

A final problem is that of misreading the lessons of 1987-90. Assertions that sacrifices have been made by employees which must now be rewarded ignore the fact, shown in Table 5, that there have been no sacrifices – pay restraint pays! Misleading statements to the effect that the 'poor', the 'disadvantaged', the 'vulnerable', etc have borne the brunt of the adjustment costs give rise to a misplaced sense of grievance. Adjustment has fuelled economic growth, not halted it, and in so doing has laid the foundation for improved prosperity and greater numbers employed. Some key social indicators have improved. This is not to suggest that Ireland's social problems have been solved: simply that the adjustment process has not made them worse. Moreover, this generalisation is obviously subject to individual exceptions, notably in the health and housing sectors.

There is also a tendency to downplay the role of domestic reform on business expectations and consumer confidence by attributing most of the post-1986 improvement to favourable external circumstances. OECD estimates reported by NESC (1990 p. 37) indicate that the oil price fall and the acceleration of export market growth added 1.5 percentage points per annum to the growth rate over the 1986-88 period. This still leaves over half of the total growth to be explained by domestic factors such as the investment boom and the rise in consumption. At this stage it seems entirely plausible to link these factors with the effects on confidence of the drive for fiscal balance – even though no Irish macro-economic model to my knowledge is designed to capture such effects.

Successful stabilisation — what next?
Suppose macro-economic stability *is* sustained, will the Irish economy stay on its recent growth path? Where will growth come from and how can efficiency and effectiveness in the public domain help the growth process?

Much of Irish industrial development has been spearheaded by foreign industry. Policy has been consistently positive towards overseas investors, although the emphasis has shifted in recent years from capital grants to labour training assistance, R & D grants and equity participation. There is more selectivity in the type of industry being targeted. Given a stable macro-economic framework, there is a reasonable expectation that Ireland's tax and other fiscal incentives, competitive labour costs and access to the fast-growing EC markets of 1992 will attract an increasing supply of overseas corporations.

Indigenous industry has performed poorly during past decades. Employment in such firms has fallen by 21 per cent between 1973 and 1988 – and in the medium- to large-size firms the rate of loss has been 40 per cent (Ruane and McGibney 1990; Foley 1990). The failure of an entrepreneurial culture to take root has been the topic of much debate. The search for an effective industrial development strategy continues.

Ireland has an abundance of English speaking intelligent young people who do well abroad but who appear to find insufficient stimulus at home. Has this something to do with heavy income taxation (among many other factors)? Government policy aims to continue the process of reducing income tax rates. This is necessary for defensive reasons – other countries, notably the UK, have done so. But will it release a new dynamism in Irish society? In particular, will it provide an extra push to the marketed services sector on which Ireland is pinning so much hope?

The Irish government, like governments in many other countries, is examining ways of obtaining better value for money in the public enterprise sector. Public enterprises have been subjected to tighter budgetary control. Deregulation has also affected them and, in the case of transport, has secured a welcome reduction in fares. Privatisation of some state-owned enterprises has already been decided.

Efficiency and effectiveness in the field of health, education and social services is an urgent theme for the Irish economy in the 1990s. As noted earlier, the Irish government, by international standards, spends liberally, relative to its income, on these areas. The combined budget of the Department of Health and the illness element of the Department of Social Welfare amounts to 7.7 per cent of GNP. Does this signify too great an emphasis on treating illness as opposed to promoting good health? With 14 per cent unemployed, there is continuing pressure to find ways of maintaining a safety-net while providing greater and more flexible incentives to work. Replacement ratios relative to low income employment – which is a more relevant basis for comparison than the average industrial earnings standard usually chosen – are high. The Irish economy is in consequence labour-abundant but not especially low-cost in terms of many types of labour. The tax and social welfare systems have still to be integrated. Tax revenue foregone is estimated at £60-£70 million in tax year 1989/90 (NESC 1990 pp. 7, 46). As Ireland's demographic structure changes, how can the composition of social expenditure be changed to take account of these new realities?

The link between efficiency in fiscal policy and proper utilisation of Ireland's external position has been mentioned more than once in this paper. Experience shows that one interacts with the other. Weak fiscal policy has been associated with high costs and poor competitiveness. A key feature of the 1987-90 period was the conjunction of fiscal adjustment with a much-improved competitiveness position. The marked deterioration in competitiveness in the early 1980s was the cause of many difficulties for the economy. With the advent of the Single European Market, and further of EMU, the efficiency/competitiveness link becomes more imperative.

Conclusion

The Irish economy has made great progress in recent years. Much of this progress is related to the improvement in public finances. External circumstances were also helpful. The distinctive feature of Irish experience is not the fact of fiscal improvement. Most OECD countries enjoyed a similar upturn in the second half of the 1980s (Table 2). The speed of recovery and its extent is what singles out Ireland – and also the degree to which it depended on expenditure cuts as distinct from an increase in tax revenue.

As we face into the nineties, the international scene has become less benign. Oil price volatility, weakening food prices and the prospect of a slow-down in our major trading partners give cause for concern, for economic growth as much as for the public finances. Against this there are the pluses: a balance of payments surplus and low inflation for four years in a row, a major injection of EC structural funds between now and 1993 to help get the country's economic infrastructure in order and a realistically-based strategy of development. An essential element in this strategy will be the continued search for measures to improve efficiency and performance in the public sector.

Notes

[1] The author is grateful to Dr Michael Mulreany for helpful comments.

[2] See NESC (1990) Chapters 11 and 12 for discussion of the management of public expenditure and

Lane (1991) for an excellent survey of issues relating to government expenditure in Ireland.

[3] The replacement ratio measures the proportion of aftertax income that is replaced by social welfare payments.

References

Bradley, J., Fanning, C., Prendergast, C., and Wynne, M., *Medium-Term Analysis of Fiscal Policy in Ireland: A Macroeconomic Study of the Period 1967-1980,* ESRI Research Paper No. 122, Dublin, 1985.

Cromien, S., 'The Implications of the Single Market for Economic Management', in A. Foley and M. Mulreany (eds), *The Single European Market and the Irish Economy,* Institute of Public Administration, Dublin, 1990.

De Buitléir, Donal, 'Budgetary Policy for the 1990s', paper to Dublin Economic Workshop Policy Conference, Kenmare, 19-21 October, 1990.

Foley, A., 'Indigenous Manufacturing', in A. Foley and M. Mulreany (eds), *The Single European Market and the Irish Economy,* Institute of Public Administration, Dublin, 1990.

Kennedy, K., Giblin, T., and McHugh, D., *The Economic Development of Ireland in the Twentieth Century,* Routledge, London, 1988.

Lane, P., 'Government Intervention', in J. O'Hagan (ed), *Economy of Ireland, Policy and Performance,* 6th edition, Irish Management Institute (forthcoming).

Lee, J., *Ireland 1912-85: Politics, Culture and Society,* Cambridge University Press, 1990.

McAleese, Dermot, 'Is There a Want of Capital in Ireland?', *Administration,* Vol. 31, No. 4, 1982.

McAleese, Dermot, 'Ireland's Economic Recovery', *Irish Banking Review,* Summer 1990.

McAleese, D., and McCarthy, F.D., 'Adjustment and External Shocks', PPR Working Papers 262, The World Bank, Washington DC, August 1989.

Maguire, M., 'Social Expenditure in Ireland and other European OECD Countries: Past Trends and Prospective Developments', in *Public Social Expenditure - Value for Money?,* ESRI, Dublin, 1984.

NESC, *The Future of Public Expenditure in Ireland,* No. 20; *Report on Public Expenditure,* No. 21; *Prelude to Planning,* No. 26, 1976.

NESC, *A Strategy for Development 1986-1990: Growth Employment and Fiscal Balance,* No. 83, 1986.

NESC, *A Strategy for the Nineties: Economic Stability and Structural Change,* No. 89, October 1990.

OECD, *OECD Economic Surveys: Ireland 1987/88,* Paris, 1987.

Ryan, Louden, 'EMU – Personal Reflections', *Irish Banking Review,* Spring 1990.

Ruane, F., and McGibney, A., 'The Role of Overseas Industry', in A. Foley (ed), *Overseas Industry in Ireland,* Gill and Macmillan (forthcoming).

Whitaker, T.K., *Interests,* Institute of Public Administration, Dublin, 1983.

Index

224